STUDIES IN AN

A PRISM FOR HIS TIMES

Late-Tudor Anglesey & Hugh Hughes of Plas Coch

ROBIN GROVE-WHITE

CYMDEITHAS HYNAFIAETHWYR A NATURIAETHWYR MÔN
THE ANGLESEY ANTIQUARIAN SOCIETY & FIELD CLUB

LLANGEFNI 2020

To Joe, through thick and thin.

Text © Robin Grove-White 2020
*Rights of reproduction of all the illustrations
are retained by their copyright holders.*
All rights reserved

Published by
The Anglesey Antiquarian Society
Llangefni, Ynys Môn

www.hanesmon.org.uk

Production
Robert Williams, Llansadwrn
robert@robertwilliams.eu

Cover
A decorated drawing of Plas Coch, *c.*1865
(*Casgliad Brynddu*)

First published in 2020
ISBN 978-0-9568769-1-1

Contents

Illustrations

Author's foreword

WHAT WAS IT LIKE to be an educated Anglesey Welshman in the sixteenth century? Most of us have only the haziest idea — hardly surprising, given how few local records, pictures or journals from the period have survived. Nevertheless, this book is a kind of response to that question.

The Elizabethan period was a momentous one for Anglesey, as indeed for Wales as a whole. Under Elizabeth's father, Henry VIII, the Welsh became equal subjects under the crown for the first time, opening up all sorts of opportunities for those who chose to take advantage of them.

The Anglesey lawyer and landowner Hugh Hughes of Plas Coch, was such an individual. He lived most of his life in Anglesey between 1548 and 1609, and it's his story that provides the focus for what follows.

As for myself, I was brought up in Anglesey from the age of ten. Though largely Anglo-Irish, I'm partly Welsh — thanks to a loved and admired Anglesey grandmother, Anna Hughes-Hunter, who was born in Llanedwen in 1884. It was through her that in 1951, my father inherited the remains of her family's centuries-old Plas Coch / Brynddu estate. One result was that in the 1950s and early 'sixties, throughout my teenage years, we lived at Brynddu as the family home.

Brynddu is on the edge of Llanfechell in the north west of the island, best known locally for its association with the celebrated diarist William Bulkeley, another ancestor. He lived here all his life, between 1691 and 1760. It was not long after his death that Brynddu became joined with Plas Coch, through the marriage in 1765 of Jane, his granddaughter and heiress, to William Hughes of that house.

In 2004, my wife and I moved back to Brynddu, having retired after varied working lives in England and north America. Inevitably, living in a 400-year-old house with the accumulated family detritus of the centuries, I was drawn increasingly into the history. From the outset, my interest gravitated towards Hugh Hughes as a pivotal figure. Initial archive searches suggested he had been a significant public presence in Anglesey and north Wales in the late-Tudor and early-Jacobean periods. This was an encouragement to pursue him through a thesis at Bangor University's Welsh History Department several years ago.

Oddly, part of Hugh's attraction arose from a sense that my own life-experience contained faint echoes of his. True, there was a gap of five centuries between us, but there were similarities. Like him, I'd combined a landed Anglesey background and an English university education, and for a time worked in political London, straddling two cultures almost without noticing. Like him, I'd had a measure of cultural attunement to Welsh-speaking Anglesey and its local workings, whilst also having learnt to operate within the very different world of the British state, absorbing and operating within London's complex hier-archies, still to this day effectively a gigantic court — at home within the codes and practices of government departments, agencies with del-egated powers, Parliamentary officials, Inns of Court lawyers... And these echoes of similar experience seemed to equip me to intuit some of the personal tensions and challenges that might have arisen for Hugh in his own dealings with the two very different worlds of metropolitan London and rural Welsh-speaking Anglesey. Five hundred years on, some of the texture and manners of Hugh Hughes's day-to-day experi-ence, in both Anglesey and further afield, felt strangely accessible, in shadowy and skeletal form.

As the research progressed, I found that Hugh Hughes's story also needed to be understood in the context of a long-running theme amongst historians of Wales. This concerned the contribution people of his class and time are sometimes implied to have made in the alleged decline of Welsh uniqueness, through their 'anglicisation'. To many critics of a cultural-nationalist bent in the nineteenth and early twentieth centuries, the Welsh gentry (*uchelwyr*) of that earlier Tudor period had begun to sell their heritage for a mess of pottage, cynically abandoning Welsh ways and forsaking the language. And if academic historians in our own times are now less censorious, a flavour of gentry betrayal and neglectful self-interest in the wake of the 'acts of union' still lingers in present-day popular communications.

The more I explored the life of Hugh Hughes, the less persuaded I was that this offered a fair or adequate picture. On the contrary, it seemed, Welsh distinctiveness continued to flourish in the sixteenth and seventeenth centuries, and indeed well down into our own times, not least because of the subtle and realistic accommodations that Hugh Hughes and people like him had made back in that earlier period.

That at least is the thrust of the narrative that follows. My argument leads down various byways of both late-Tudor and early-Jacobean Wales and England, sometimes necessarily where direct documentary sources are uneven. Hugh Hughes played a role in a variety of local and regional institutions in the north Wales of his time, and by using him as a prism I've tried to clarify something of the fabric of the routine public life of the period both in Anglesey and further afield. This has involved a fair degree of historical imagination in R.G. Collingwood's sense, making the most of what are sometimes limited written records.

Hugh Hughes was a fresh kind of hybrid, thoroughly Welsh, whilst also educated in England and active professionally in what was in the process of becoming a British state. His tale has resonance for present-day discussions about Welsh identity — as I trust this Anglesey-based inquiry confirms.

ROBIN GROVE-WHITE
Brynddu, Llanfechell
February 2020

Glossary

Escheat The procedure whereby the tenement of a tenant who died without heirs, or in rebellion, or who was convicted of felony reverted to the lord.

Gwely (pl: **gwelyau**) Family or kinship group owning the collective rights to a holding, hence also the holding itself.

Hendre (pl: **hendrefi**) Homestead, or habitation

Maenol (pl: **maenolau**) A 'free' social and tenurial unit with dependent hamlets. After the 1282 conquest, because of their apparent similarities, *maenolau* tended to become manors in the English sense.

Maerdref The unfree township in each commote attached to the royal court there for its maintenance which corresponded, more or less, to the desmesne.

Rhaglaw Chief official of the commote (later, the 'hundred'), of which Menai was one of six on Anglesey. The post was carried over from the time of the princes following the 1282 conquest, with diminished administrative responsibilities, but lucrative perquisites in the form of fines on most legal actions within the commote.

Rhingyll In Gwynedd until the 'acts of union' (1536 and 1543), the *rhingyll* was the executive arm of royal government in the commote, responsible to the Auditor for crown rents and renders, with associated personal financial perquisites which were substantial. After this, the equivalent post was the bailiff of the hundred, subordinate to the sheriff.

Tref / Township Small settlement with several dwellings, acting (under old Cymric law) as a single community as regards cattle and ploughing.

Uchelwr (pl: **uchelwyr**) Literally, high one(s), equivalent to a gentry class, generally claiming gentility through lineal descent from (Welsh) royalty or its senior administrators.

Abbreviations

APC	Acts of the Privy Council
Arch.Camb.	*Archaeologia Cambrensis*
BBCS	*Bulletin of the Board of Celtic Studies*
BL	British Library
BM	British Museum
CUP	Cambridge University Press
HLQ	*Huntington Library Quarterly*
LI	Lincoln's Inn
NLW	National Library of Wales
ODNB	Oxford Dictionary of National Biography
OUP	Oxford University Press
RHS	Royal Historical Society
RCAHMWM	Royal Commission on Ancient & Historical Monuments in Wales and Monmouthshire
STAC	Star Chamber
TAAS	*Transactions of the Anglesey Antiquarian Society*
TCHS	*Transactions of the Caernarvonshire Historical Society*
THSC	*Transactions of the Honourable Society of Cymmrodorion*
TNA	The National Archives
UB	University of Bangor
UWP	University of Wales Press
WHR	*Welsh History Review*

> *"History buries most men, and exaggerates
> the height of those left standing"*
>
> John Updike, *Memories of the Ford Administration*

Plas Coch, Llanedwen, in 2020

Preface

LATE SIXTEENTH-CENTURY ANGLESEY may have been geographically remote from
the centre of the Elizabethan state. But it was subject nevertheless to influences
and pressures that were leading to the emergence of a new kind of political nation across mainland Britain – increasingly unified, yet also increasingly devolved in the distribution and exercise of power in the regions. This book
explores the experience of a single Anglesey individual caught up in these processes in the circumstances of late-Elizabethan and early-Jacobean north Wales.

The specific focus is the life and career of Hugh Hughes of Plas Coch, who
was born in Llanedwen in south-east Anglesey in 1548,[1] and died in London
in June 1609.[2] Hitherto largely unstudied, he was a successful lawyer and Anglesey landowner in the times of the first Queen Elizabeth and James 1st.

The book has a more ambitious aim than biography alone. The intention
has been to use this one man's personal experience to throw light on ways in
which Wales, and north Wales in particular, was being governed in the late-
Elizabethan and early-Jacobean periods, and for reflection on the evolving relationship between the Welsh and the English across the period.

Hugh was born shortly after the so-called 'acts of union' (1536 and 1543)[3]
had transformed the formal connection between Wales and England. He was
of the first generation of Welshmen to have been raised from the outset as an
unambiguously equal subject of the crown, with the associated 'rights and liberties', and indeed expectations, such standing entailed. He grew up culturally
an Anglesey Welshman and lived there for much of his life, yet his public life
and career were shaped throughout by English educational and wider cultural
influences.

---

1 In the absence of a confirmed date for Hugh's birth, the likely year has been inferred from the
 known date of his matriculation, 1564, at Trinity College Cambridge (W.W.Rouse Ball &
 J.A.Venn (eds), *Admissions to Trinity College* (Macmillan, London, 1911), 1:2, p.426) on the
 assumption that, in line with practice of the time, he would have gone to university at around
 the age of sixteen.

2 UB Plas Coch 184, the Inventory of his goods and chattels, dated 16 June 1609.

3 27 Hen VIII c.26 (1536) and 34-35 Hen VIII, c. 26 (1543), in I.Bowen (ed), *The Statutes of
 Wales* (London, Fisher Unwin, 1908).

The story could be of interest simply as that of a talented Welshmen who took full advantage of the educational and professional opportunities opening up in the late-Tudor period in the new federated polity crystallised by the 'union'. But it also has a richer significance. Like a number of his north Wales contemporaries, Hugh found success in the law, and this led to his becoming deeply involved in the machinery of government in the region at a number of levels. By tracking his commitments as a crown official and lawyer, it becomes possible to glimpse some of the ways in which, by the time of the troubled last decades of Elizabeth's reign, sophisticated bicultural Welshmen of his kind were indispensable for the smooth running of the by-then well established settlement.

Scrutiny of this kind may well have implications for a subtler appreciation of aspects of the Welsh-English relationship overall – perhaps down even to our own times. There are still those in Wales who believe that 'the fundamental purpose of the [1536] Act was to merge Wales in England, to assimilate the Welsh, to destroy their separate national identity ... [such that] every aspect of the menial status of the Welsh nation demonstrated Cymru to be a colony'.[4] If, on the contrary, the legal and administrative dispensation fostered by the 1536/1543 administrative changes, with the subsequent Elizabethan Protestant settlement, can be seen to have had a less aggressive or oppressive design, that same set of arrangements might be pictured as having contributed to the remarkable survival of the Welsh language and its associated culture into our own times. Examination of the experience of a key individual like Hugh in helping make such processes work during the late-sixteenth and early-seventeenth centuries may enhance understanding of that possibility too.

There has been a tendency in recent historical commentary to depict the approach to public office of Welsh 'gentry' individuals of this period as overwhelmingly self-serving. Glanmor Williams for example suggested that such 'officials, from highest to lowest, were all the while apt either to neglect their official responsibilities or else to exercise them in pursuit of their own advantage. They continued to react instinctively, in the first instance, as interested individuals and only secondly, if at all, as representatives of a distant government',[5] whilst G. Dyfnallt Owen has argued that 'with only a distant monarch, and the strictures, but not always enforceable penalties, of the Council of Wales, to restrain them, they were in a commanding position to regulate the affairs of the community in conformity with their interests and the requirements of their status as the dominant social class'.[6] David Williams has even gone so far as to

---

4   G. Evans, *The Fight for Welsh Freedom* (Talybont, Ceredigion, Y Lolfa Cyf, 2000), pp.99-100.

5   G. Williams, *Recovery, Reorientation and Reformation: Wales c.1415-1642* (Oxford, OUP, 1987), p.345.

6   G. Dyfnallt Owen, *Wales in the Reign of James I* (London, Royal Historical Society / Boydell Press, 1988), p.113.

suggest that the house of Gwydir, headed by the rapacious Sir John Wynn, was 'the prototype of all the gentry of Wales'.[7] Sound evidence can of course be produced to support such claims.

However an implication of the arguments developed in the following pages is that such disparagement of those engaged actively in government in Wales during this period should not be taken too far. Something rather different was also going on. In the decades following the acts of union, a new polity was beginning to consolidate across England and Wales, on a basis of what A.H. Dodd has called 'federation rather than fusion'[8] – that is to say, a political and social settlement in which key dimensions of Welsh distinctiveness were maintained under the umbrella of a new shared national jurisdiction. Nor could this have worked if there had not been at least a measure of integrity in the system. The discussion that follows shows how Hugh Hughes, like others of his kind, became a significant figure in the engine room of the new evolving entity. This involved not only legal skills and social sensitivity, but also a personal commitment to the changing social and political order across England and Wales.

The role of highly trained individuals like Hugh in these developments is one which has been examined only imperfectly in treatments of the period to date. Indeed, to the reader coming fresh to the literature, even the most impressive accounts of late-Tudor and early Jacobean Wales – by Glanmor Williams, Penry Williams, G. Dyfnallt Owen, G.H. Jenkins[9] and others – offer a tantalisingly incomplete picture of how the institutional matrix of the new 'Britain' implied by the union settled down to actually work. W.P. Griffith's authoritative study of higher education and professional training for Welshmen of the period[10] is an exception for the light it casts on the values and accomplishments of the Welsh intellectual classes of the time – as indeed are studies by J. Gwynfor Jones,[11] which have enriched understanding of the cultural norms and aspirations of the sixteenth-century North Welsh gentry. Nevertheless, for the most part the histories of the period choose to lay repeated stress on the escalating litigiousness of the sixteenth-century Welsh in general and gentry in particular, the self-serving behaviours of members of the new gov-

7   D.Williams, *A History of Modern Wales* (London, John Murray, 1965 edn), p.86

8   A.H.Dodd, 'The Pattern of Politics in Tudor Wales', *THSC* (1948), p.8.

9   G.Williams, *Recovery, Reorientation and Reformation*; P.Williams, *The Council in the Marches of Wales under Elizabeth I* (Cardiff, UWP, 1958); G.Dyfnallt Owen, *Elizabethan Wales, the social scene* (Cardiff, UWP, 1958); *Wales in the Reign of James I*; G.H.Jenkins, *Concise History of Wales* (Cambridge, CUP, 2007).

10   W.P.Griffith, *Learning, Law and Religion: Higher Education and Welsh Society c.1540-1640* (Cardiff, UWP, 1996).

11   J.Gwynfor Jones, *The Welsh Gentry 1536-1640: Images of Status, Honour and Authority* (Cardiff, UWP, 1998); *Law, Order and Government in Caernarfonshire 1558-1603: Justices of the Peace and Gentry* (Cardiff, UWP, 1996).

erning class, and the ruthlessness of the latter's scrambles for local office and social recognition.[12]

All of this is doubtless well-justified. Yet at the same time, in parallel with such emphases, there is recognition that somehow the new system produced relatively effective, and even popular, government – certainly, if such things can be measured, a significant improvement on that which had prevailed previously in Wales. George Owen was just one of those to express this view at the time (in 1594), 'No countrey [county] in England so flourished in one hundredth yeares as Wales hath don sithence the government of Henry VII to this tyme...' [13] At the very least there is a paradox here inviting explanation. Is it plausible that the complex machinery of the post-'acts of union' legal and political institutions could have been made to work satisfactorily by individuals who were overwhelmingly acquisitive and self-seeking? Is it not also likely that many of those involved were groping to uphold social codes and principles shaped by religious commitments, humane Renaissance values and growing respect for law, as well as distinctively Welsh cultural ideals of leadership?[14] Did not many of them also have an intellectual training combining rigour, breadth and depth in the terms of the time, as well as, in many cases, an energetic commitment to hard and even unselfish work in the public realm – reflecting in turn codes of civility and service of the kind articulated by renaissance humanists such as Erasmus and Castliglione, and, closer to home, Sir Thomas Elyot in *The Boke named the Governour*? [15] Indeed, what frequently appears understated alongside the well-justified criticisms of the early-modern Welsh ruling caste by Glanmor Williams, G. Dyfnallt Owen and others is allowance for the presence of a degree of moral seriousness in its individual members – which is to say, recognition of the extent to which such individuals may also have been attempting to enact, however erratically, an ethic of political responsibility involving 'coherence between intention and action'.[16] As will be seen, much of Hugh Hughes's life appears to manifest a seriousness of commitment of much this kind, however marked by occasional lapses.

The argument that follows is developed in two stages. The first two chapters seek to piece together the evidence concerning Hugh Hughes's personal origins, and his lifelong rootedness in the Welsh social milieux of late-Elizabethan

---

12 Dyfnallt Owen, *James I*, pp.176-179; J.Gwynfor Jones, *Wales and the Tudor State* (Cardiff, UWP, 1989), pp.59-66.

13 George Owen, *The Dialogue of the Government of Wales* (1594), in H.Owen, *The Description of Pembrockshire*, Vol 3 (London, Bedford, 1906), p.56.

14 See note 11.

15 W.P.Griffith, *Civility and Reputation: Ideas and Images of the 'Tudor Man' in Wales* (Bangor Studies in Welsh History, 1985).

16 A.Judt, *The Memory Chalet* (London, William Heinemann, 2010), p.31.

and early-Jacobean Anglesey. The subsequent four chapters then investigate his largely English education and legal training, and subsequent public career on both sides of Offa's Dyke.

Thus chapter one examines first his family's origins in pre-conquest Menai, the long history of its *gwely*, and the slow emergence of the Plas Coch estate from the mid-fifteenth century onwards. It is a picture with similarities to those of other Gwynedd *uchelwr* families of the period – the Maurices of Clennenau, for instance, or the Meyricks of Bodorgan. However, like every family history, it has its idiosyncratic features, in this case a lineage and adjacent kinsfolk leading back directly to the twelfth-century Porthaml strong man, Llywarch ap Brân. Hugh Hughes's identity as an increasingly prominent presence in early-modern Anglesey is thus shown to have derived from membership of a family that had been conspicuous in the south-east of the island since the medieval period, if not substantially before that.

> **Gwely** (pl: **gwelyau**)
> *Family or kinship group owning the collective rights to a holding, hence also the holding itself.*
>
> **Uchelwr** (pl: **uchelwyr**)
> *Literally, high one(s), equivalent to a gentry class, generally claiming gentility through lineal descent from (Welsh) royalty or its senior administrators.*

Chapter two pursues further the theme of Hugh's local embeddedness in an Anglesey which by the late sixteenth century was undergoing significant social, cultural and economic change, driven by population expansion, inflation, and a brutally dynamic land market. Like others of his kind, Hugh was engaged on his own account in the increasingly keen struggle for land during the century's later decades, and close examination of a particular protracted dispute with one of his Anglesey neighbours – the Rhydderchs of Myfyrian – throws light on prevailing patterns of routine social relationship within his social class, as well as showing how up-to-date legal and political insight was coming to have advantages in the new forms of struggle characteristic of the time. Reflecting the fluctuations in fortune of local families, Plas Coch with Hugh as proprietor rose in the 1580s, at the expense of the formerly more prestigious *gwely* of Myfyrian. The key protagonists were neighbouring kinsmen of the *uchelwr* class, and their struggle also hints at differences then crystallising within that class, as the needs of government in Wales within the post-union framework elevated some and reduced others.

Chapter three then considers Hugh's education, his professional training and practice as a lawyer, and his marriage. Through each of these life-stages, the English influence was strong. After early schooling, and probably grammar school, he matriculated and graduated at Cambridge in the mid-1560s – following which he qualified for the bar at Lincoln's Inn, an entity with which he retained an active personal association throughout his adult life, rising to Bencher and ultimately Treasurer, the top office of the society, at a time when

the Inns of Court were at the intellectual centre of debates of mounting constitutional significance. A relatively late marriage at the age of forty to Elizabeth, of the influential Montagu family of Northamptonshire, reinforced
Hugh's English connections. Indeed certain of his wife's male relatives remained important to him for the remainder of his life.

Nevertheless, as chapter four goes on to show, most of Hugh's mature years
were spent as a native Welshman in north Wales, where he was involved not
only in extending the family estate, but also in the machinery of government
of the region, at multiple levels from the local to the national. Both personally
and professionally he developed as a man who straddled two cultures, equally
at home in both. And through snapshots of his public roles in late Elizabethan
and early-Jacobean north Wales, the chapter seeks to provide insight into some
of the ways in which government in the region was working over the period –
as increasingly part of a larger British whole, yet also durably Welsh. The interlocking nature of his various posts is explored, including reflections casting
fresh historiographical light on the detailed workings of local government
within Anglesey.

Chapters five and six then focus on Hugh's wider involvements in governance at the national level. Chapter five takes as its focus three further key appointments of his mature years, as the Anglesey Knight of the Shire (county
MP) in the 1597 Parliament, as a member of the Council in the Marches from
1601, and as putative Chief Justice of Ireland in 1609. Discussion of his experience in these posts locates Hugh within some of the key political and constitutional concerns of the late-Tudor state, throwing further light on the ways
in which authority was working both within Wales and further afield.

Finally, in chapter six, his multiple accomplishments are considered in the
round and an attempt made to conceptualise his role and intentions in the
light of the recent historiography of post-union Wales and the late-Tudor English state. The integrated nature of the institutions of government for Wales
at the time, reflected directly in Hugh's own person and experience, is highlighted especially. Brief reflections are also offered on implications of the findings for present-day understanding of the Welsh-English relationship in the
twenty-first century.

Overall, this book examines the way in which Hugh Hughes developed as a
particular kind of bilingual actor in the evolving institutional fabric of the late-
Elizabethan nation, during what was a turbulent and creative period for British
governance and political culture. From the late 1570s onwards, his legal
promise and accomplishments gained him recognition, resulting in appointments to positions at local, regional and latterly national levels. And this appears to have put him in a position to contribute in a modest way to the
evolution of the union settlement.

In developing the analysis, it has been important from the outset to avoid unduly narrow or anachronistic understandings of two very different terms – 'lawyer' and 'Britain'. In present-day parlance, 'lawyer' tends to connote a professionally qualified specialist in legal knowledge and advocacy. Indeed in our own time, though lawyers come in many shapes and sizes, they tend to be pictured collectively as trained specialists in a circumscribed, if rigorous and intellectually esoteric, occupational space. Such a 'sectoral' conceptualisation is hardly adequate for the period with which we are concerned here. In the sixteenth century, whatever the specialist professional roles of particular individuals, lawyers and the law itself were carrying a deeper and more dynamic social significance. As W.J. Bouwsma, Christopher Brooks and others[17] have shown, throughout the sixteenth-century secularised legal discourse and mechanisms were moving rapidly to the centre of the political and social organisation of new forms of nation state in western Europe. The inexorable cultural momentum of this shift was reinforced by a far-reaching 'crisis of social order and belief'[18] throughout the century, a crisis manifested not only in the Reformation itself, but also in religious wars, intense international conflicts, inflation and depression, and recurrent social tensions and dislocation. The cultural response to such pressures and uncertainties in much of sixteenth-century Europe, suggests Bouwsma, was 'a singular exaltation of law as an antidote to disorder'.[19] Thus lawyers carried a distinctive social significance in Post-Reformation Britain as on continental Europe. They were political actors and philosophers of constitutional government, as well as mere jurists.

Certainly, the growing significance of the law can be seen in Tudor Britain. From early in the sixteenth century, there was continuous growth in the body of statute law in England (and Wales), paralleled by adaptations and reforms to the common law, in response to changing economic and social needs. The enactment and implementation of the innovative Elizabethan Poor Law, passed in the 1597-98 Parliament, in which Hugh himself was Anglesey's MP, is just one landmark example. What is more, in the fields of what we now understand as 'public administration' and 'local government', the boundaries between law on the one hand and politics and public policy on the other had yet to be distinguished, or even fully conceptualised. In such a context, the language and concepts of law came increasingly to shape and guide social experience and the interpretation of public life and events.

---

17 W.J.Bouwsma, 'Lawyers and Early Modern Culture', *American Historical Review* 78 (1973), pp.303-327; C.W.Brooks, *The Law, Politics and Society in Early Modern England 1450-1800* (Cambridge, CUP, 2008); C.Thorne, 'Tudor Social Transformations and Legal Change', *New York University Law Review*, 26 (1951), pp.10-23.

18 Bouwsma, 'Lawyers & Early Modern Culture', p.316.

19 Ibid., p.317.

As to the second term, 'Britain', this is used in what follows from time to time as a shorthand way of referring to the over-arching, post-union constitutional entity embracing England and Wales, in which the Welsh had become fully equal citizens with the English. It is intended, for the purposes of the argument, to refer to an entity that was still in Hugh Hughes's time in the process of *becoming*, a matter discussed more extensively in chapter six. This coinage of the term 'Britain' had substantive historical grounding, reflected both in the persistence of medieval myths of Welsh origins in an earlier Brythonic people descended from Brutus (and subsequently felt to be embodied in Henry Tudor, scion of Wyrion Eden),[20] and in parallel, deeply-embedded English political dreams from an earlier period. As Professor Rees Davies has observed, 'The idea of Britain exercised a powerful hold over the medieval mind. It had a depth, a resonance, a precision, and an incontestability which did not belong to its imprecise, contestable, and Johnny-come-lately competitors – England, Scotland, Wales ... It was also, throughout the early Middle Ages, a political aspiration. It presented a prospect of unity and simplicity in what was a fragmented and fissile world of ethnic divisions and short-lived hegemonies.'[21] Moreover, in the post-Reformation period the idea of Britain began to take on practical political plausibility and by the 1570s it had gained a powerful hold on the Elizabethan imagination, taking forms to which, as will be shown, Welsh intellectuals like John Dee were able to make a powerful contribution. The book is thus suggesting that it makes sense to see Hugh's career as being acted out in an emerging entity transcending simply 'England' or 'Wales', or some literal legal amalgam of the two. There was now also a new national community, both 'imagined'[22] and increasingly real, being brought into being, best thought of as 'Britain'.[23] The significance of this matter is discussed more fully in chapter six.

Within Wales, the formal institutional arrangements introduced by the 1536 and 1543 Acts were a striking instance of the creative use of statute already referred to. Those arrangements had three principal elements, each dovetailing with the others. At shire level, the 1536 Act[24] introduced county government

20 J.Davies, *A History of Wales* (London, Penguin, 1994), p.219.

21 R.R.Davies, The *First English Empire: Power and Identities in the British Isles 1093-1343* (Oxford, OUP, 2000), pp.35-36.

22 B.Anderson, *Imagined Communities: Reflections on the Origin and Spread of Nationalism* (London, Verso, 1983).

23 G.A.Williams, *When Was Wales?* (Bury St Edmonds, Black Raven Press, 1985), pp.121-131; A.Grant & K.J.Stringer, *Uniting the Kingdom? The Making of British History* (London, Routledge, 1995); J.S.Morrill & B.Bradshaw, *The British Problem c.1534-1707: State Formation in the Atlantic Archipelago* (London, St Martin's Press, 1996).

24 27 Henry VIII c. 26.

on the long-established English model, with Commissions of the Peace and Quarter Sessions, across Wales.[25] The marcher territories all became shires, like Anglesey, Caernarfonshire, Merioneth, Pembroke, Carmarthen, Flint and Cardigan under the pre-1536 arrangements. Above this, under the 1543 Act,[26] were the new Courts of Great Sessions, four in number and each with a circuit covering three or more counties. And at regional level, the revamped Council in the Marches took on an expanded role as a quasi-Privy Council for Wales as a whole. This customised system of interlocking judicial and administrative bodies was peculiar to Wales. In important respects, through its personnel, it offered a significant degree of what might be called home rule, under the over-arching jurisdiction of Westminster and the Crown.

There is evidence that within a generation the new system had achieved positive social and cultural impacts. In an officially commissioned appraisal,[27] William Gerard[28] felt able to report to Secretary of State Walsingham in 1576 that, whilst before the acts of union most of Wales had 'lived as a country of war and not as ... a country governed by law', now 'in Wales universally are as civil a people and obedient to law as are in England'. Thanks to early strong enforcement by Rowland Lee and his successor Presidents of the Council in the Marches of Wales, and (though Gerard does not mention it) the undramatic success of local government by county justices, the law was now generally observed across Wales, crucially including the former Marches, 'except in 3 or 4 petty corners', stated Gerard. There had been a drastic reduction in numbers of murders and highway robberies, such that the outstanding remaining problem was now 'cattle-stealing'. The new courts, especially the Council in the Marches, which though first established in 1473 had been given statutory recognition only in the 1543 Act, were proving an unquestionable success, as integral elements of the new administrative framework. Indeed they were becoming almost too successful, since their popularity across Wales was now resulting in an increasingly unmanageable volume of small suits and counter-suits.[29] Nor was such improvement simply a matter of more effective handling of disputes between individuals. Because most initiatives relating to what we would now understand as 'public administration' or 'local government' of the period were handled through this same three-tiered court system,

---

25 Under the 1536 Act.

26 34 & 35 Henry VIII c. 26.

27 'William Gerard's Discourse – Special Memorandum to Secretary of State Thomas Walsingham' reproduced in D.L. Thomas, 'Further Notes on the Court of the Marches, with Original Documents', in *Y Cymmrodor*, Vol XIII (1900), pp.97-164.

28 Gerard had been Vice President of the Council in the Marches between 1562 and 1568 under Sir Henry Sidney's Presidency.

29 Gerard, *Discourse*, p.148.

the growing popular acceptance of the authority of these bodies may also have reflected recognition of their relatively greater efficacy as vehicles of active government. This matter is discussed further in chapter four.

Overall, for many Welsh people, a notable feature of the acts of union settlement was the extension of opportunities available to Welshmen in the day-to-day running of their communities, largely in their own language,[30] through the county Commissions of the Peace, juries, constables, coroners, bailiffs and the like, as well as, more selectively, through service in the Council in the Marches or in the routine processes of the Courts of Great Sessions. The holders of many of these offices were from native families some of whom had been prominent in their areas in the period before the rearranged settlement (albeit the Great Sessions justices remained exclusively English till the following century). The evidence is that, as the tentacles of the multi-tiered system spread, for example at hundred and parish level, it incorporated a growing range of individuals from less obviously advantaged origins. At county level, the proliferating breadth and complexity of the justices' duties in the later years of the century, together with rising official expectations of their efficiency, created a pressing need for competent, educated individuals in key positions. In the late-Elizabethan context, this meant, increasingly, individuals whose property stake in the area was supplemented by legal training and skills. Hugh Hughes was one such.

He makes only fleeting appearances in recent histories of the period. Aspects of his career, as a lawyer specifically, are unravelled usefully in W.P. Griffith's above-mentioned *Learning, Law and Religion*,[31] in the context of a more general analysis of the experience of educated Welsh lawyers and churchmen of the period. But neither there nor in other studies of the period has his career been given sustained attention. He has tended to be sidelined as simply a Welsh gentry-lawyer, devoid of wider significance. Not only does he go unmentioned in the Dictionary of Welsh Biography,[32] but he makes no appearance in any of the key nineteenth-century biographical dictionaries either.

Any passing mentions in more recent journal articles tend to reflect a single source – the late Thomas Richards's introductory essay to the Plas Coch

---

30 Notwithstanding the 'language clause' making English the formal language of judicial and administrative record-keeping, Welsh continued to be used routinely at all levels of the courts system. See for example, R.Suggett, 'The Welsh Language and the Court of Great Sessions', and P.R.Roberts, 'Tudor Legislation and the Political Status of "the British tongue" ' – both in G.H.Jenkins (ed), *The Welsh Language before the Industrial Revolution* (Cardiff, UWP, 1997)

31 W.P.Griffith, *Learning, Law and Religion*, pp. 43, 149, 152, 154, 155, 158, 183, 184, 190, 196.

32 *Dictionary of Welsh Biography / Bywgraffiadur Cymreig* (Oxford, Blackwell / Hon Soc of Cymmrodorion, 1959).

manuscripts,[33] which offers a regional university archivist's perspective, written in 1937, on Hughes as 'the real founder of the fortunes of Plas Coch'.[34] Grounded though that essay is in extensive understanding of local genealogy and power networks, it predates the significant body of more recent historical research relevant to early-modern north Wales, by A.D. Carr, W. Ogwen Williams, J. Gwynfor Jones and others.[35] There is thus scope for a reappraisal of his role and significance in the light of the more recent historiography of the period.

---

33 The Plas Coch manuscripts (PC MSS) are held in the Bangor University Archives.

34 UB Plas Coch Vol I, *Introduction*, p.1.

35 *e.g.* A.D.Carr, *Medieval Anglesey* (Llangefni, Anglesey Antiquarian Society, 2011 revised edition); W.Ogwen Williams, *Tudor Gwynedd* (Caernarfon, Caernarvonshire Historical Society, 1958); Gwynfor Jones, *Law, Order and Government in Caernarfonshire.*

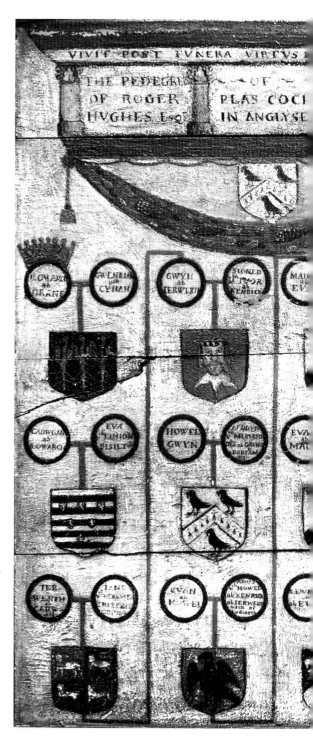

This genealogy, hand-painted by Owen Hughes for his brother Roger in 1697, shows the Plas Coch Hughes family lineage back to Llywarch ap Bran (left, top) in the twelfth century.

The late-Tudor Hugh Hughes of the present study is shown at the bottom of the fourth column.

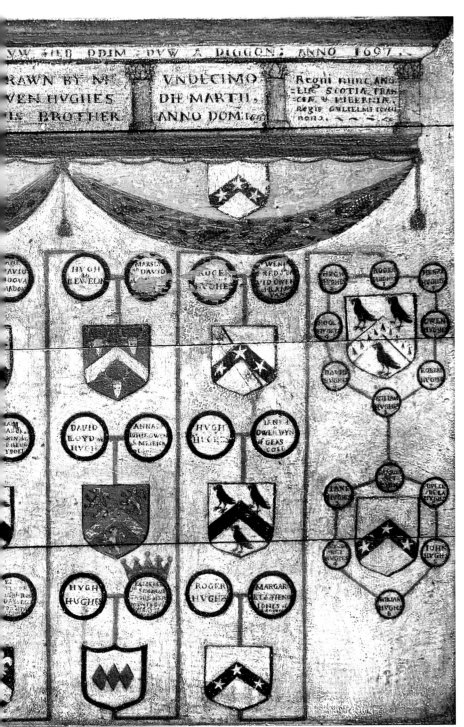

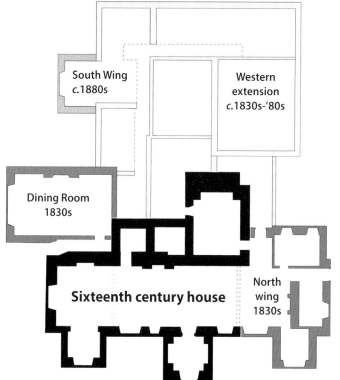

The Plas Coch ground plan shows the original sixteenth-century core of the house to have been the elements on the left of the photograph. The North Wing was a later addition, in the 1830s, skilfully mimicking the earlier 'Flemish' architectural style.

I *Porthaml and the Hughes of Plas Coch*

THE MOST VISIBLE remaining trace of Hugh Hughes today is Plas Coch – known as Porthaml Isaf until the late-sixteenth century – close by the Menai Strait at Llanedwen.[36] This striking mansion, with its Elizabethan neo-gothic exterior of pink limestone, has a stone surround above the front porch bearing the inscription, 'In the yere of Lord God 1569 DH mad this hou'. The 'DH' refers to Hugh Hughes's father, Dafydd Llwyd ap Huw, whose original 1569 construction was subsequently enlarged and reworked in the 1590s, apparently to Hugh's specification,[37] to create the impressive Flemish exterior which meets the eye today.[38] The flamboyance of this still-existing exterior clearly reflected an intention to create an 'outward symbol' [39] of the successful rise of a native Anglesey family.[40]

To appreciate Hugh, and the public roles he came to play in Anglesey and further afield, it is important first to have an understanding of his family origins and genealogy, and of the sense of himself these would have brought with them. The architectural flamboyance of Plas Coch in the context of late sixteenth-century Anglesey appears to have been an expression of Hugh's own self-belief, which this chapter suggests was grounded significantly in awareness of his family's standing in local Welsh society. Hence the central aim of this first chapter is to examine the origins and rise of the family, and the gradual build-up of material resources which made possible the construction of the mansion in the

---

36 Plas Coch is at British National Grid Reference SH 512684.

37 Royal Commission on Ancient & Historical Monuments in Wales and Monmouthshire, *An Inventory of the Ancient Monuments in Anglesey* (London, HMSO, 1937), p.55.

38 The house was expanded further on the west and north sides in the early nineteenth century, in closely matching style. The interior is largely of this later period.

39 G.Williams, *Religion, Language and Nationality in Wales* (Cardiff, UWP, 1979), p.155.

40 Investigation by Dr David Longley, former Director of the Gwynedd Archaeological Trust, has discovered beams and windows in the present Plas Coch mansion dating from the 1530s. This implies that Dafydd Llwyd's house incorporated elements of a substantial still earlier dwelling on the same site (D.Longley, personal communication, May 2011). These findings have yet to be published. The house exterior was sensitively restored *c.* 2010 under the tenure of James McAllister. It is currently owned by Park Leisure.

late-sixteenth century. In the process, the account touches on aspects of the medieval social history of Anglesey, and in particular patterns of land acquisition and tenure in the south-east corner of the island. This is important not only for what it reveals about the origins of Plas Coch, but also for an appreciation of the complexities of kinship and community which would have informed Hugh's self-understanding, as his career developed on both sides of the Welsh-English border.

Hugh's antecedents had an intimate association with Porthaml – and indeed with the very ground on which Plas Coch itself came to stand – reaching back to at least the twelfth century. Convergent documentary sources[41] show that the Plas Coch Hughes were direct male heirs and descendants of Llywarch ap Brân, a high official in the service of Owain Gwynedd (1137-1170).[42] Moreover, there are indications that antecedents of this Llywarch had been dominant figures in the Porthaml area for a number of generations prior to that. Henry Rowlands, writing in 1710,[43] pointed to field and rock names close to the Plas Coch site referring to Llywarch's father, Brân, and his grandfather, Dyfnwal – and research by David Longley[44] tends to confirm that Llywarch's forebears had probably been dominant free-holders in the neighbourhood during a lengthy earlier period.[45] Indeed, Longley's research appears implicitly to challenge Jones-Pierce's seminal proposition[46] that key Anglesey free townships were created *de novo* by political fiat of Owain Gwynedd in the mid-twelfth century, suggesting instead that such free-holding lordships had probably already had a long existence prior to Owain's reign, making the later twelfth-century formalisation of township boundaries a matter of accommodation to existing political fact, rather than royal patronage pure and simple. However, Henry Rowlands's further suggestion[47] that the Plas Coch family could trace its descent directly from Tudwal Gloff, son of the ninth-century Rhodri Mawr, is too tenuous to be secure.[48]

---

41 These sources include UB Baron Hill 6714 – the 1352 *De Delves* Extent, reproduced in A.D.Carr, 'The Extent of Anglesey, 1352', *TAAS* (1971-72), pp.150-272; Revd H.Rowlands, 'Antiquitates Parochiales, XII & XIII', *Arch.Camb.* 4 (1849); and the Hughes family records – *Pedigree of Hughes of Plas Coch* (1869, original uncatalogued manuscript held at Brynddu, Llanfechell,Ynys Môn).

42 Llywarch is identified as a 'prominent minister of the prince's *curia*' in D.Stephenson, *The Governance of Gwynedd* (Cardiff, UWP, 1984), p.125.

43 Rowlands, *Arch.Camb.* 4, XII.

44 David Longley, personal communication, December 2008.

45 Ibid.

46 T.Jones-Pierce, 'Medieval Settlement in Anglesey', *TAAS* (1951), pp.1-33.

47 Rowlands, *Arch.Camb.* 4.

48 G.P.Jones, 'Notes on Some Non-Dynastic Anglesey Clan-Founders', *TAAS* (1923), pp.35-48.

Llywarch ap Brân's descendants

> **Maenol** (pl: **maenolau**)
> A 'free' social and tenurial unit
> with dependent hamlets. After
> the 1282 conquest, because of
> their apparent similarities,
> maenolau tended to become
> manors in the English sense.

Henry Rowlands suggested the further likelihood that, before 1282, Porthaml had been a *maenol*, a small and consolidated free township (*tref*) with a court and dependent bond hamlets (*rhandiroedd*) including Llanedwen, Bodlew, Bodowyr, Myfyrian, Berw Uchaf, Cefn Poeth, and Tresgawen.[49] [Map, page 22]. He cited as supporting evidence wording in a 1317 charter marking a property transfer between two of Llywarch ap Brân's great-grandsons, one of them Hugh Hughes's direct ancestor, Gwyn ap Iorwerth ap Cadwgan.[50] More recently, A.D. Carr has confirmed the probability of a Porthaml *maenol* vested in 'a prominent figure in twelfth-century Gwynedd',[51] presumably Llywarch, as both a top official of Owain Gwynedd and local strong man in the area – a suggestion consistent with present understanding both of Llywarch's role as leader of one of the key free Anglesey kindreds,[52] and of political-administrative initiatives by Owain Gwynedd in mid twelfth-century Anglesey, whereby he consolidated favoured local lordships of key allies.[53]

As the 1352 extent confirms, three of Llywarch's sons – Cadwgan, Iorwerth and Madog – established separate *gwelyau* in Porthaml in the late twelfth century, consistent with the Welsh inheritance law of *cyfran*.[54] Iorwerth's line appear to have settled at Porthaml Uchaf, at or close to the site of the present Porthaml Hall, whilst Madog established a second *gwely* within the township, close by 'in the commote of Menai'.[55] The second son, Cadwgan, based himself at what subsequently became known as Porthaml Isaf, closest to the ancestral site, now Plas Coch.[56] Hence it was Cadwgan's line which grew to become, eventually, the Hughes family of Plas Coch, his descendants staying the course both procreatively and topographically. Henry Rowlands commented in 1710,

49 There is however no confirmation of this in the 1352 extent, which states simply of Porthamel, 'this township is free'. Carr, 'The Extent of Anglesey', p.254.

50 Rowlands, *Arch.Camb.* 4, XIII.

51 Carr, *Medieval Anglesey*, p.155.

52 E.Gwynne Jones, 'Some Notes on the Principal County Families of Anglesey in the Sixteenth and Early Seventeenth Centuries', *TAAS* (1939), p.66.

53 J.Beverley Smith, 'Owain Gwynedd', *TCHS* (1971), pp 8-17. Also, D. Longley, 'Medieval Settlement and Landscape Change in Anglesey', *Landscape History* 23 (2001), pp.39-60.

54 *Cyfran*: the native Welsh inheritance law of partible succession, akin to gavelkind in English terms.

55 Rowlands, *Arch.Camb.* 4, XII.

56 Ibid.

'which is rather unusual, it is found that males alone, in the family line, have inherited [Plas Coch] throughout such a long space of time'.[57] Indeed, the Porthaml Isaf / Plas Coch line was to continue unbroken, at the same site, over the 800 years between the mid-twelfth and mid-twentieth centuries. As will be shown, the Plas Coch estate which accumulated around the Porthaml Isaf *gwely* was slow to develop, but its rump survives vestigially to this day.

Rowlands also recorded that in 1710 his Rectory held records of at least twelve families descended from Llywarch's three sons, each with its own property in Llanedwen or a neighbouring parish. As will be seen, the relationships between these families and Porthaml Isaf / Plas Coch ran anything but smoothly, as the period of estate assembly accelerated in the late fifteenth and sixteenth centuries.

To clarify the nature of the obstacles as well as the opportunities which had to be negotiated in the early development of *gwely* Cadwgan, it is useful first to outline the evolving shape of land tenure patterns as they developed within pre-conquest Welsh and post-conquest English customary and legal frameworks. The key social and political division within medieval pre-conquest Gwynedd society was that between 'free' and 'bond' status. Porthaml and its dependent hamlets were free townships, abutting on the south and east sides onto crown lands attached to the royal *maerdref* of Rhosyr, which included a number of bond *trefs*, hamlets and *gwelyau*. Under native inheritance law in free communities, rights in land gave a life interest only. Land was vested in the kindred group rather than the individual person. It was thus an entitlement to a lifetime share rather than absolute possession of the land itself which passed to an occupant's heir. What is more, if an individual died without an heir within four degrees of consanguinity, or was convicted of a felony, his share escheated to the lord. In such cases the land tended then to be leased to a further individual for an annual rent, to be paid to the lord in addition to the lessee's share of the *gwely*'s overall annual obligation – which increasingly came to take the form of a monetary commutation of former food renders and services, a pattern which was hastened by the 1282 conquest. On the ground, the pattern of agricultural organisation was the open field, with each occupant holding a number of scattered strips, as well as a share of the *gwely*'s common pasture and waste.

Maerdref   *The unfree township in each commote attached to the royal court there for its maintenance which corresponded, more or less, to the desmesne.*

Escheat   *The procedure whereby the tenement of a tenant who died without heirs, or in rebellion, or who was convicted of felony reverted to the lord.*

---

57 Ibid.

Spreading out

Jones-Pierce's groundbreaking studies[58] of the evolution of tenurial and land accumulation practices in medieval Anglesey and Caernarfonshire suggest how such matters may have evolved in practice. For example, his Llysdulas (in the Anglesey commote of Twrcelyn) study[59] shows how, from the twelfth century, individual families deriving from a free kindred spread out from the originating *hendrefi* [60] over successive generations, to colonise fresh areas within the township, creating new hamlets in ever more dispersed fashion. Much of this pattern can be seen to have also taken place in Porthaml, where the workings of *cyfran* led to accumulating dispersal of younger siblings from each generation to holdings in hamlets within and beyond the township. Thus for example by the time of the 1352 Extent,[61] at least four *gwelyau* founded by descendants of Iorwerth ap Llywarch's son, Maredudd, were in existence.[62] Jones-Pierce argues in a further Caernarfonshire-based study[63] that over successive generations such processes inevitably generated their own tensions. In particular, *gwely* lands distributed in a variety of increasingly distant hamlets tended to become seen by the families working them as effectively their own individual holdings. In part, this was a 'natural' process, flowing from the close working familiarity of such individuals with the places in which they lived and sustained a livelihood, and from their new, less interdependent relationships with neighbours similarly detached from their originating *gwelyau*. Within Porthaml, such processes can be seen in hamlets spun off from the Porthaml Isaf / Plas Coch family, such as Berw and Myfyrian. In each case, younger siblings of Cadwgan ap Llywarch's descendants became established at locations distant from the antecedent *gwely*, at sites which evolved over subsequent centuries to become the consolidated individual farms still evident to this day. Thus for example, descendants of Llewelyn, the youngest son of Iorwerth ap Cadwgan ap Llywarch, established themselves at Myfyrian from the early-twelfth till the late-sixteenth century.[64] Similarly, at Berw, a further (later) Iorwerth ap Llywarch descendant, Hywel ap Llewelyn ap Dafydd ap Ieuan, was in the preliminary stages of estate-build-

58 T.Jones-Pierce, 'Medieval Settlement in Anglesey', *TAAS* (1951), pp.1-33; 'Some Tendencies in the Agrarian History of Caernarvonshire during the later Middle Ages', *THCS* (1939), pp.18-36.

59 Jones-Pierce 'Medieval Settlement', *passim*.

60 **Hendref** (pl: *hendrefi*): habitation.

61 UB Baron Hill 6714. Also, Carr, 'Extent of Anglesey'.

62 Ibid. See also Stephenson, *Governance of Gwynedd*, pp.110-11. The *gwelyau* in question were at Ysceifiog, Llanfigel, Trelywarch and Clegyrog.

63 Jones-Pierce 'Some Tendencies', pp.18-36.

64 Griffith, *Pedigrees*, pp. 109, 119, 309.

ing in the early fifteenth century, following several generations of his antecedents' residence in the hamlet.[65]

By the mid-fourteenth century, a range of hard-edged economic and social realities were reinforcing and accelerating these developments.[66] A crucial consequence, as Jones-Pierce suggests, was that the 'reciprocal rights and duties' which had been the defining features of the *gwely* in and around Porthaml, as elsewhere in free Anglesey and Caernarfonshire townships, were being steadily eroded. Communal ownership was yielding increasingly to patterns of individual accumulation through the media of purchase, mortgage and exchange, leading inexorably towards concentrations of holdings under single proprietorships.[67] These dynamics manifested themselves at different rates in different parts of Gwynedd and elsewhere in Wales; the forcefulness and ambition of particular individuals was clearly a key determinant in the exploitation of such opportunities, as will be seen in the next section in relation to the Porthaml Uchaf family.

Black Death and Glyndŵr rebellion

The economic and social realities referred to immediately above were of diverse kinds. Under native Welsh law, alienation could only occur through a licence from the lord, and after the conquest such licenses became ever easier to obtain.[68] Legal fictions such as the *tir prid* form of unredeemed mortgage became increasingly well used, as the impetus towards rationalisation of impracticably small and dispersed *cyfran* strips grew steadily. Such tendencies were given added momentum by the conspicuous daily examples of neighbouring colonists entitled to operate within English legal doctrines of inheritance (*i.e.* primogeniture) and land tenure. However, across the post-conquest period as a whole, the most crucial factor affecting land markets was the calamitous impact of the Black Death (1348-1350) which, by decimating the populations of both free and bond communities across the region, made substantial swathes of land available for encroachment and sale. And compounding the effects of this natural disaster, the wave of escheats and crown confiscations following the Glyndŵr rebellion of the early 1400s brought still more land onto the market.

Hence, in Anglesey as elsewhere, through a variety of contingencies in the fourteenth and fifteenth centuries, it was becoming possible for native individuals to accumulate and pass on increasingly significant, if still at this stage mod-

---

65 Carr, *Medieval Anglesey*, p.129.

66 The realities in question are elaborated in the section following.

67 Jones-Pierce, 'Some Tendencies', pp.29-35.

68 L. Beverley Smith, 'The gage and the land market in late medieval Wales', *Economic History Review* 29 (1976), pp.537-541.

est, personal estates, despite the formal persistence of *cyfran*. Jones-Pierce's close analysis of the Clennenau estate and family in the fifteenth and sixteenth centuries[69] shows a comparably aspiring family in south Caernarfonshire exploiting such opportunities in a fashion with apparent similarities to the acquisition patterns of Hugh Hughes's antecedents. Jones-Pierce shows how, through *tir prid* acquisitions of the tenurial rights of neighbouring *priodorion* in small, increasingly fragmented holdings, and subsequently, in the early decades of the sixteenth century, a succession of direct purchases of tenements, cottages, plots, and mill leases, as well as encroachments on crown lands, Morris ap John ap Maredudd and his son Elise were laying the foundations of what was to become the substantial estate of Clennenau, in Eifionydd. The Plas Coch papers contain at least one indication of a *tir prid* transaction by one of Hugh Hughes's antecedents.[70] Probably the device was also being used by his ancestors Madoc ap Ieuan ap Hywel between 1438 and 1447, and the latter's son Ieuan ap Madoc and grandson Llewelyn ap Ieuan between 1448 and 1500, alongside the more conventional 'releases' and grants-in-fee for which documents have survived.[71] What is more, there is also evidence of crown land encroachments by the last-named of these individuals in the fine and pardon by Arthur, Prince of Wales, dated 20 September 1495, for the Llewelyn ap Ieuan's stated 'intrusions on lands in Porthaml and Bodronyn.'[72]

Gwely Cadwgan & Gwely Iorwerth

A further useful perspective on the emergence of the Porthaml Isaf / Plas Coch estate, and hence on the gradual processes of resource assembly enabling eventual construction of the 1569 mansion, can be gained through consideration of the relative fortunes of, and interactions between the two primary Porthaml *gwelyau* in the late medieval and early-modern periods. Plas Coch, formerly Porthaml Isaf, and Porthaml Hall, formerly Porthaml Uchaf, are next-door neighbours to this day (in 2020) with grounds abutting onto one another's. In the medieval period, the two families, living in the same close proximity, albeit in the radically different communal and agricultural circumstances of the period, would have been acutely aware of their shared ancestry. It is plausible to speculate that a mixture of pride and rivalry would have obtained between them. Marriages and land sales between the two occurred sporadically. For ex-

---

69 T. Jones-Pierce, 'The Clennenau Estate', in T. Jones-Pierce (ed) *Introduction to Clennenau Letters and Papers in the Brongyntyn Collection*, NLW Supplement Series Pt.I (Aberystwyth, 1947).

70 UB Plas Coch 12 – a four-year 'assignment' of lands in Gwydryn.

71 *e.g.* UB Plas Coch 1, 2, 7, 8, 9, 10, 13 & 14. See also the Table on page 11.

72 UB Plas Coch 22.

ample, Arddun, daughter of Maredudd Ddu ap Goronwy of Porthaml Uchaf, married Hywel ap Gwyn ap Iorwerth of Porthaml Isaf in c. 1350;[73] and Maredudd Ddu's great-granddaughter Mallt married Ieuan ap Madog of Porthaml Isaf in c. 1440-50.[74] And, as noted previously,[75] there is at least one example from the fourteenth century of a land transfer between the two *gwelyau*.

In the fourteenth and fifteenth centuries it was Iorwerth ap Llywarch's line, at Porthaml Uchaf, which flourished especially. Iorwerth's eldest son, Maredudd, continued in the style of his grandfather, Llywarch. He was a beneficiary of significant land grants in the mid-thirteenth century from Llewelyn ab Iorwerth,[76] as well as being (like his grandfather Llywarch) a prominent minister in that prince's *curia*.[77] In the wake of the 1282 conquest, this Maredudd's grandson, Maredudd Ddu ap Goronwy, was *rhaglaw* of Menai and, as a leading man of Anglesey, had done homage and fealty to the new English Prince of Wales at Caernarfon, in 1301.[78] Two generations later, Maredudd Ddu's own grandson, Maredudd ap Cynwrig, built further on this legacy, both before and after the Glyndŵr rebellion, in which he was active, and for which he was subsequently fined and pardoned in 1406.[79] Swiftly rehabilitated as an indispensable local leader, he then became steward of the borough of Newborough, approver of the manor of Rhosyr, and under-sheriff of the county,[80] and in 1417 was also appointed the king's sergeant-at-arms in Anglesey.[81] In parallel he became farmer of the manors of Cemaes, Penrhosllugwy, the Llannerch-y-medd tolls, and subsequently Newborough, Rhosyr and the Llanidan ferry.[82] In Carr's words, Maredudd ap Cynwrig was 'perhaps the greatest accumulator of farms and offices in medieval Anglesey'.[83]

> **Rhaglaw** *Chief official of the commote (later, the 'hundred'), of which Menai was one of five on Anglesey. The post was carried over from the time of the princes following the 1282 conquest, with diminished administrative responsibilities, but lucrative perquisites in the form of fines on most legal actions within the commote.*

---

73 P.C.Bartrum, *Welsh Genealogies AD 300-1400* (Cardiff, UWP, 1974), Llywarch ap Brân 3.

74 Ibid.

75 Jones-Pierce 'Medieval Settlement', passim.

76 Stephenson, *Governance of Gwynedd*, p.98.

77 Ibid., p.110-111.

78 TNA SC 6/1170/ & 1227/7.

79 G.Roberts,'The Anglesey submissions of 1406', *BBCS* 15 (1952), p.57.

80 TNA SC 6/1152/4 6a.

81 *Calendar of the Patent Rolls 1416-1422*, p.101.

82 TNA SC 6/1152/5 2a, 4a.

83 Carr, *Medieval Anglesey*, p.211; and 'Maredudd ap Cynwrig: a medieval public person', *TAAS* (1988), pp.13-21.

The indications are that, by contrast, the family of *gwely* Cadwgan at Porthaml Isaf were left far behind their successful kinsmen during this period. By 1352, *gwely* Iorwerth is recorded as including six bovates of escheat land, reckoned as a twenty-fourth part of the whole, which must thus have been around 576 acres. By contrast, *gwely* Cadwgan held half a bovate of escheat, implying just forty acres.[84] Seventy years later, by the time of Maredudd ap Cynwrig's death in *c.*1428, the gap in terms of both land and influence was increasing still further – and further afield. In other words, at this stage the Porthaml Isaf family, despite occupying the 'founder' Llywarch's ancestral site, were very much in the shadow of their Porthaml Uchaf kinsmen.

It was not until after the Glyndŵr rebellion, in which the heads of both households had participated, that *gwely* Cadwgan began to expand significantly. Unlike Maredudd ap Cynwrig, who, as already mentioned, had been pardoned in 1406, Madog ap Ieuan ap Hywel of Porthaml Isaf was still in rebellion in 1408-9; he is assumed to have made his peace soon afterwards.[85] The dislocation of the economy of north Wales in the decades following the Glyndŵr rebellion and the subsequent upheavals of the Wars of the Roses, helped create drastically new conditions in land markets in Anglesey, as the century advanced.[86] A sense of individual proprietorship was becoming increasingly the norm with the waning of collective social bonds, at the very time when the workings of *cyfran* were creating an excessive fragmentation of holdings, to the point where the latter were becoming progressively too small to sustain individual livings. Probably reaping the opportunities created by this situation, the earliest documented purchases of land by the Porthaml Isaf family took place in 1438[87] and 1439,[88] by Madog ap Ieuan ap Hywel, Cadwgan ap Llywarch's direct lineal descendant. And from that point on (as the Table on page 11 shows), for the next 180 years, there was a steady increase in the rate of the family's acquisition of lands and associated income in Porthaml township and beyond, as has already been indicated.

In contrast to this burgeoning expansion of Porthaml Isaf, the momentum of accumulation associated with the Porthaml Uchaf family appears to have stabilised by the mid-fifteenth century. Four generations after Maredudd ap Cynwrig, the sons of his descendant Hwlcyn failed between them to produce

---

84 UB Baron Hill 6714.

85 TNA SC 6/1233/1. Also Carr, *Medieval Anglesey*, p.172.

86 Williams, *Tudor Gwynedd*, pp.39-40.

87 UB Plas Coch 1. This purchase was made in Porthamel by Madog ap Ieuan ap Howel, Cadwgan ap Llywarch's direct descendant.

88 UB Plas Coch 2.

any male heirs, and chose to sell their shares in the Porthaml Uchaf lands (including what is now Plas Newydd).[89] By 1482, all of these Porthaml properties had been purchased by William Griffith of Penrhyn (also known as 'Gwilym Fychan' and 'Gwilym ap Gruffudd').[90] Subsequently, in *c.*1550, Porthaml Uchaf and the residue of its lands passed to the extensive Bulkeley estates through the marriage of the Griffith heiress, Elin ferch Risiart ap Llewelyn, to Rowland Bulkeley of Llangefni.[91] Thus during precisely the period in which the fortunes of the Porthaml Isaf family were beginning to rise, the resources of the previously more dynamic Porthaml Uchaf family were being absorbed into the larger estates of the two most powerful Carnarfonshire and Anglesey families.

Porthaml Isaf becomes Plas Coch

By the late fifteenth century, Llewelyn ap Ieuan ap Madoc, the grandfather of the Dafydd Llwyd who was to initiate the construction of Plas Coch, was becoming a significant landowner and public office-holder. Between 1476 and 1500, he acquired at least nine properties in or close by Porthaml, largely grants in fee from other free Porthaml residents[92] – probably individuals who were finding it impossible to sustain a living on such small holdings, in what was becoming increasingly a cash economy.[93] Moreover, with such land resources came prestige and significant local office. In January 1478-9, Llewelyn was appointed a *rhingyll* of Menai commote.[94] The fortunes of the Porthaml Isaf family were advancing.

> **Rhingyll** *In Gwynedd until the 'acts of union' (1536 and 1543), the rhingyll was the executive arm of royal government in the commote, responsible to the Auditor for crown rents and renders, with associated personal financial perquisites which were substantial. After this, the equivalent post was the bailiff of the hundred, subordinate to the sheriff.*

The Table opposite summarises the geographical patterns of land accumulation through six generations of Llewelyn's antecedents and descendants. The emphasis evident in this Table on acquisitions in Porthaml township between 1438 and 1500 is confirmed by a crown rental undertaken in the late 1490s for Menai, documenting properties then in individuals' possessions across the commote.[95] This shows that whilst Llewelyn's holdings in the township at that

---

89 Rowlands, *Arch.Camb.* 4, XII. Also Carr, *Medieval Anglesey*, pp.209-210.

90 Ibid.

91 Griffith, *Pedigrees*, p.56.

92 UB Plas Coch 7, 8, 9, 10, 13, 14, 18, 19, 20, 21.

93 Williams, *Tudor Gwynedd*, p.40.

94 UB Plas Coch 11.

95 NLW Carreglwyd 135.

stage were still modest in relation to those of, for example, his neighbour Robert Gruffudd at Porthaml Uchaf, they were nevertheless significant. Moreover, after 1500, his reach can be seen from the Table to have broadened into Talybolion[96] and across the Strait into Caernarfonshire.[97]

The pattern of cumulative land acquisition, 1430 to 1609

Source: *Schedules of Plas Coch Manuscripts, Volumes I & II*

FAMILY HEAD	Documented acquisitions and locations	*… and offices at the time*
1430 — 1450 **Madog ap Ieuan**	**2** Porthaml (1) Gwydryn (1)	
1450 — 1475 **Ieuan ap Madog**	**1** Porthaml (1)	
1475 — 1500 **Llewelyn ap Ieuan**	**9** Porthaml (7) 'Menai com.' (1) Tre'r-beirdd (1)	*Constable/Guardian of the Peace, Menai com.* 1481
1500 — 1548 **Hugh ap Llewelyn**	**13** Porthaml (11) 'Talybolion com.' (1) 'Menai com.' (1)	*Rhingyll, Menai com.* 1499 *Bailiff, Menai com.* 1513, 1518-23(?)
1548 — 1570 **Dafydd ap Hugh**	**17** Porthaml (11) Bodlew (1) 'Menai com.' (1) Caernarvon (1) *plus mills:* Pensynllys, Celli Ddu and Rhos y Cerrig	
1570 — 1609 **Hugh Hughes**	**42** Porthaml (20) Ysceifiog (4) Alaw (3) Gwydryn (2) Bodlew (1) Maesoglan (1) Bodrida (1) Nancoll, Caerns. (1) Newchurch, Kent (1) London (1) 'Dindaethwy com.' (1) 'Talybolion com.' (1) Rhosfair (1) Cleifiog (1) *plus mill:* Rhosfair / *plus ferries:* Talyfoel and Porthaethwy	*Seneschal of Rhosfair manor* 1580, 1603 *Seneschal of manors of Celleiniog, Cornewey, Penmynydd, and Bodgaewith* 1586, 1603 *Deputy Steward of 'manors & land of the Bishop of Bangor'* 1595 *High Sheriff of Anglesey* 1581,1592,1600 *Deputy Attorney General for North Wales* 1589 *Attorney General for North Wales* 1596 *MP Anglesey* 1597 *Council in the Marches* 1601

96   UB Plas Coch 25.

97   UB Plas Coch 74.

Building for the future

Llewelyn's son and heir Huw appears have been a further quietly important figure in the family's progress. He continued to build up the family's land assets in the surrounding area,[98] whilst also holding significant office in the commote for a lengthy period between 1500 and the mid-1520s, as *rhingyll*.[99] Tax records for the 1540s – relating in particular to the subsidy collections of 1546 and 1547 – point to his having been relatively modestly placed amongst Menai property-owners of the time, listed twentieth in the commote in terms of income from land, and sixth or seventh in terms of goods.[100] Nevertheless, the latter in particular represented significant wealth, pointing possibly to sources of income – from trade in cattle for example – over and above the accumulating land rentals. In fact, in July 1544, just before these subsidy assessments, he had formally sold all of this estate to his son Dafydd, whilst retaining its use during his own lifetime.[101] Earlier, probably in the late 1530s, he had sent Dafydd to be educated in England at Hereford Cathedral School,[102] a decision hinting at strategic aspirations for the family, around the time of the acts of union.[103] Perhaps Huw's wife Marsli was a particular influence in this regard. She was a sister of the locally powerful Rhydderch ap Dafydd of Myfyrian, the latter a former *gwely* with strong ancestral connections to the Porthaml Isaf clan,[104] and a notable nest of local high achievers.[105] Both Marsli and Huw appear to have been well respected. They were mourned on their deaths, in 1557 and 1562 respectively, in elegies (*marwnadau*) by the bard Lewis Menai.[106] These suggest that Porthaml Isaf was known as giving hospitality to poets, and more particularly that Huw himself was modest and altruistic in reputation:

> Didrwst oedd, da'i dryst y wan,
> Diwyd, iach oedd, di-duchan,
> Ni ddymunai ddim enwir.

---

98   *e.g.* UB Plas Coch 25, 33, 35, 36, 39, 42.

99   UB Plas Coch 23, 24, 26, 27, 28, 29, 30, 31.

100   TNA E 179/219/4 (37 Henry VIII) and E 179/219/5 (38 Henry VIII). The respective values were 40 shillings p.a. (land) and £9 6s 8d (goods)

101   UB Plas Coch 50.

102   UB Plas Coch 55.

103   The issue is discussed in more detail in Chapter 2.

104   See note 74.

105   The Myfyrian family were to feature prominently in Hugh Hughes's life later in the century, a matter addressed in Chapter 2.

106   Lewis Menai graduated as an 'apprentice of the master craft' at the Caerwys Eisteddfod of 1567 (G. Thomas, *Eisteddfodau Caerwys*, Cardiff, UWP, 1968), p.97.

Ni funnai swydd a fewn o sir.
Ei goel drwy hwsmonaeth a gad,
Duwoliaeth ac adeilad …[107]

> ' Unpretentious, good in his dealings with the weak,
> Diligent, sound as he was, uncomplaining,
> He did not desire any falsehood.
> He did not seek appointment in his county.
> His trust was got through husbandry,
> Godliness and tenancy … '

Allowing for the usual hyperbole, such lines hint at an individual standing somewhat apart from the acquisitive and competitive drives of some of his neighbours, attracting respect (as well as office) for personal competence and decency, complementing the far-sightedness evident in early recognition of the potentials of an English education for his eldest son and heir, Dafydd.

Dafydd's ambitions

Thomas Richards claims in his 'Introduction to Volume I of the Plas Coch manuscripts' that 'the real founder of the fortunes of Plas Coch was Hugh Hughes'.[108] However, that ascription more properly belongs to Dafydd, as Hugh's father. It was Dafydd (in adult life known generally as Dafydd Llwyd) who built up the resources which permitted the 1569 construction of the new Plas Coch mansion, as well as those needed for the extended English education of at least two sons, Hugh and Owain – at Trinity College Cambridge and Lincoln's Inn for the first, and at Jesus College Oxford for the other.[109] There is a problem however in establishing quite where his money came from, even allowing for the fact that he was building on the fruits of his antecedents' efforts. He was not an ostensibly wealthy man – better off than his father had been, but still no more than comfortable by the local standards of the time. The Anglesey subsidy collection for 1568 lists him ('dd ap hugh ap lln ap ieuan') as having land worth forty shillings per annum, ranked ninth in Menai commote,[110] and three years later in 1571 he is rated at the same level, though this time ranked eighth.[111]

---

107 Lewis Menai, 'Marwnad Huw ap Llewelyn ab Ifan o Borthamel Isaf (Plas Coch) 1557' in
     D. Wyn Wiliam (ed), *Y Canu Mawl i Rai Teuluoedd o Gwmwd Menai* (Llandysul, Gwasg
     Gomer, 2007), p.10.

108 UB Plas Coch Manuscripts Vol I, T. Richards, 'Introduction', p.1.

109 Jesus College has no record of Owain's matriculation, as its records do not extend back
     beyond *c*.1600. However, in UB Plas Coch 154 & 2993, he is referred to as MA and LLB of
     Jesus College.

110 TNA E 179 219/13 (9 Eliz).

111 TNA E 179 219/16 (15 Eliz).

It appears however that Hereford-educated Dafydd was in a position to gen-erate significant liquid assets, sufficient to be able to have become a lender of cash to friends, neighbours and other associates. This liquidity – unusual amongst Anglesey *uchelwyr* of the time – is a pointer to entrepreneurial activi-ties of some kind. His will, made and witnessed on 11 March 1574, lists by name thirty-two individuals owing him sums ranging from 12 pence ('Medd ap John ap Rob') to £34 6s 8d ('Rolland Bybie') – a total of well in excess of £70.[112] Some of the debtors were local kinsmen or neighbours of substance – for example 'Rowland Bulkeley of Porthamall' (£5 15s), 'Richard ap Rhytherch' (£4), 'Roland ap Medd of Bodowyr' (£4) and 'Maurice Gruffudd' (7s 6d), all four of whom had held the office of High Sheriff of the county by this stage, and were also to play roles of various kinds in the life of Dafydd's son Hugh, as will be seen below.[113] But frustratingly, the two individuals owing the largest sums – the 'Rolland Bybie' mentioned above and 'George Wattishe' (£6 8s 4d), both apparently English surnames – have proved impossible to identify. The likelihood is that they were business associates of some kind. The Inventory attached to Dafydd's will lists farming stock in his ownership at the time of death, including seven oxen and 42 cows, bullocks and heifers of various ages, pointing to a degree of involvement in cattle trading. However this seems barely sufficient to account for the capacity to act as informal local banker and funder of his sons' extended terms of higher education. When it is borne in mind that fees and battels at both Cambridge and Oxford would have been in excess of £20 per annum each[114] – albeit Hugh at least held a sizarship at Cambridge – and that 'the accepted minimum cost of maintaining a student at the [Inns of Court] was about £40 a year' in the late sixteenth century,[115] it seems clear that Dafydd had developed sources of income additional to those it has proved possible to identify here. Possibly he was involved in trading by sea, out of Beaumaris or Caernarfon – but no evidence for this has been discovered. Apart from cattle trading and rental income from land, the only other traceable source of revenue is that from his interests in three mills. One of these was Y Felin Bach in Pensynllys township, which he leased from Dafydd ap Howel ap Dafydd ap Tudur for eight years in 1549, at a rent of forty shillings per

---

112   UB Plas Coch 93. An approximate 2009 equivalent of £70 in 1600 is £16,700, using the
        retail price index as comparator. (L.H.Offering, *Purchasing Power of British Pounds for 1264
        to the present* : MeasuringWorth, 2011 – www.EH.net, an educational website run by the US
        Economic History Association).

113   All four of these individuals are discussed further in Chapters 2 & 4.

114   L.Stone, 'The Educational Revolution in England, 1560-1640', *Past and Present* (1964), p.71.

115   W.R.Prest, *The Inns of Court under Elizabeth I and the Early Stuarts, 1590-1640* (London,
        Longman, 1972), p.27.

annum; [116] the second, Melin Bryn Celli (a moiety) on which he took a 28-year lease in 1557 for 20 shillings and a 'consideration' of £6 to the owner, Richard ap John ap Howe ap Robyn of Bodlew, in 1557; [117] and the third, at Rhos y Cerrig, Bodowyr, leased from Rowland Meredith of Bodowyr for 21 years at a rent of 2*d* per annum in 1565.[118] Again, significant though the returns from these activities would have been, they seem unlikely to have been sufficient to account for all of the resources evidently at his disposal. A further curiosity about Dafydd is that, unlike either his father or paternal grandfather, he appears to have held no public office in Anglesey, an anomaly for which it is hard to suggest an explanation. Nevertheless, his energy and determination – reflected in multiple property acquisitions,[119] the entrepreneurialism implied by his mill interests, the commitment to his family's advancement, and the bringing to fruition of the first phase of construction of Plas Coch – suggest an enterprising and resourceful individual.

Enter Hugh

With Dafydd's death in 1574, the growing estate and recently built hall-house passed to the Hugh of this study, who was by then aged 26 and still a student at Lincoln's Inn (as is elaborated in chapter three below). With Hugh's advent, a further acceleration in the pace and geographical reach of the family's property acquisitions and associated landed wealth becomes evident.[120] By 1581, on the evidence of the tax records for the year, Hugh's land income had grown rapidly to the point where it was rated as identical with that of Rowland Bulkeley of Porthaml Uchaf and Maurice Griffith of Llwyn y Moel (now Plas Newydd).[121] And by 1600, he had risen to be listed third amongst landowners in the whole of Anglesey, with only Sir Richard Bulkeley 3rd of Beaumaris and William Lewis of Presaddfed above him.[122] The overall pattern of this estate expansion can be seen in the Table on page 11.

Developments on these lines were not unusual at the time amongst landowners and freeholders in north Wales, many of whom were coming to benefit from the continuing inflation of the later sixteenth century. In an increasingly competitive land market, rents were on the rise under new forms of

---

116 UB Plas Coch 53.

117 UB Plas Coch 66.

118 UB Plas Coch 76.

119 UB Plas Coch 43, 50, 53, 57, 65, 66, 67, 76, 85, 87.

120 UB Plas Coch 85-177.

121 TNA E 179/219/17. The land income figure is recorded as 60 shillings p.a.

122 TNA E 179/219/17a. The figure had risen still more sharply to £16 3 4*d* p.a., compared to the £40 p.a. and £20 p.a. of Bulkeley and Lewis respectively.

leasehold, and possession and exploitation of land offered ever more substantial returns, as well as social prestige. The pressure for expansion was probably driven in many cases as much by the wish not to be bested by more successful neighbours, as by acquisitiveness *per se*.

Nevertheless ruthless means were being use to gain possession of this most basic resource. Amongst the most lucrative of Hugh's new properties from the 1580s was 500+ acres of crown land south-west of Llanedwen at Gwydryn, Bodrida and Maesoglan, which he acquired in controversial circumstances leading to no fewer than three cases before the Court of Exchequer, involving *uchelwyr* plaintiffs who were his neighbours and kinsmen.[123] The rich details of this saga, sociological as much as legal and personal, are explored in the next chapter. They throw light on some of the ways in which land ownership and power in late-Elizabethan Anglesey were shifting decisively in favour of the legally sophisticated, at the expense of what might be understood as the more traditional order.

The redesign and extension of his father's original Plas Coch mansion by Hugh in the 1590s was made possible partly by the resources flowing from this enhanced land income. But the latter would have been dwarfed by the substantial fees and perquisites flowing from his professional activities by this stage as a hard-working barrister and senior crown official. Chapters three to five discuss his various public roles in closer detail, though the precise income from these has been impossible to pin down, as no relevant personal financial records have survived. However, given that his post as deputy and, from 1596, full Attorney General for the two North Wales circuits of Great Sessions, coupled to a thriving legal practice at Lincoln's Inn,[124] at least two Anglesey manorial stewardships, and *quorum*[125] membership of three county Commissions of the Peace,[126] would have put him well up the pecking order of lawyers' incomes of the time, it is reasonable to rely on Prest's judgement that individual lawyers of his kind could well have been earning upwards of £200 p.a.[127] With anything like such resources, the financing of the Plas Coch refurbishment would have

---

123   G.Jones, *Exchequer Proceedings Concerning Wales: Henry VIII – Elizabeth* (Cardiff, UWP, 1939) 58-16, 58-21 & 58-32.

124   UB Plas Coch 340-355: a variety of bonds, land conveyances and deeds of title arising from business handled through his Lincoln's Inn chambers.

125   **Quorum**: The select small group within a Commission of the Peace, principally lawyer-justices, with particular authority on issues of law and policy.

126   Details of these various appointments and Hugh's experience in them are examined in Chapters 3 & 5.

127   W.R.Prest, *The Rise of the Barristers: A Social History of the English Bar 1590-1640* (Oxford Clarendon, 1986), pp. 148-151, 173-183. This is a rough equivalent of £70,000 p.a. in 2020 terms.

been straightforward, as comparison with the construction costs of the even more imposing Plas Mawr in Conwy in the 1560s indicates. The total bill for the latter has been estimated at £500.[128] Even allowing for inflation, such sums would have been well within Hugh's reach by this stage.

Hugh's money and property

Of equal significance for tracking the development of the estate and its income in this phase is the inventory of Hugh's 'goods, cattell and chattels' made immediately following his death in June 1609.[129] This reveals both significant cereal production and involvement in cattle- and horse-trading. Thus the inventory details resources of 'corne and grayne' valued at £30; 47 steers and heifers at £33; 50 milk cows and calves at £40; 22 oxen ('eleavon yoke') at £43; and 22 horses of various kinds at £54 3s 8d. These and other pointers suggest both a thriving home farm and a rental estate enterprise of an improving kind, consistent with practice of the time – enclosing fields to rear animals for sale into mainland, almost certainly English, markets, and employing teams of ox-ploughs to convert recently acquired open land to cereal-growing, perhaps also for the growing English market in such products.[130] There is confirmation of this in eye-witness testimony offered in a 1593 Exchequer Court hearing, reporting that Hugh, following acquisition of the crown lease, had already built 'severall houses upon parte of her Maj landes...beinge in Mossoglyn and Gwydryn and hathe required the hedginge...of the same to his and their greate charges [constructing] houses, farmes and inclosures newlie made, with oxe-houses...' [131]

By the time of his death, Hugh's total landed estate is likely to have been in excess of 1,400 acres, a figure derived from the earliest surviving Plas Coch rental of 1792, almost two centuries later.[132] Moreover, the 1609 inventory made after his death shows he left movable assets of a total value of £261 2s 8d, over and above the Plas Coch mansion and its farms, and unknown liquid, but probably also substantial, cash resources. In the will he made handsome lifetime provision for his widow, Elizabeth, and provided for dowries of £300 and £344 to his daughters, Miriam and Elenor respectively.[133] The rest of what was

---

128 R.C. Turner, 'Robert Wynn and the building of Plas Mawr, Conwy', *National Library of Wales Journal* 29 (1995-96), pp.177-203.

129 UB Plas Coch 184.

130 F.E. Emery, 'The Farming Regions of Wales: Regional Economies', in J. Thirsk (ed), *The Agrarian History of England and Wales*, Vol IV, 1540-1640 (Cambridge, CUP, 1967), p.199.

131 TNA E 134/35&36Eliz/Mich 18. Statement of William ap Hugh ap Owen of Gwydryn, 10 August 1593.

132 UB Plas Coch 703.

133 UB Plas Coch 173 – See Appendix B below.

now a substantial estate passed to his only son, Roger. Furthermore, in line with custom of the time, he chose to make personal gifts of rings, of values between £1 and £5, to several individuals, including the Lord Chancellor, Lord Ellesmere (formerly Sir Thomas Egerton) and Mr Justice Warburton. The significance of the last two of these is explained in a later chapter.[134]

It should be acknowledged that there is a certain artificiality in this chapter's virtual isolation of the historical emergence of Plas Coch and its estate from the larger narrative of Hugh's personal and professional life in and beyond Anglesey. However this limitation, if such it be, will be repaired in the chapters that follow. As stated at the beginning of the chapter, the purpose has been first to piece together as rigorously as possible the ways in which Hugh was building on foundations laid down over several centuries by his direct family antecedents, on both sides of the 1282 conquest.

Plas Coch *(Joseph Nash, watercolour, c.1850)*

---

134 See pages 68-72 & 125 .

Lineage and standing

That he would have been acutely conscious and indeed proud of his free Porthaml lineage and the accomplishments of at least some of his direct ancestors is shown by steps taken in 1594 to have this lineage formally and publicly confirmed by the College of Arms. A Visitation Pedigree tracing direct descent from his twelfth-century ancestor 'Llywarch ap Brân, Lord of Menai' onwards, 'deduced by Llwys Dunn, Deputy Herald of Arms under the authority of Clarencieux & Morrey King of Arms' was certified by Hugh himself on 14th August of that year (36 Eliz).[135] Similarly, two *cywyddau*,[136] the first by Lewis Menai on the occasion of Hugh's first term as Sheriff of the county in 1580-81, and a second by Huw Pennant to Hugh and his wife in 1604, show – in conventionally unctuous and fulsome terms – how the social memory of his family forbears was translated into respect and admiration for Hugh himself in hierarchical Welsh society. For example:

> *… Pel aur a glain piler gwlad,*
> *Post mawr ei gost ym mrig iaith,*
> *Pen teulu, impyn talaith,*
> *Pais ddur Hwfa bur a'i barch*
> *Pengwern llu, pen grawn Llywarch,*
> *Penrhyn, Lliwon Glyn a'i glod*
> *Pel Fawl clau pur Fwlcleiod …*[137]

> ' … A golden orb and the jewel and pillar of the country,
> A valuable support at the head of the language,
> The head of the nation, the scion of the region,
> The steely tunic of good Hwfa and his respect
> The forces of Pengwern, head of Llywarch's line,
> Penrhyn, Glynllifon, and their praise
> The swift fair praise of the Bulkeleys … '

and

> *… O iach Llywarch alluawg*
> *Ap Brân hen, wyd bur iawn hawg,*
> *Iach y deiliodd eich dylwyth*

---

135 Sir S.R.Meyrick, *Lewis Dunn's Heraldic Visitations of Wales* (folio) Vol. 2 (Llandovery, Welsh Manuscript Society, 1846), p.142.

136 **Cywydd** (pl: *cywyddau*): a key metrical form in traditional Welsh poetry, consisting of a series of several seven-syllable lines in rhyming couplets, with strict requirements of internal stress and alliteration (*cynhangedd*).

137 Lewis Menai, 'Moliant Huw Huws Pan Oedd yn Siryf (1580-81)' in Wyn Wiliam (ed), *Menai*, p.15.

Irddewr lain o Iarddur lwyth,
A haelwaed diwehilion
Mae iwch o Llwydiarth ym Mon.[138]

> ' You are very truly of the long and mighty line of old
> Llywarch ap Brân.
> Your family, brave jewel, issued soundly
> From the stock of Iarddur,
> Of generous, unsullied blood
> From Llwydiarth in Anglesey. '

All of this would have both shaped and reflected his self-understanding. Indeed, the likelihood is that he would have been encouraged from an early age to see himself rightfully, by virtue of long inheritance so to speak, as a potential leader in the community, with his father Dafydd prodding him in addition to set sights on the wider opportunities beyond Anglesey flowing from the legal and administrative reorganisation of 1536 and 1543. And beyond this, the evidence of Hugh's continuing, indeed lifelong, involvement in the expansion of the Plas Coch estate and parallel embeddedness in local continuities of Anglesey life and culture suggest that his personal ties to the island remained strong, even as his career took him far further afield.

Later chapters examine the multiple ways in which Hugh's education and legal ambitions led to involvement in wider political and social developments affecting both England and Wales. But it is central to the argument throughout that, despite such broader-ranging commitments, he never lost touch with his Anglesey roots. Hence before passing to consider the crucial English-influenced dimensions of his career and how he may have been able to keep these different loyalties in balance, it is useful first to gain a further richer flavour of the local social networks in which he continued to be embedded on the island.

---

138   Huw Pennant, 'Moliant Huw Huws ac Elisabeth ei Wraig (tua 1604)' in Wyn Wiliam (ed),
       Menai, p.16.

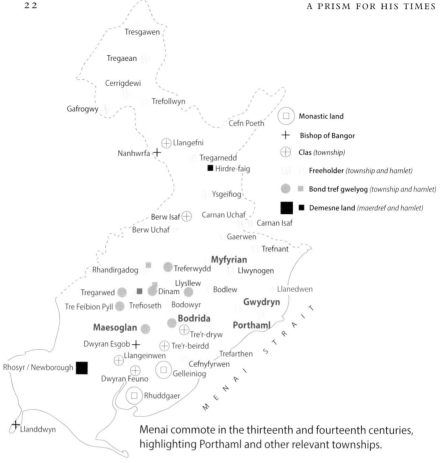

Menai commote in the thirteenth and fourteenth centuries,
highlighting Porthaml and other relevant townships.

The protracted dispute In the 1580s between Hugh Hughes and his Myfyrian
neighbours and kinsmen, the Rhydderchs, involved formerly bond land covering the
present-day farms of Maesoglan, Bodrida, Cefn Maesoglan and Gwydryn Newydd,
close to Dwyran and Brynsiencyn. (Adapted from Ordnance Survey Map 114, 2001 edition)

2 *The Maesoglan–Bodrida Saga*

THE PREVIOUS CHAPTER has traced Hugh's origins and family inheritance in the ancient free township of Porthaml, close to the Menai Strait in south-east Anglesey. The essentially agricultural community of which he was part in the later decades of the sixteenth century was one which had been shaped by strong kinship relations and continuing interactions between neighbours over many centuries, not least amongst those claiming descent from the clan founder, Llywarch ap Brân.[139] An attempt is now made to cast further light on the patterns of social interaction and relationship in which Hugh would have been involved as a significant member of this community.

Land was the currency of power in late sixteenth-century Wales. Wealth, social prestige and political influence flowed from its possession, as well as longer term family security. Moreover, between 1460 and 1550, there had been an unfolding 'revolution in landownership'[140] in Anglesey and Caernarfonshire, as the disintegration of bond townships[141] and the dissolution of monasteries and chantries created fresh land acquisition opportunities for those from free townships with the guile and energy to challenge for them. With population expanding throughout the century and a cash economy ever-more pervasive, the material gulfs between landowning and the landless classes were widening steadily. Continuing inflation[142] aggravated the position of the latter – whilst for the former, competition in an increasingly tight land market became progressively fiercer. These were the circumstances in which the Porthaml Isaf estate had been expanding over the four generations preceding Hugh, and by the last two decades of the sixteenth century, the tensions were becoming increasingly acute.

---

139   Carr, *Medieval Anglesey*, pp.52-53.

140   Williams, *Tudor Gwynedd*, pp.37-49.

141   Under the Charter of Privileges granted to North Wales inhabitants in 1507. (J.Beverley Smith, 'Crown and community in the Principality of North Wales in the reign of Henry Tudor', *WHR* 3, 1966).

142   C.Russell, *The Crisis of Parliaments: English History 1509-1660* (Oxford, OUP, 1971), pp.3-11.

Upsets in Menai

Between 1580 and 1595 Hugh was at the centre of a bitter dispute with close neighbours concerning leases of crown land in Menai hundred. The protracted row that resulted throws light not only on aspects of his local social world and modus operandi, but also, more generally, on ways in which balances of cultural and political power in late sixteenth-century Anglesey were evolving, as the reverberations of the union settlement[143] penetrated ever deeper. It also confirms Hugh's routine embeddedness in the day-to-day life of the island, even as his expanding public career was requiring a presence in locations well beyond the Menai Strait. Whilst at one level what was involved was a straightforward struggle about land, the episode also has significance for the light it casts on shifting patterns of cultural difference between native Welshmen of different outlooks at this historical juncture, with entrenched local prestige and influence coming up against the power of new English-trained legal skills and political sophistication. Indeed, the case offers illuminating glimpses of tensions within the local *uchelwr* class itself, at a time of social, economic and cultural change. At the most obvious level Hugh won the argument, but the resentments this victory aroused rumbled on well into the following century.

The immediate nub of the conflict was as follows. In 1573, just two years into his legal training at Lincoln's Inn,[144] Hugh acquired the reversion[145] of a crown lease for 30 years, covering the (formerly bond) townships of Maesoglan and Bodrida, both of them close to Dwyran, the mill at Rhosyr, and extensive tracts of other farmland ('viij frythes'), some of it escheat, in Porthaml. This meant that, on the expiry of the existing lease, the future interest in these lands would reside with Hugh for the duration of a new term. Quite how this lease in-reversion came into his hands, and what this meant from the perspectives of the different individuals involved in the episode, is discussed later. The immediately important point is that over the previous several decades, the crown lease-holders – with the entitlement to farm[146] these lucrative assets – had been Hugh's kinsmen and close neighbours, the Rhydderchs[147] of Myfyrian, the lat-

---

143 The details, and implications, of the 1536 and 1543 legal and administrative changes in Wales are discussed in detail in Chapters 4 & 6.

144 His education is examined in detail in Chapter 3.

145 **Reversion**: On the expiry of a crown lease, a leased property would return to the original owner, *i.e.* the Crown. A Grant (or Lease)-in-Reversion could then start.

146 'Farm' in the Elizabethan sense of 'exploit to derive income from'.

147 The liberty is taken here of assigning the Myfyrian family an English-style surname, 'Rhydderch'. In fact, at that stage, they were still using the Welsh style 'ap'. But Rhydderch is the constantly recurring Myfyrian family name in the period of concern here, so it is used for simplicity's sake.

ter a locally significant farm, today named Myfyrian Isaf, standing barely a mile to the north of Plas Coch.[148] Unsurprisingly, the Rhydderchs, for whom the land in question had been a valued part of their estate, did not take the reversal lying down. Nor did some of the long-established under-tenants from the Rhydderch regime, in particular Huw ap Rees Wynn of Maesoglan, who objected that part of the land now claimed by Hugh had historically been part of his own family's long-held freehold. A succession of negotiations, court cases and other inquiries ensued, precipitated by the Myfyrian and Maesoglan families. But by the end, Hugh's legal right to the bulk of the land had been conclusively confirmed.

The shape of the controversy has been pieced together from previously unanalysed Exchequer Court reports, Commission patents and other papers in the National Archive, as well as Hugh Hughes's own papers and Anglesey praise poetry concerning the principal actors.[149]

Protagonists

It is helpful first to know the families involved. The three were neighbours and kinsmen. Each had a long-established territorial stake in the area, all of them tracing descent from Llywarch ap Brân. As already noted,[150] the Myfyrian *gwely* had its medieval origins as a spin-off from Porthaml Isaf. There would have been continuing links between the families, refreshed from time to time over the previous two or three centuries through marriages, dispute arbitrations[151] and the like. It appears to have been a conflict in which the principal actors knew one another well, being from families who had lived cheek by jowl in the Porthaml vicinity for many generations.

The individuals of particular concern here are: at *Myfyrian*, Rhydderch ap Rhisiart (1540-1606) and his redoubtable father and grandfather, respectively Rhisiart ap Rhydderch (*c.*1502-76) and Rhydderch ap Dafydd (1475-1562); at *Maesoglan*, Huw ap Rees Wynn (1542-1600); and at *Plas Coch*, Hugh Hughes (1547-1609) and his father and grandfather, respectively Dafydd Llwyd ap Huw (*d.*1572), and Huw ap Llewelyn (*d.*1558), all of whom have already been discussed in chapter one.

One especially significant illustration of the likely familiarity between the

---

148   Present-day Myfyrian Uchaf and Myfyrian Isaf lie along a side road close to the Gaerwen level-crossing. (See Map p.22)

149   The research of Dr Dafydd Wyn Wiliam, evident in his invaluable volumes of praise poetry associated with more than thirty individual Anglesey houses and families (assembled over the past 35 years and published by Gwasg Gomer), has been especially appreciated.

150   See note 74.

151   *e.g.* UB Plas Coch 51.

Myfyrian and Plas Coch families is that Hugh Hughes and Rhydderch ap Rhisiart, the two principal protagonists in the 1580s and '90s, were close cousins as well as neighbours. Rhydderch ap Dafydd's sister, Marsli ferch Dafydd (d.1562), had been the wife of Huw ap Llewelyn, and hence Hugh Hughes's grandmother. Indeed, in an elegy on Marsli's death in 1562, the poet Lewis Menai laid particular stress on her hospitality and close family connections on both sides.[152] A pointer to the trusting relationship prevailing between the two families prior to the falling-out is the fact that in April 1552 Risiart ap Rhydderch stood as surety for Dafydd Llwyd, a £10 bond in relation to a forcible entry indictment against the latter.[153]

Myfyrian, Gaerwen, in the 1920s
The powerful Rhydderch family lived at Myfyrian throughout the Tudor period, and held local offices over several generations — including the first Anglesey borough MP, as well as justices of the peace, sheriffs and subsidy commissioners.

152 Lewis Menai 'Marwnad Marsli, Gweddw Huw ap Llewelyn ab Ifan', in Wyn Wiliam, *Menai*, p.10.
153 W.O.Williams, *Calendar of the Caernarvonshire Great Sessions Records, Vol 1, 1541-1558* (Caernarfon, Caernarvonshire Historical Society, 1956), p.218.

The Rhydderchs of Myfyrian

In the middle of the sixteenth century, before the controversy broke out, the Myfyrian family was one of the most prominent in Menai hundred, if not in the county of Anglesey as a whole. Siôn Brwynog, an Anglesey poet writing in 1545, addressed Rhydderch ap Dafydd (Rhydderch ap Rhisiart's grandfather) as *rhywolwr Môn* [154] ('ruler of Anglesey'), inquiring rhetorically *Pa wr mwy pwer ym Môn…?* [155] ('What man more powerful in Anglesey…?').

Around the time of the acts of union, this Rhydderch ap Dafydd had found crown favour, reflected in his appointment to a variety of privileged crown posts, as King's Surveyor (1544)[156] and as Sewer (1542),[157] and subsequently Gentleman of the Royal Chamber (1545).[158] Locally, he also came to hold such influential Anglesey positions as Sheriff (1544),[159] and justice in the newly created Commission of the Peace from its inception in 1543.[160] These posts, and the fact that he was a Commissioner for Anglesey in relation to three crown Benevolence and Subsidy collections between 1546 and 1549,[161] point to high local standing, as a powerful presence. Such an impression is reinforced by the evidence of the Subsidy rolls for the 1540s, which show him repeatedly as one of three wealthiest landowners in Menai, some way behind William Bulkeley of Porthaml Uchaf and Rowland Gruffydd of Llwyn y Moel (Plas Newydd),[162] but way ahead of the family at Porthaml Isaf.[163]

It has not been possible to pin down conclusively why Rhydderch had benefited so significantly under Henry VIII, but there was a widespread local belief, reflected in witness depositions made in one of the later court proceedings (in 1593[164]), that he had been granted leases in Porthaml and Gwydryn, and perhaps also the crown sinecure posts mentioned above, in recognition of services to the crown in France. For example, Rhydderch's witness Daniel

---

154 Siôn Brwynog, 'Moliant Rhydderch ap Dafydd 1544/5' in D. Wyn Wiliam, *Y Canu Mawl i Deulu Myfyrian* (Llandysul, Gwasg Gomer, 2004), p.12.

155 Ibid., p.75.

156 *Letters & Papers Foreign and Domestic H VIII* ii, 443.

157 *Calendar of the Patent Rolls 1557-8* (1939), 25.

158 Ibid.

159 H.F. Richards, *New Kalendars of Gwynedd* (Denbigh, Gwasg Gee, 1994), p.51.

160 J.R.S. Phillips, *The Justices of the Peace in Wales and Monmouthshire 1541 to 1689* (Cardiff, UWP, 1975), p.1 ('Roderick ap David').

161 TNA E 179 219/4 (1547), E 179 219/5 (1548), E 179 219/6 (1549).

162 Ibid.

163 TNA E 179 219/5, which shows that in 1548 Huw ap Llewelyn was ranked twentieth in land in Menai.

164 TNA E 134/35&36Eliz/Mich 18.

Llwyd claimed he 'hathe h(e)ard yt crediblie reported the same was first be-
stowed on rhydd ap d(afyd)d his grandfather in consideracon of s(er)vice
donne unto kynge henry the eighthe', whilst John Owen had heard such services had been performed 'in France and elsewhere in the tyme of her
Ma(jesty)'s progenitors…' [165] Indeed he may well have won distinction on the
battlefield.[166] Quite apart from any royal patronage however, Rhydderch's lineage was a regionally significant one by the social codes of the time. His mother
Mallt had been a direct descendant of the Maredudd ap Cynwrig of Porthaml
whose accomplishments in the acquisition of offices and lands had been second
to none in early fifteenth century Anglesey.[167] And several generations of her
other antecedents had served variously as *rhaglaw*, *rhingyll* and constable in
Menai during the fourteenth and fifteenth centuries.[168] Rhydderch's grandfather on his father's side, Ieuan ap Ednyfed, had come from south Wales in the
early fifteenth century in the wake of the Glyndŵr rebellion, in which he and
his brother had played active roles.[169] Benefiting from the general pardon, he
had then married Gwenllian, the heiress to Myfyrian, probably in the 1430s.

Rhydderch ap Dafydd's own wife Marsli also came from a leading Gwynedd
uchelwr family, being daughter of William ap Gruffudd ap Robin of Cochwillan,
who had been Sheriff of Caernarfonshire between 1475 and 1500.[170]

Overall then, the Myfyrian family line was a weighty one in Anglesey terms
– and over an unusually long life Rhydderch ap Dafydd consolidated and developed the family's position. This was a man of cultural as well as political
substance. There are indications he had practised as an attorney early in the
century,[171] possibly even in London.[172] But still more tellingly, his household
at Myfyrian was notable as a continuing centre of bardic activity throughout
the sixteenth century. At least thirty-five *cywyddau* are known to have been
written to Myfyrian family members, by upwards of fourteen bards,[173] several
of the highest levels of accomplishment, between 1523 and 1592. These included Wiliam Cynwal (*d.*1587) and Wiliam Llyn (1534-80), both leading bards

---

165 Ibid.

166 Siôn Brwynog (in Wyn Wiliam, *Myfyrian*, p.13) implies this: *Da prifiaist drwy hap ryfel…* ('It
        is well you succeeded by accident of war…')

167 See page 8.

168 Carr, *Medieval Anglesey*, pp. 52-53.

169 Griffith, *Pedigrees*, p.115.

170 Griffith, *Pedigrees*, p.186.

171 H. Owen, *The Plea Rolls of Anglesey 1509-1516* (1927), pp. 28, 51.

172 Gwynne Jones ('Some Notes', p.65) suggests that Rhydderch may have acted as an attorney
        in London around the time of his appointment as High Sheriff of Anglesey. It has not been
        possible to trace this further.

173 Wyn Wiliam, *Myfyrian*, pp.7-8.

who had been protégés of the celebrated Gruffudd Hiraethog – as well as Huw
Pennant (*fl.*1565-1619), Rhys Cain (*d.*1614), Huw Machno (1560-1637) and
Lewis Menai (*fl.*1557-81).[174] After Rhydderch ap Dafydd's death in 1562 at the
age of 87, he was mourned in elegies by Siôn Brwynog, Dafydd Alaw, Lewis
Menai and Huw Cornwy, all of whom appear to have been regular presences
at Myfyrian over the preceding decades, and who had previously sung his
praises in other cywyddau.[175] At a time when wider *uchelwr* patronage of bards
was beginning to fray for social and economic reasons,[176] there was no such
waning of support at Myfyrian, as the poets were quick to affirm:

> *Af 'fory i Fyfyrian*
> *Ar frys i lys Ifor lân...*[177]

> ' Tomorrow I shall go to Myfyrian
>   with haste to the court of the genial Ifor [i.e. Rhisiart] ... '

and

> *Awn ni a gawn yno i gyd*
> *Aur a gwin awr ac ennyd ...*[178]

> ' Let us all go, we shall receive there
>   gold and silver every hour and second ...'

Rhydderch's eldest son and heir, Rhisiart ap Rhydderch – a central actor in
the frictions with the Plas Coch family, as will be seen shortly – appears to
have been quite as impressive a figure as his father. He too had been made a
justice of the new Anglesey Commission of the Peace on its inception in
1543,[179] a striking father-and-son arrangement, pointing again to the degree of
political and intellectual authority the family had gained across the island. He
continued as a justice for the rest of his life. Moreover, almost certainly,
Rhisiart was one of Anglesey's original members of Parliament – for the borough of Newborough in the 1541 Parliament,[180] the first such following the
1536 Act, which had granted all Welsh shires the new right to direct representation in the House of Commons. The local prestige attached to election to
this position by Rhisiart's *uchelwr* peers on the island, at such a significant historical moment, scarcely needs underlining. Moreover, his independent stand-

---

174   Ibid. Also, M.Stephens, *The New Companion to the Literature of Wales* (Cardiff, UWP, 1998).

175   Ibid.

176   C.W.Lewis, 'The Decline of Professional Poetry', in R.Geraint Gruffydd (ed), *A Guide to
      Welsh Literature. 1530-1700* (Cardiff, UWP, 1999), Vol 3, Chap 2.

177   Dafydd Alaw, 'Moliant Rhisiart ap Rhydderch' in Wyn Wiliam, *Myfyrian*, op cit, p.35.

178   Huw Cornwy, 'Moliant Rhydderch ap Dafydd, in Wyn Wiliam', *Myfyrian*, op cit, pp. 21, 27.

179   Phillips, *Justices of the Peace*, p.1.

180   W.R.Williams, *The Parliamentary History of Wales* (Brecknock, 1895), pp.8-9.

ing in parallel with that of his long-lived father also is confirmed by the evidence of the subsidy rolls. For example, in the 1548 Subsidy, in which, as already noted, Rhydderch ap Dafydd was listed as a Commissioner and third highest payer, Risiart is listed separately, just after his father in fourth position. Unsurprisingly, Rhydderch also married within his class. His wife Catrin was daughter of Owen ap Meurig of Bodeon; her brother, also Owen, was twice Sheriff and a justice of the Commission of the Peace for forty years in the middle of the century.[181]

Like his father, Rhisiart appears to have actively maintained the bardic culture and enthusiasms of Myfyrian. No fewer than seven elegies, by different poets, were composed to mark his death in 1576, alongside an impressive body of other praise poetry.[182] The internal evidence of this poetry is that Myfyrian was something of local cultural hub throughout Rhisiart's life. Indeed it may be no coincidence that, raised in such a household, his eldest son and heir, Rhydderch ap Rhisiart (1540-1606), grew up to have aspirations to be himself a serious poet within the tradition,[183] though composing perhaps for pleasure rather than gain.

Overall then, the Myfyrian household in the period 1540-70 represents a striking instance of an *uchelwr* family which had seamlessly sustained its local dominance across the period straddling the 'acts of union'. The Rhydderchs appear to have been precisely the kind of family recent historians have had in mind when pointing to the way in which the 1536/1543 settlement relied for much of its success on local Welsh power elites with long prior experience of local administration under pre-acts of union conditions.[184] The accumulated public experience and prestige of Rhydderch ap Dafydd and Rhisiart ap Rhydderch, the dense web of Anglesey and Gwynedd marriage networks and connections, the relatively comfortable income through land,[185] and the sustained encouragement of indigenous poetry and cultural traditions must have attracted wide local respect. Indeed in the native Welsh terms of the time, they must have appeared to be a family that had it all.

However, with such well-grounded advantages, it would not be surprising

---

181   Gwynne Jones, 'Some Notes', p.63. Catrin was not only Rhisiart's wife, she also became his step-mother-in-law! Rhisiart's redoubtable father Rhydderch took Catrin's daughter, Eva (from her first marriage) as his second wife (Griffith, *Pedigrees*, pp. 58, 115).

182   Wyn Wiliam, *Myfyrian*, pp.31-54.

183   Wyn Wiliam (*Myfyrian*, p.104) identifies a number of *cywyddau* by Rydderch ap Rhisiart, over and above Rhydderch's general reputation as a 'bard' (*e.g.* Griffith, *Pedigrees*, p.115)

184   *e.g.* H.Thomas, *A History of Wales 1485-1660* (Cardiff, UWP, 1991), pp.52-53; A.H.Dodd & J.G.Williams (eds), *Aspects of Welsh History* (Cardiff, UWP,1969), pp.304-318; Gwynfor Jones, 'Law, Order and Government in Caernarfonshire', pp.79-107.

185   TNA E 179 219/13 (1568); TNA E 179 219/16 (1571).

if, by the time the bitter land dispute with Hugh Hughes flared up in the early 1570s, a measure of family complacency had not begun to creep in.

The Plas Coch family

By contrast, as will already be clear from the account in chapter one, in the 1550s and '60s the Plas Coch / Porthaml Isaf family would have had little to visibly rival the prestige of the Rhydderchs at Myfyrian. Hugh Hughes's paternal grandfather, Huw ap Llewelyn, appears to have been a modest and self-possessed individual, who at some point in the 1520s married Rhydderch ap Dafydd's sister, Marsli, a union which may have had implications for the social aspirations of the Porthaml Isaf family. Certainly the couple would have been aware of the growing distinction attained by her brother Rydderch over the subsequent three decades. Perhaps this awareness, coupled to knowledge of her earlier forbears' accomplishments at Porthaml Uchaf,[186] fed Marsli's ambitions for her own children, including their schooling. Certainly, as shown in the previous chapter, the couple's eldest son, Dafydd Llwyd, proved to be resourceful and energetic – attuned, by virtue of a costly English education, to the growing individualism flowing from social and economic changes on both sides of the border. Indeed, as has already been seen,[187] it was Dafydd who had initiated the construction of Plas Coch in the mid-1560s. Nevertheless at the beginning of the period relevant to the dispute between the two families, the *gwely* of Myfyrian probably possessed a social and cultural lustre unmatched by that of Porthaml Isaf.

The dispute itself

The crown lease on which the dispute turned related to the townships of Maesoglan and Bodrida, the mill ('gryndinge myle') at Rhosyr, eight 'frithes' in the township of Gwydryn, and various fields and tenements within Porthaml itself. For the most part, this was land which previously had either been bond or escheated to the crown,[188] or where title was simply unclear. Whilst precise measurements are impossible from the available evidence, at least several hundred acres must have been involved.[189]

---

186 Especially Maredudd Ddu and Maredudd ap Cynwrig in the previous three centuries – see page 8.

187 See pages 1 & 13-15.

188 The escheat lands resulted from the outlawing for felonies of the previous owner, Meredith ap Llewelyn Colye of Porthamel (UB Plas Coch 130).

189 The present-day farm of Cefn Maesoglan is *c.* 300 acres, Bodrida 170 acres, and Gwydryn Newydd 70 acres. All of these acreages were within the disputed lands, as were assorted further fields and tenements, suggesting a total of more than 600 acres. (See Map, p.22)

The Disputed lands

The several hundred acres attached to the present-day farms Maesoglan (in foreground), Cefn Maesoglan (in middle), and Bodrida (behind), were owned by the Crown throughout the sixteenth century. Their 'lease-in-reversion' was the prize fought over in the fierce Myfyrian–Plas Coch dispute of the 1580s and '90s. The Menai Strait and Brynsiencyn village are in the top-right corner.

These lands at Gwydryn, east of Brynsiencyn, also came into Hugh Hughes's hands in the late 1580s, following the bitter legal fight with the former crown lease-holders. Some of this land was still in the Plas Coch–Brynddu estate till the early twenty-first century.

These lands had been in the hands of the Rhydderch family for a number of years when the dispute arose. Whilst there are circumstantial suggestions in witness depositions on behalf of Rhydderch ap Rhisiart in the 1593 Exchequer Court suit[190] that the original lease had been granted by Henry VIII to Rhydderch's grandfather, Rhydderch ap Dafydd – and thus that the lands in question had been in his family's possession since the 1530s or '40s – the earliest *traceable* reference is to a crown lease granted to the latter's son, Rhisiart ap Rhydderch, a number of years later – in 1557,[191] This appears to have been a 25-year lease, terminating in 1582.[192] Whatever the details, it appears that by the early 1570s Rhisiart was becoming anxious to secure any subsequent reversion, in order to ensure his continuation as the crown farmer. And according to repeated later claims by his son Rhydderch, it was at this point that Rhisiart purportedly asked Hugh Hughes, presumably on the strength of his presence in London, to use his best efforts to ensure that the lease-in-reversion did not pass into other hands.[193]

Yet that is precisely what happened in 1572. The reversion was acquired by one Thomas Gower esq, who then quickly sold it on, that same year, to 'James Armorer gent of Furnivall's Inn'.[194] By the following year it had found its way into the hands of none other than – Hugh Hughes. The precise means by which this had happened became a key bone of contention in the wrangles that ensued. It is considered below. At the time of James Armorer's sale of the reversion to Hugh Hughes, the original lease still had nine years to run. During the period that followed, unsurprisingly, relations between the Plas Coch and Myfyrian families became increasingly fraught. Rhisiart died in 1576, leaving his son and heir Rhydderch as holder of the now-expiring original lease.

Some time around 1580, Rhydderch made a move, submitting the first of several petitions to the Court of Exchequer. According to a later deposition, he contended Hugh had abused knowledge imparted to him in confidence as an adviser to the late Risiart, in order to acquire the reversion of the lease for himself [195]. The implication was that Hugh's interest should be invalidated on grounds of dishonest practice. In parallel, Rhydderch appears to have done what he could to physically obstruct Hugh from taking possession of at least one of the properties now formally his.[196]

---

190 TNA E 134/35&36Eliz/Mich 18.

191 LP 4&5 Ph & Mary.

192 This 25-year term is an inference.

193 TNA E/134/35&36Eliz/Mich 18. Interrogatories ministered on the behalfe of Rhydderch ap Risiart against Hugh Hughes esq defft.

194 Ibid., Deposition of James Armeror.

195 Ibid., 'Interrogatories ministered'.

196 Ibid.

Though no records survive pointing to counter-petitions or complaints by Hugh at this stage, it is highly likely he used his legal know-how and contacts to fight back hard. By now he was a practising barrister,[197] as well as steward of Rhosyr manor,[198] and in 1581 he became Sheriff of the county for the first time. As a professional lawyer and landowner on the rise, he is unlikely to have been reticent in asserting his rights in appropriate quarters. It may well be that local negotiations and attempts at non-judicial arbitration ensued over the next two or three years. There are several instances in Hugh Hughes's papers of such quasi-formal lay processes, with associated 'bonds of obligation' on the key parties, in relation to local land-title disputes, albeit generally in cases less substantial than the one under consideration here.[199] No documentary evidence of anything of this kind has survived but it appears that at some point around 1582 or 1583, Hugh's title was confirmed by certificate by Thomas Hanbury, the Crown Auditor for North Wales.[200]

Nevertheless, with stakes so high for both parties, the controversy surrounding the lease rumbled on with such intensity that on 22 June 1586, Letters Patent were issued from the Court of Exchequer under the Lord Treasurer's name, creating a Commission of crown officials and heavyweight Anglesey gentry, ten in all, to investigate the lands at issue.[201] This step must have reflected the local significance of the dispute – as indeed did the composition of the Commission itself. Its most prominent members were Thomas Hanbury himself (as Auditor), Edward Hughes esq, the Receiver for North Wales, and Sir Richard Bulkeley. The others were Rowland Thomas, Dean of Bangor; Robert Turbridge esq, Surveyor of Crown Lands in Anglesey; John Heymys gent, Deputy-surveyor of Crown lands; William Maurice esq of Clennenau; John Griffith esq; Thomas Bulkeley esq; and Maurice Griffith esq – the last four all weighty local *uchelwyr*, well known personally to Hugh and probably to Rhydderch also. For example, Thomas Bulkeley was not only Hugh Hughes's next-door neighbour at Porthaml Uchaf,[202] but also his exact contemporary at Lincoln's Inn and later a fellow Bencher at that Inn;[203] Maurice Griffith of

---

197 He had been called to the bar on 25 November 1579. *LI Black Books, The Records of the Honourable Society of Lincoln's Inn*, Vol I (Lincoln's Inn, 1897), p.416. This is discussed further in Chapter 3.

198 UB Plas Coch 99. The significance of this local legal-advisory post is discussed below in Chapter 4.

199 For example, UB Plas Coch 51 (1545), 60 (1555), 2917 (1559), 80 (1569), 2954 (1582).

200 The certificate is referred to in an Exchequer Court decree of 11 July 1589 (TNA E 123/12), in the context of a subsequent challenge to its validity by Hugh ap Rhys Wynn.

201 UB Plas Coch 2968.

202 Griffith, *Pedigrees*, p.12.

203 *Lincoln's Inn Admissions Register 1420-1799* Vol I (Lincoln's Inn 1896), 20 March 1571.

Llwyn y Moel (now Plas Newydd) was a fellow JP who had been Hugh's under-sheriff when Hugh held the shrievalty in 1581;[204] and John Griffith, a neighbour at Chwaen Wen, was also a fellow justice.[205] Collectively the commissioners were charged to 'survey the lands called Ffrydd Kenwrick ap Eignon, Ffrydd Philip, Ffrydd Trosglin, Ffrydd David bobig, Ffrydd Midache, Ffrydd Corsglyne, Ffrydd Bodower and Ffrydd Mifirian in the township of Gwydryn; the townships of Bodvreda [Bodrida] and Mossoglin [Maesoglan]; and those lands in the township of Porthaml formerly in the possession of Meredith ap Llewelyn Colye, outlawed for felony and all lands in the township of Gwydryn found by the Inquisition to be of the value of 3/2'.[206]

The Commission worked quickly, concluding its work at Conwy on 11 October 1586.[207] This is clear from a later deposition of John ap Rees of Llanedwen, stating that he attended the Beaumaris arbitration meeting before proceeding to Conway for the Commission's final proceedings the following day. No evidence of a breach of trust by Hugh Hughes was found,[208] and title to the lease-in-reversion then appears to have been confirmed once more in a subsequent certificate from the Auditor, Thomas Hanbury.[209]

No let-up

However, this was far from the end of the matter. Not only did Rhydderch continue to protest to the courts that Hugh's title was invalid, but a second, quite separate action was initiated in 1584/5 by Huw ap Rees Wynn, Rhydderch's principal under-tenant for part of Maesoglan. This suit appears to have challenged the Auditor's original certificate at the very time the issue was being investigated quite separately by the Commission.[210] Huw ap Rees Wynn argued that the lease obtained by Hugh Hughes, while purportedly covering the whole township of Maesoglan, in fact bore on only two-thirds of its area, the remaining third being freehold which had been in his own family's possession over the previous 140 years. It should therefore remain in his possession, he argued. On the face of it, it is puzzling that this particular Maesoglan property should have been caught up in the controversy in the first place. As Dafydd Wyn Wiliam has shown,[211] Huw ap Rhys Wyn's *uchelwyr* forbears had been long-estab-

---

Hugh was admitted seven weeks later on 3 May 1571.

204 UB Plas Coch 2950; Phillips, *Justices of the Peace*, p.3.

205 Phillips, *Justices of the Peace*, p.3; Griffith, *Pedigrees*, p.14; UB Baron Hill 26.

206 UB Plas Coch 2968.

207 TNA E 134/35&36Eliz/Mich 18. Deposition of John ap Rees.

208 TNA E 123/19(b), Decrees & Orders of Exchequer Court, Anglesey.

209 TNA E 123/12(a). Decrees and Orders of Exchequer Court.

210 Ibid. The decree includes a summary of Huw ap Rees Wynn's plea.

lished at the farm, which boasted a particularly splendid garden designed for the family by one Robert Bangor, who had been a prominent priest in the Bangor diocese before his death in 1518. This is known from an *englyn* by Robert ab Ifan in the period with which we are concerned.[212] Huw ap Rhys Wyn's claim against Hugh was examined in 1586 – whilst the Commission referred to above was actually sitting – by a judge appointed by the Exchequer Court, Mr Baron Gent. The latter's findings led the court then to order, on 11 July 1587, that he should be granted time to produce evidence of the claimed title.[213]

It appears he was able to do so successfully. Though it has not been possible to find documentary confirmation, the physical evidence on the ground to this day suggests that a separate 140-acre farm unit was brought into being at that stage at Maesoglan, even while the other two-thirds of the township – what is now the quite separate 300-acre farm of Cefn Maesoglan – became part of Hugh Hughes's (and his descendants') estate.[214] There is circumstantial confirmation of this in witness depositions made at a later (1593) hearing in the neighbouring village of Llanddaniel Fab, to the effect that since his adoption of the lease in the previous decade, Hugh had built 'severall houses uppon parte of her Maj landes…beinge in Mossoglyn and Gwydryn and hath required the hedginge…of the same to his and their greate charges',[215] constructing 'houses, farmes and inclosures newlie made, with oxehouses…' on the lands in question.[216] Such processes of land improvement, enclosure and farm consolidation – creating a sharply reconfigured pattern of land holdings which was to last through the following three centuries – were becoming increasingly common in late sixteenth-century Anglesey. Cefn Maesoglan appears to have been such a new entity, replacing the multiple late-medieval holdings of the former Maesoglan township, whilst an adjacent farm consolidated at Maesoglan itself, under the continued separate ownership of Huw ap Rees Wynn and his successors.[217]

But if the latter was able to prevail in his case against Hugh Hughes, Rhydderch ap Rhisiart continued to be less successful. As ordered by the Exchequer court in 1587, he allowed Hugh to take possession of most of the lands at Maesoglan, Bodrida and Gwydryn, as well as of the Rhosyr mill – whilst continuing to fight an attritional battle over the ownership of two major blocs of pasture

211   D. Wyn Wiliam, *Y Canu Mawl i Deulu Mysoglen* (Llangefni, O.Jones, 1999), p.7.

212   Ibid., pp. 7, 16-17.

213   TNA E 123/12a, Decrees & Orders of Exchequer Court.

214   Plas Coch Estate maps for 1805 and 1875 – originals at Brynddu, Llanfechell, Ynys Môn.

215   TNA E 134/35&36Eliz/Mich 18. Statement of William ap Hugh ap Owen of Gwydryn, 10 August 1593 – see also note 131.

216   Ibid. Statement of 'William Roberts of Llanedwen, weaver', 10 August 1593.

217   Griffith, *Pedigrees*, p.83.

lying broadly between Myfyrian and Plas Coch, known as Ffridd Myfyrian and Ffridd Kenwrick ap Eignon.

In October 1586, as the original Commission was concluding its investigation, these fields had been the subject of side meetings, culminating in an arbitration conducted by Sir Richard Bulkeley and Hugh Owen of Orielton, Pembrokeshire, the latter 'kinsman to both the plaintiff and the defendant [who had] travelled most earnestlie to effecte an agreement between them'.[218] Hugh Hughes and Rhydderch ap Rhisiart were present in person at Sir Richard's Beaumaris home. In a memorandum agreed at that meeting,[219] the final fate of the two ffridds was deferred, pending their valuation by the two arbitrators. However, the documents are damaged and the precise details obscure – including the question of who, at that stage, was stated to have right of occupation. The implication appears to have been that they were Hugh's, but should be 'assigned' to three of his Montagu relatives, rather than remaining in his direct possession.[220]

However, Rhydderch continued to hang on grimly. He persisted in occupation and use of much of the land, whilst continuing to submit not only further petitions to the Exchequer Court on his original 'breach of trust' claim against Hugh, but also 'an English Bill' in the autumn of 1592, again asserting ownership of the two *fridds*. Later that year, the court ruled that he should be entitled to occupy the one nearest his home (Ffridd Myfyrian), subject to being able to produce proof of title. The other, Ffridd Kenwrick ap Eignon, close to Plas Coch, should be handed over to Hugh,[221] but this was clearly a temporary expedient. As the feud continued, Rhydderch physically obstructed his rival's use of even Ffridd Kenwrick ap Eignon. According to a later deposition by one of Hugh's witnesses, his brother John ap Dafydd Llwyd gent, 'the pl[aintiff] dyd occupie the landes in variance about v or vi yeares without painge aney rente to the def[endent] … sithens the commencement of the def[endent's] lease nowe in effect, the plaintiff do interrupt the def[endent] in occupac[i]on of fryth Kenwrick sundry times this yeare'. And a second witness, William Roberts, 'weaver', confirmed the position: 'The pl[aintiff] hathe interrupted the def[endent] and this deponente in the occupant[i]on of the said frith divers tymes by turning oute of the cattell continuallie'.[222] Hugh applied for, and was granted, an Information of Intrusion against Rhydderch, but the latter again

---

218 TNA E 134/35&36Eliz/Mich 18. Deposition of Hugh Owen, 10 August 1593.

219 The memorandum is attached to a statement by Sir Richard Bulkeley seven years later (19 October 1593) in evidence to the subsequent 1593/4 Exchequer Court trial (in TNA E 134/35&36Eliz/Mich 18).

220 Ibid.

221 TNA E 123/19(b).

222 Both on 10 August 1594, in TNA E 134/35 & 36Eliz/Mich 18.

countered, this time with a further motion to delay proceedings until his 'English Bill' had been heard.

Apparently in an attempt to resolve matters conclusively, the following year, 1593, a further trial then took place.[223] Indeed, it is largely from the copious surviving written interrogatories and witness depositions from this trial that it has been possible to trace the vagaries of the dispute overall. This time the Exchequer court ruling was conclusive: All of the matters in Rhydderch's petitions and English Bill had been dealt with. The various hearings and Commissions had established that the land was Hugh's. The encroachments were to stop. Not only was Hugh 'to remove (Rhydderch) out of the possession of' the *ffridds* in question, but he was absolved from obligation to respond to any of the outstanding allegations in Rhydderch's Bill.[224]

In due course, Hugh received Letters Patent from the crown, granting him, on 26 November 1598, the freeholds of all the properties confirmed in the judgement – a 120-year term, to commence in 1618 on the expiry of the exisiting lease-in-reversion.[225]

What had really happened?

Throughout the dispute, the key plea of the Myfyrian family had been that back in 1573 Hugh had used underhand means to acquire the lease-in-reversion. This claimed breach of trust was the recurrent theme of Rhydderch ap Rhisiart's successive petitions to the courts between 1580 and 1593. Questions posed in the latter's interrogatories on the point at the 1593 trial summarise his contention: '...Have ye not h[e]ard Richard ap Rhytherche the plaintiff's father say that Hugh Hughes faithfully promised to observe and to deale for him concerning his farme and did you heare the sayd Ric. saye that the sayd Hugh Hughes against the truste reposed dealt falsely with him?'[226] Twenty years after the event, Rhydderch's witnesses[227] were indeed ready to confirm that all of them had heard the latter's father say such things – although not, it should be noted, able to offer first-hand evidence that Rhisiart's allegation itself was well-grounded. For instance, John Owen ap Daniel of Llanddaniel Fab stated in evidence that he had 'h[e]ard that the plt father had reposed a p[er]sonal trust in the def[enden]t so that noe other man wold possess eney

---

223   TNA E 134/35 & 36Eliz/Mich18.

224   TNA. Exchequer Court: Decrees and Orders for Hilary 34th and Mich 35th, Vol 19, Folio 11.

225   See Appendix B, 'Hugh Hughes's Will', page 35 below.

226   TNA E 134/35&36Eliz/Mich 18. Interrogatories ministered on behalf of Rhydderch ap Richd plt against Hugh Hughes esq defft.

227   Ibid. The witnesses in question were: John Owen ap Daniel of Llanedwen; John ap Rees of Llanedwen; and Daniel Lloyd, clerk, of Trefdraeth.

lease of the same fearme. And h[e]ard that Mr Hughes promised to forsee the same accordinglie. And that he hathe h[e]ard afterwards that the def[enden]t had abused Ric ap Rhudd therein in that he had paste the same unto himselfe contrary to the former promise' [228] [emphases added]

Taken literally, this account would seem to imply the claim that, whilst still a largely untrained law student, in the second year of a long and arduous training as a barrister at Lincoln's Inn, Hugh had been entrusted by Rhisiart ap Rhydderch, a leading Anglesey figure in late middle age – hard-bitten, shrewd and a long-serving justice and former MP – with professional responsibility for securing the crown lease-in-reversion for lands constituting a key element of the Myfyrian estate. Cast in such terms, the suggestion seems far-fetched. Not only was Hugh at the time merely a neophyte law student from the provinces, with no influence at court, but Rhisiart himself would surely have suspected that the acquisition of crown lease-reversions was an arcane and specialist activity requiring inside knowledge and court contacts probably not (yet) available to the young man.

Hugh's account of the events of 1572-3 on the other hand was sharply different. He had bought the lease, he claimed, from one James Armorer, who in turn had purchased the original patent the previous year from one Thomas Gower. What is more, he (Hugh) had only purchased it from Armorer after the latter had first offered it, unsuccessfully, for sale back to Rhisiart ap Rhydderch.

According to Armorer's deposition to the 1593 trial:[229] 'After he [Armorer] had bought the same of the sayd Mr Gower metynge in London with the sayd pl[aintiff] Rhydderche ap Richard offered the same for a reasonable gayne to sale to the sayd pl[aintiff] farre better cheape than he hathe afterward sold the same to the Defenden[t]...' But Rhydderch had been infuriated by this offer, 'grately disputing the same to [Armorer] and threatened hym that he wold make yt not to be worthe to hym yf he kept yt, not worth fortie powndes, yet fortie powndes he wold gyve for yt having in reasonable tyme, to pay it and no more.' It appears however that Armorer was not prepared to wait. He got an (unnamed) Anglesey friend to approach some of Rhydderch's under-tenants with a view to possible individual sales, but the friend reported that 'non[e] of them durste kepe with hym for feare of the pl[aintiff] & his father who were tenantes then of the premises...' At which point, Armorer appears to have decided to complete a sale to Hugh and his father Dafydd Llwyd.

According to Hugh, even after their purchase of the lease in 1573, he and his father had bent over backwards to try to accommodate the Rhydderchs.

---

228   Ibid. Deposition of John Owen, 10 August 1593.

229   TNA E133/8/1126 (Part I), Baron's Depositions, 1593 Hilary (36 Eliz). Deposition of James Armorer.

Twenty years later, one of Hugh's witnesses, William ap Hugh ap Owen, recalled that Hugh and Dafydd 'did send this deponent to the compl[ainan]t's
father to offer the sale of the premises...for the like some of money as the
def[endent] had paid unto the said James Armorer'.[230] But Rhisiart ap Rhydderch declined, pointing out that the original lease still had ten years to run at
that stage, and that 'yf he lived longer than those yeares [he] hoped the def[en-
dent] should not enjoie the same'. But there, it seems, the politenesses ended.
The tensions bubbled on, and later in the decade, Rhydderch, his imposing
father now in his grave, launched the first of his sequence of pleas to the courts.

Explanation demanded

So what had *really* happened back in 1572-3? Successive Exchequer court inquiries and Commissions had found in Hugh's favour, reporting that no breach
of trust of the kind alleged by Rhydderch had been proved. On the other hand,
the fact that the reversion-lease ended up in Hugh's hands so soon after he
had been alerted to its possible availability demands a fuller explanation. Perhaps something more questionable did take place. For example, it is plausible
that, in the course of friendly family exchanges around the fire at Myfyrian or
Porthaml Isaf between a patriarchal Rhisiart and his bright young cousin
Hugh, the issue of the Maesoglan-Bodrida lease and Rhisiart's concern to secure the reversion in the near future could have been touched upon, with Hugh
perhaps contributing up-to-date gossip from the Inns of Court about mounting
speculative activity in such leases in the capital.

Shenanigans in Westminster

A thriving trade in leases-in-reversion was indeed developing in and around
Westminster by this time.[231] Most of them were being granted to medium-level
crown officials rather than sitting tenants, as, from the Exchequer's perspective,
a relatively painless way of increasing crown servants' incomes at a time when
the privy purse was ever more squeezed for hard cash. It was taken for granted
that any such lease granted would be quickly sold on for a profit; by the concluding decades of the century, Madeleine Gray suggests, 'reversionary (crown)
leases were normally designed not for exploitation by the nominal lessee but
to allow him to profit from the difference between unimproved rents and actual
land values by selling the reversion'.[232] Gray further shows how these circum-

---

230 Ibid. Deposition of William ap Hugh ap Owen.

231 D. Thomas, 'Leases in Reversion on the Crown's Lands, 1558-1603', *Economic History
     Review* 30 (1977), pp.67-72; Russell, *Crisis of the Parliaments*, pp.30-38.

232 M. Gray, 'Mr Auditor's Man: the Career of Richard Budd, Estate Agent and Crown Official',
     WHR (1985), pp.307-323.

stances created growing opportunities for officials in the Exchequer's bureau-cracies, such as the various Auditors' offices where information about relevant crown properties was monitored and assembled, to use their insider knowledge to speculate, either for themselves or for land-hungry clients around the coun-try, in the buying and selling of such reversions.

It is not hard to imagine Rhisiart responding to news of such developments by urging his intellectually sophisticated young kinsman to keep an ear open for any developments that might bear on the Maesoglan-Bodrida reversion specifically. Nor is it hard to imagine Hugh, back in London, his interest piqued, raising the matter with Lincoln's Inn friends, and catching the atten-tion, deliberately or otherwise, of potentially interested figures like Thomas Gower.[233] For Hugh, at this early stage of his career, to actively monitor the Maesoglan-Bodrida reversion would have required him to ask people in the know, with the inevitable risk that such folk might choose to take up the op-portunity for themselves.

Or another way of looking at it

That is one possibility, implying relative innocence and purity of intention in Hugh. But a somewhat darker reading, closer to the Rhydderchs' suspicions, may also be worth considering. As we have seen in chapter one, Hugh's father, Dafydd Llwyd, was a dynamic and ambitious individual, active in developing the interests of the family and its Plas Coch estate. His completion of the first stage of the new mansion in 1569, and his investment in sending Hugh to Cam-bridge and the Inns of Court, and his brother Owen to Oxford,[234] are powerful testimony to this. He would have been aware of the enviable power and prestige of his nearby Rhydderch kinsmen, and the free and easy, even somewhat deca-dent, way in which they were exploiting their position as the crown's farmers at Rhosyr and Maesoglan-Bodrida. Indeed, in the 1587 trial, Hugh alleged that Rhydderch had encouraged the under-tenants to withdraw their suit from the Rhosyr crown mill and had accepted private contributions in lieu of that suit – whilst also 'suffering divers of his friends to erect mills of their own within half a mile of the said Crown mill', meanwhile encouraging destruction of the latter's associated channels and watercourses.[235] So overall it is reasonable to

---

233   It seems possible this 'Thomas Gower of Yorkshire' was the abrasive soldier Sir Thomas
       Gower 'of Yorkshire' (fl. 1530-1577), noted as having played a major role in the Scottish
       wars of the mid-sixteenth century (ODNB, Vol 23, pp.141-142), and probably the individual
       of that name referred to in David Thomas's article (op.cit note 231) as having obtained
       several leases-in-reversion for crown lands in Lincolnshire and twelve other counties in the
       1570s. (TNA E 310/41/16 mss. 583-595).

234   See note 109.

235   G. Jones, Exchequer Proceedings concerning Wales: Henry VIII – Elizabeth (Cardiff, UWP,

assume that Hugh would have discussed with his father any fireside conversation with Rhydderch concerning the reversion issue – and not inconceivable that the two of them could then have seen an opportunity, and worked out a scheme whereby the lease could be made to become available for sale back in Anglesey, with a fair chance of their being able to wrest it from their, perhaps overbearing, relatives. Through the family networks, Dafydd (who was of course Rhisiart's first cousin) would probably have known about the state of the Myfyrian finances. There were grounds for believing these were not as healthy as they might once have been. The evidence for this is circumstantial, but intriguing. During the 1593 trial,[236] one of Hugh's witnesses, the 70-year-old Thomas Hughes of Llanedwen, reported that in about 1569, when he (TH) had been a haberdasher in London, Rhisiart ap Rhydderch 'dyd pawne a boxe with writing wherein (were) two patents leases of the premises…for a certaine sum of money'. The lender was Thomas Hughes himself, and Rhisiart repaid him, and reclaimed the boxes, after an unspecified interval. Strikingly, this appears to have been the only matter on which Thomas Hughes was asked to make a deposition on Hugh's behalf. The incident occurred just three years before Thomas Gower took his decisive initiative on the Maesoglan-Bodrida lease. A possible implication was that across that period Rhisiart may have been financially stretched. On the strength of that, Hugh and his father could have judged the Rhydderchs unlikely to be able to afford purchase of the lease from Armorer, whereas, presumably, they themselves would.

The plan, if such there was, would have involved tipping-off some likely London acquaintance – perhaps James Armorer of Furnival's Inn (a Lincoln's Inn adjunct) – who would then, in the fashion outlined by Madeleine Gray,[237] urge Gower to act as his 'insider' agent in acquiring and passing on the patent. Armorer would then come to Anglesey, secure in the knowledge that he had a potential buyer in Hugh and Dafydd, once he had gone through the motions of offering the lease for sale back to the Rhydderchs. There is indirect confirmation of this hypothesis in the perhaps hyper-scrupulous way in which Dafydd and Hugh offered the lease back to Rhydderch once it was securely theirs. James Armorer had already done this at a slightly earlier stage, and been given a flea in his ear for his pains. What is more, Rhydderch's circumstances had not changed. So Dafydd and Hugh may well have been confident he would say no again; they certainly would not have wanted to lose the property now that it was in their hands. Perhaps it is not unfair to put the gesture to Rhydderch down to an uneasy concern to cover their tracks. After all, they were

---

1939), p.13. (TNA E 5/36/7).

236   TNA E 134/35 & 36 Mich 18.

237   Gray, 'Mr Auditor's Man'.

going to have to live cheek by jowl with the Myfyrian family into the indefinite future, and would have been concerned to head off any prospect of an enduring family feud. However, as will be seen shortly, a feud is what they got.

Two 'mentalités'

The Plas Coch and Myfyrian families were of the same *uchelwr* social class, and, it may be inferred, equally well-disposed towards the 1536/1543 administrative changes in Wales. In their different ways, each had continued to benefit from the resources and opportunities these changes offered – the Rhydderchs through crown patronage of material kinds, which had bolstered their local standing, Hugh Hughes and his father through educational and professional opportunities which turned out to have similar consequential effects. However, these same benefits also had the effect of reinforcing important differences between the two families.

In the Rhydderchs' case, the crown lease for Maesoglan-Bodrida, Rhosyr Mill, and the other associated lands had enabled successive generations to perpetuate Myfyrian's role as a prominent local political and cultural presence, within a recognisably late-medieval Welsh framework. Though the days of land held in common based on kindreds had largely dissolved over the previous century in the face of an increasingly pervasive individualism – indeed Myfyrian was itself an example of an estate which had developed by by-passing the *cyfran* system of inheritance from the mid-fifteenth century onwards – in other respects the Rhydderchs maintained many of the old ways. Well into the later decades of the sixteenth century, the household at Myfyrian was being celebrated by bards as a mecca of traditional culture and hospitality, where poetry, music and feasting were a norm:

> ... *aur a gwin*
> *a pharadwys gyffredin* ... [238]

    ' ... gold and wine
       and a common paradise ...'

and

> *i bob rhai, i bawb y rhydd*
> *bara can a brig gwinwydd.* [239]

    ' ...To all manner of people, she [Catrin] gives to all
       white bread and the choicest wine '

---

238   Lewis Menai, 'Marwnad Rhydderch ap Dafydd 1562', in Wyn Wiliam, *Myfyrian*, p.26.

239   Huw Cornwy, 'Marwnad Rhisiart ap Rhydderch', in Wyn Wiliam. *Myfyrian*, p.54.

The veteran poet Wiliam Cynwal was an indicative presence in this regard.[240] A former apprentice to Gruffudd Hiraethog, he was noted as a highly traditional upholder of the medieval bardic conventions, reflected in his celebrated and protracted verse exchanges with Edmund Prys throughout the 1580s concerning the future direction of Welsh poetry.[241] The attractiveness of the household to creative individuals of Cynwal's culturally conservative leanings, as much as the highly praised local leadership practices of Rhydderch ap Dafydd and Rhisiart ap Rhydderch, suggests that the Myfyrian family identified itself with historic continuities of Welsh culture and social relationship. Any benefactions they had received from the English crown provided a base for perpetuating their position in that regard. It is not insignificant that Rhydderch ap Rhisiart, Hugh Hughes's contemporary and a key protagonist after Rhisiart's death in 1576, appears to have identified personally with this background to such an extent that he himself became known as a poet of some accomplishment within the tradition.[242] During his proprietorship however, the family's former political role dipped. Unlike his father and grandfather, this Rhydderch was appointed to no public posts, and with the estate reduced by the loss of the crown lease, the family's overall standing appears to have been diminished.[243]

The Plas Coch / Porthaml Isaf family, by contrast, were looking outwards, engaging with new social forces and possibilities opening up in the late-Tudor 'Britain' of which Wales was now part. They were equally conscious of local cultural implications of their lineage, but also keen to reach beyond the limitations of their inherited circumstances. Huw ap Llewelyn took a bold initiative in sending Dafydd to be schooled at Hereford in the 1530s. It paid off. By the time of the Maesoglan-Bodrida controversy in the last two decades of the century, and benefitting from Dafydd's active paternal encouragement, Hugh was on the way to local and regional eminence of a kind distinctly different from that the Rhydderchs had enjoyed. As will be seen, Hugh's education and accomplishments as an English-trained lawyer and crown official, coupled to native roots in Anglesey and the north Wales region, were having the effect of turning him into a hybrid of a novel kind.

---

240 Marwnad Rhisiart ap Rhydderch 1576 reflects Cynwal's appreciation of Myfyrian's atmosphere (Wyn Wiliam, *Myfyrian*, pp.61-63).

241 Lewis, 'Decline of Professional Poetry', pp.40-42. Prys, the Cambridge-educated humanist Archdeacon of Merioneth, castigated Cynwal for his lack of responsiveness to wider Renaissance visions of poetic possibilities. Cynwal defended perpetuation of the historic bardic conventions and preoccupations.

242 Wyn Wiliam, *Myfyrian*, p.8. Griffith, *Pedigrees*, p.59.

243 Things improved for them in the next generation however with the professional brilliance of Rhydderch's son, Richard Prydderch of Llanidan, who became a Justice of the Chester circuit and member of the Council in the Marches. He also became a thorn in the flesh of Hugh Hughes's son, Roger, as will become clear later in this chapter.

Contrasting values

One is tempted to detect such differences of value and aspiration between the two households in their respective approaches to the Maesoglan-Bodrida trials themselves. Consider, for example, the morally questionable skill of Hugh and Dafydd's successful manoeuvres to acquire the lease (if that hypothesis is accepted). This reflected not only a cunning and well-calibrated understanding of the interplay between Westminster actors' self-interest and local outcomes, but also an ability to preserve the appearance that they themselves were squeaky clean, should there be any subsequent legal challenge (as indeed there proved to be). Compare this with the clumsiness of Rhisiart ap Rhydderch's initial emotional, even violent, response to James Armorer's offer, and Rhydderch's later refusal physically to vacate lands the courts had already ruled were Hugh's. The one approach, setting aside its ethical ambiguities, reflected legal and political subtlety, the other, habits and patterns of parochial dominance.

The comparative forensic quality of their respective selections of witnesses and interrogatory questions is equally suggestive. In the 1593 trial, Rhydderch ap Rhisiart's witnesses were all exposed, through Hugh's targeted questions, as close relatives or indebted familiars of Rhydderch himself, throwing doubt on their reliability. Rhydderch's own interrogatories were erratic and sometimes diffuse, lacking the focus of Hugh's, which strike the reader as crisp and logical. The depositions of his witnesses are equally clear. Or again, Rhydderch's multiple petitions repeated, again and again, allegations on which rulings had already been made, eventually exasperating the Exchequer judges:

> '... Forasmuch as Her Ma[jesty]'s Attorney Generall hathe upon the examininge of the whole matter shewed unto this honourable courte divers former proceedings in the said cause that the def[endan]t had at sevrall tymes before the sayd Bill exhibited by way of complaint against the said Hughes seven sevrall petitions to the Right Honorable the Lo[rd] Chancellor of England alledginge and charginge hym with the sayd trust. His Lordshipp referred the sevrall examinacon thereof to the Right Honorable Mr Baron Gent, Mr Auditor Hanbury, Mr John Morley, Mr Hughes her Ma[jesty]'s forryster ... [who] severally certified that they coulde finde no seche trust at all reposed in Hughes ... And ... the sayd English Bill against the sayd Hughes dothe conteyne no other matter than was conteyned in the sayd sevrall petitions...' [244]

Hugh's approach, by contrast, appears to have been to be patient, professionally confident perhaps that he would win any contest in the courts.

---

244 TNA 123/19. Exchequer Court Decrees & Orders for Hilary 34th and Mich 35th, Vol 19, folio 11.

It is useful here to keep in mind that by 1592-3, when the crucial court proceedings took place, Hugh was a busy and successful advocate in his own right,
not least as Deputy Attorney General in the Court of Great Sessions.[245] Doubtless he crafted his approach to the trial proceedings for himself, explicitly or
otherwise. Rhydderch on the other hand was probably reliant on the serviceof
local attorneys, at an accumulating cost which can only be guessed at.

Not so straightforward

The contention here is that such apparently unremarkable differences between
the two key protagonists also have a richer significance. They offer pointers to
a contrast of *mentalités* between the Plas Coch and Myfyrian families, reflecting
cultural differences, and indeed tensions, within the Welsh landowning classes
at this historical moment. There has been a tendency in even the best histories
of the period to treat the late sixteenth-century Welsh 'gentry' as largely a ho-
mogeneous whole, with shared values and aspirations – taking up the reins of
local power, competing for land to build up their estates, litigating one with
another, marrying their own kind, and selectively adopting English ways. To
be sure, there is recognition that different individuals and families varied in
their attachments to historic Welsh manners and mores or the opportunities
for advancement that had opened up in England, but nevertheless the general
picture offered is one of a social caste sharing broadly consistent interests and
outlooks.[246]

Through the prism of the Maesoglan-Bodrida dispute, it is possible to dis-
cern the outlines of something more complex, whereby differences of personal
experience were producing differences of outlook amongst Welshmen of similar
backgrounds. Hugh Hughes's years of immersion in London and English legal
institutions had equipped him not only with the specialist skills and insider
knowledge to prevail in judicial disputes, but also with what might be pictured
as a returning outsider's sense of the ways in which previously entrenched patterns of local power and influence in Anglesey, were no less open to change
than in other parts of the Wales and England where seriously competitive land
markets were developing.

It is hard to tell how typical of Hugh's behaviour this particular episode may
have been. It should be borne in mind that the original acquisition of the reversion had taken place in 1572, when he was still only 24, with the crucial
legal proceedings not occurring till upwards of fifteen years later, by which
time he was well on the way to becoming a regional eminence. Possibly in ret-

---

245   See pp. 124-125.

246   Dyfnallt Owen, *Elizabethan Wales*, Chapter 1 passim; J Davies, *History of Wales*, pp.219-
      225; Gwynfor Jones, *Welsh Gentry*, passim.

rospect he found the experience and its fallouts disconcerting, because of the depth of the resulting split with the Myfyrian kinsmen. Certainly the Plas Coch papers contain no hints of similar cases of sharp practice over subsequent years, though that may simply mean Hugh was able to cover his tracks with legal polish. Perhaps he chalked up the whole reversion episode to youthful experience – knowing anyway that the land was now securely Plas Coch's – and decided not to risk more such upsets? His other major crown land acquisition, the Nantcall purchase discussed below in chapter four,[247] was an altogether subtler affair, more the result of being in the right place at the right time than of sleight of hand.

Continuing tensions

Be that as it may, the Rhydderchs' bitterness at the loss of properties they continued to think of as rightfully theirs, and the Hughes's determination to hold onto their gains, continued well into the next century, unappeased by the deaths of Hugh (in 1609) and Rhydderch ap Rhisiart (in 1606). Their respective sons, Roger Hughes and Richard Prydderch, themselves both lawyers, perpetuated the bad blood. Prydderch rose to greater professional heights than Roger, as mentioned above,[248] and used his skills to initiate at least two Bills of Complaint against the latter in the Council in the Marches – one in c.1620, another in 1641.[249] The first of these referred back explicitly to parcels of land acquired by Hugh several decades earlier during the original reversion row. The forty acres in question had not been part of the crown property under contention, Prydderch claimed, but were in fact 'a messuage, gardens and meadowes' which had properly belonged to his father, Rhydderch ap Rhisiart, in his final years. Prydderch alleged that 'Hugh Hughes deceased being the late Queene and Kinge's Attorney in North Wales and by that meanes of great power in this countie did by color of some conveyance made unto him by the sisters of the said John ap Robert [a previous lessee] who had noe right to the premises wrongfully entered into the said premises and lands…' [250] More than thirty years after the original event, he demanded the court require Roger to produce deeds proving title to the property, apparently confident that the latter would not be able to do so. Unfortunately it has not been possible to establish how the case turned out, as no further surviving documents can be traced. However, there is no mistaking the flavour of a continuing vendetta in the very posting of a Bill in this public fashion.

---

247 See page 121.
248 See note 251.
249 UB Plas Coch 222.
250 UB Plas Coch 3017.

Similarly in a second case twenty-one years on – by which time Prydderch
had risen to the heights of Puisne Justice of the Chester circuit, and hence a
lawyer member of the Council in the Marches[251] – the mutual animosity was
still evident. This time the complaint focused on 'Ffrith Philipp' in Gwydryn,
which, it will be recalled, had been one of the portions of land investigated by
the specially convened Commission in 1586 at the height of the original dispute.[252] Evidently, the title to this land too was still in contention more than
fifty years later. Prydderch, who by this stage was living at Llanidan Hall in
the parish adjacent to Plas Coch, claimed it had been conveyed to him recently
in two parcels, one from Lewis Williams, the other from Lewis ap William Pugh
(conceivably the same individual), and furthermore – a colourful detail – that
the former had left him 'compost to the value of five shillings' in one of the
fields. The new allegation was that on 11 January 1640 Roger and his servants
Owen John ap Euan, John Williams and Rowland ap Hugh had 'enter[ed] in
and upon the said p[ar]cell of land and take[n] and cast away the said compost
and plow[ed] the said p[ar]cell of lands ...who beinge resisted by two of [Pry-
dderch]'s servants...did enter upon the same p[ar]cell of land on the 12th and
13th dayes of the month and divers other dayes, did likewise enter...breaking
the meares thereof...' [253] The implication appears to be that Roger's aggressive
actions reflected a conviction that the land was his rather than Prydderch's.
Indeed, in the initial 'answeres and demurrers' offered by Roger and his servants, Prydderch's complaint was scorned as 'devised and contrived of malice'
and designed only 'to putt the said defendant [sic] to greate trouble and ex-
pences in the lawe'. If Prydderch believed he had a case against them, which
he didn't, claimed Roger and Co., he should pursue it at common law in the
normal fashion, rather than in the Council in the Marches, where the com-
plainant himself was 'one of the judges of the said Courte'.[254] The outcome of
this suit too is unknown, but again what is important is its suggestion of an
unbroken attritional struggle between the families at least a generation after
the demise of the original two litigants.

There is also the puzzling matter of a four-line *englyn*, the only trace of which
is its appearance as part of an *Anecdote of the ancient House of Plas Coch, in the
Island of Anglesey* in the Cambrian Register of 1795.[255] The text of this poem,
with a translation by the Revd Evan Evans of Cardiganshire, a noted Welsh
scholar and translator of the time, appears there as follows (although the translation appears rather milder in tone than conveyed in the Welsh original):

251   W.R.Williams, *The History of the Great Sessions in Wales, 1542-1830* (Brecknock, 1899), p.57.

252   UB Plas Coch 2968 – see p.37.

253   UB Plas Coch 222.

254   Ibid.

255   *Cambrian Register* (1795), p.440.

Plasau, Parlyrau, pur loywon dyrau
A dyfrad fendithion
Os gwyrwyd ais y gwirion
A fai tai yn y fut hon?

> ' Ye stately palaces and princely towers,
> And all the wealth that luxury devours;
> If by the poor man's sweat and wrongs you rise,
> Can you last long? and Heaven not hear his cries? '

The Cambrian Register's short accompanying text explains that 'Hugh Hughes, of this house, was Queen Elizabeth's attorney in North Wales, a lawyer, and reputed a great oppressor; therefore upon his building of Plas Coch [*i.e.* in the 1590s] a certain poet made this *englyn*... The poet was sued in the Star Chamber, by the said Hugh Hughes, for a libel, but saved himself by the dubitative conjunction *Os* [if]'.[256] Frustratingly, it has proved impossible to track down this Star Chamber case. There seems to be no reference to it in the court's records of the time.[257] However, given the target and the timing, it is tempting to suggest a possible poet – 'the bard' Rhydderch ap Rhisiart, still smarting from the loss of Bodrida, Maesoglan and the other crown properties, and writing perhaps on behalf of the dispossessed under-tenants as much as himself.

These various episodes in the wake of the original dispute tend to confirm the likelihood that Hugh's success in outmanoeuvring the Rhydderchs would not have won him many friends in Llanedwen or the surrounding districts. For most, it may be surmised, the historical legacy of local power and prestige of the Rhydderchs, and their continuing association with the encouragement of vernacular cultural pursuits and customs, would have been respected as part of the familiar social fabric of the area. Moreover, the Myfyrian family members appear to have been lax and perhaps indulgent landlords vis a vis the long-established under-tenants at Maesoglan and Bodrida.[258] The major improvements initiated by Hugh once he took possession[259] suggest that by contrast the Rhydderchs' farming practices had probably been of a more casual 'traditional' kind. Hugh as an improving landlord was already initiating transformations which would almost certainly have been experienced as locally unsettling, of benefit to fewer tenants than under the previous regime as a consequence of the creation of larger individual farms. New brooms are rarely

---

256 Ibid.

257 I. ab O. Edwards, *Catalogues of Star Chamber Proceedings relating to Wales* (Cardiff, University Press Board, 1929).

258 See pp. 41-42.

259 See p.36.

popular in settled rural areas even to this day, and it seems reasonable to suppose that his 'victory' would have resulted in increased social distance between himself and at least the less fortunate of his neighbours, during what appears to have been a period of growing deprivation and impoverishment for many former small-holders.[260]

The saga as a whole can thus be seen to have been significant in several respects. It was characteristic of the unsettling developments in rural economy arising at this time in many parts of Wales as well as in England, as new legal skills and commercial resources came to be applied increasingly widely to the competition for land.[261] It illustrates the ways in which a new generation of legally sophisticated gentry was gaining prominence in some rural areas, within a wider context in which confidence in the law was increasingly widespread amongst the Welsh gentry generally (as Rhydderch ap Rhisiart's persistence tends to confirm). The dispute also shows how in Wales specifically, English educational influences were acting to feed, and indeed exacerbate, differences of outlook between Welsh-speaking *uchelwr* land-holders themselves. Most significant of all however, in the context of this book, the saga offers glimpses of the hierarchical and conservative Welsh social world in which Hugh was operating as proprietor of Plas Coch, and some of the ways in which he chose to deal with it. This was the world in which he had chosen to live, notwithstanding the sophistication of his educational and legal training – and it is important not to lose sight of that fact when it comes to considering Hugh's sense of himself in the round later in these pages. Before that however, it is appropriate to consider his education and public career, to begin to gain a picture of his wider affiliations and accomplishments. The next three chapters attempt this.

---

260   Williams, *Tudor Gwynedd*, pp.53-56.

261   Thorne, 'Tudor Social Transformation & Legal Change'.

3 *English Influences*

HUGH HUGHES was rooted, by origins and upbringing, in south-east Anglesey. But his adult life was moulded deeply by English influences, and this chapter explores some of these. It might be tempting to see Hugh as simply an aspiring Welshman of the period, following paths which others of his kind were also cultivating in the late Tudor period. But that would be to over-simplify. The road from north Wales to London and the Inns of Court was indeed becoming well-worn by this time. For example, three successful lawyer contemporaries of Hugh, all fellow-Benchers at Lincoln's Inn, were his already-mentioned close neighbour Thomas Bulkeley of Porthaml Hall (formerly Porthaml Uchaf) (*d.*1593), William (later Sir William) Jones of Castellmarch, Caernarfonshire (1566-1640), and Peter (later Sir Peter) Mutton of Llanerch, Denbighshire (1565-1627). The career patterns of the four contain both similarities and differences, as will emerge below. Nevertheless it is the particularities of Hugh's personal experience which are of greatest significance for the present inquiry, which concerns the developing attitudes and sense of personal identity of an educated Welshman who became involved directly in the governance of Wales in the period following its major statutory reconfiguration under Henry VIII.[262]

In the chapter's analysis, there is somewhat greater reliance on secondary source materials than in the previous two – necessarily, since the aim is to track the principal through a web of educational and professional contexts, despite the fact that personal primary documents of his own are generally lacking.

Using the Tudor road system

The discussion that follows places Hugh at various points in such English cities as Cambridge, Hereford, Ludlow, and most of all London. This being so, a preliminary word about his likely modes of travel from Anglesey to (and within) England may be helpful.

Almost certainly – there is no clinching personal documentation – Hugh's journeys to England were made on horseback, with possible occasional resort, for brief stretches, to vessels using inland or coastal waterways. His most probable way into England would be the by-then well-established route between

---

262 The detail of the resulting institutional reorganisation is discussed in Chapter 4.

Beaumaris and Chester, and thence to parts east or south in England.

This would have involved initially a sea crossing from Beaumaris, either by ferry to Abergwyngregyn or coastal carrier to Conwy, and thereafter on horseback along the road through Rhuddlan to Chester. Recent research has confirmed that from the 1570s, official postal communications between Dublin and London were passing by this long-established north Wales route.[263] Hugh's most likely road from Chester on to London would have included Lichfield, Coventry and St Alban's, much of it along stretches of the ancient Watling Street. For Hereford, there would have been the option of horseback to Shrewsbury, followed by passenger ferry down the Severn to Worcester, and then a further brief stage by road.

In the late-Tudor period, highway use by travellers of many kinds was growing in parallel with commercial opportunities and multiplying administrative and cultural activities.[264] Contrary to many modern assumptions, most arterial routes of the time were maintained in conditions adequate for routine use, with the frequently-publicised exceptions reflecting concern to maintain standards in circumstances of increasing density of road use. 'Over-privileging of reports regarding the poor state of certain stretches of particular stretches of public highways has created a perception that such conditions were more widespread than was really the case', Brayshay suggests.[265] The landmark 1555 Highways Act (2 & 3 Philip & Mary c. 8, 1555, An Act for the Amending of the Highe Wayes) across the country should be seen as the first of a succession of late-Tudor measures aimed at standardising new parish-based road repair and maintenance obligations, reflecting mounting pressures from steadily-increasing road use.

In parallel, the increasing levels of road travel were also sustaining a complex ad hoc infrastructure across much of the country of taverns and 'post-houses', at intervals of between twelve and twenty miles, offering accommodation and horses for hire in response to better-off travellers' needs. This was particularly true of the midlands and along the key arteries towards London.

In short, the possibilities for travel between Anglesey and major English cities during the late-Elizabethan period were well-established, albeit arduous and challenging in their physical demands on the individual traveller. A personal journey between Anglesey and London undertaken would have taken up to a week, involving several overnight stops – albeit recent research has shown that the mean time for conveyance of letters between Chester and the capital by the later sixteenth century was just forty hours.[266]

263   G.Ayres, *History of the Mail Routes to Ireland until 1850* (www.lulu.com, 2017).

264   M.Brayshay, *Land Travel and Communications in Tudor and Stuart England: Achieving a Joined-Up Realm* (Liverpool University Press, 2014).

265   Ibid., p.121.

266   Ibid., p.287, fig 89.

Hugh's school and university

Humphrey Llwyd, writing in 1572, observed of Elizabethan Wales, 'there is no man so poore but for some space he setteth forth his children to schole, and suche as profitte in studie sendet them unto the universities where for the most part they enforce them to studie the civile law'.[267] There are echoes here of the Porthaml Isaf / Plas Coch family.

Hugh's father, Dafydd Llwyd, wanted a good education for his eldest son. Though there is an absence of evidence pin-pointing Hugh's attendance at any specific school, two credible possibilities suggest themselves. One is the Friars Grammar School at Bangor, which was founded in 1557,[268] when Hugh was

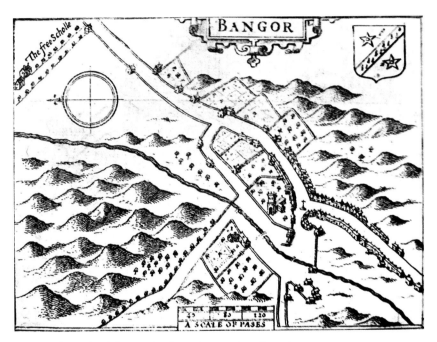

Friars free school, Bangor, in the early seventeenth century
Founded in 1557, Friars (*'The free Scholle' in John Speed's town plan*)
possibly provided part of Hugh Hughes's early education. It was
one of many grammar school foundations created across England
and Wales in the Tudor period, aimed at fostering the development
of a new protestant clerisy in post-Reformation Britain.

---

267   Humphrey Llwyd, *Commentaroli Descriptionis Britannicae Fragmentum* (Cologne 1572) tr. Thomas Twyne, *The Breviary of Britayne* (London 1573), fo. 606.

268   H.Barber & H.Lewis, *The History of Friars School, Bangor* (1901)

aged nine. Like most establishments of the new 'grammar school' type, it offered a humanistic education of the kind used to prepare pupils for university
at Oxford or Cambridge. The curricular focus was on classical grammar and
linguistics, alongside religious instruction, leading to a selective acquaintance
with the languages and literature of the ancient world [269] – a body of knowledge
held suitable for entry into both the universities and Inns of Court. Situated
just six miles from Hugh's home in Llanedwen, Friars would have been the
nearest of the host of such new secondary schools across England and Wales
in the mid / late sixteenth century, many of which (like Friars itself) had been
locally endowed.

A second possibility is Hereford Cathedral School. This was a far earlier
foundation, across the border in England. It had been attended by Dafydd
Llwyd himself, probably in the late 1520s and early 1530s. This is known from
a hand-written letter by one Hugh Roberts to Dafydd's father, Huw ap Llewelyn, reporting on Dafydd's progress in his studies and reminding the father of
the need to pay the school fees.[270] Though the letter is undated, it can be inferred to have been written in about 1529-30.[271] The 'Hugh' in question was a
godson and nephew of Huw's, living in or close to Hereford, and had evidently
been deputed to keep an eye on the young Dafydd during term-times, a
boarder a long way from home.

The original decision of Huw ap Llewelyn to send his eldest son and heir
to be educated at Hereford in the late 1520s suggests a degree of prescience
about the coming importance of attunement to English language and culture
for the family's welfare in the new world then being consolidated through the
acts of union. Later in the century, the trickle of Welsh adolescents being sent
to England for secondary schooling developed into a steady stream,[272] but at
the time Huw took his decision for Dafydd, probably in the mid-1530s, it would
have been an adventurous, as well as a financially demanding, commitment
for a native Anglesey family of relatively limited means. The spirit in which
such a decision would have been taken was probably not dissimilar from that
of a present-day EU citizen on the continental mainland choosing to learn English; there was no intention of renouncing the sense of Welsh identity – almost

---

269 W.P.Griffith, 'Schooling and Society' in Gwynfor Jones (ed.), *Class, Community and Culture*,
     p.92.

270 UB Plas Coch 55.

271 The archivist Thomas Richards, in the 1937 Plas Coch manuscript catalogue, suggests that
     the (undated) letter is from around 1550. However as Dafydd was already active in the
     property market in his own right by the mid-1540s (*e.g.* UB Plas Coch 50, 53, 54), this is
     clearly far too late. The inference for a date several years earlier rests on the internal evidence
     of the letter itself, pointing to his then-levels of academic attainment.

272 Dyfnallt Owen, *Elizabethan Wales*, pp.206-207.

certainly the aim was become equipped for future participation in the dynamic wider worlds of the professions, commerce or public life, for which English was already the *lingua franca*, often supplanting Norman-French or Latin, including, increasingly, in Wales.

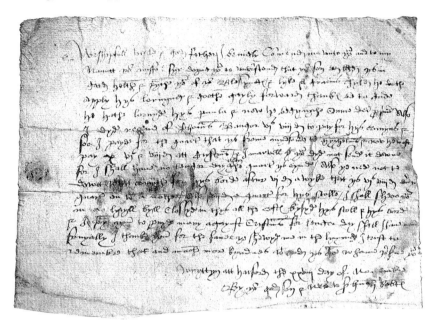

School report of the 1520s. This letter to Hugh's grandfather, Huw ap Llewelyn, from a relative resident in Hereford, reports on the educational progress of Dafydd Llwyd ap Huw (Hugh Hughes's father) at Hereford Cathedral School, where the latter was a boarder in Henry VIII's reign. Up-to-date payment of the fees is shown as a central concern. The letter implies the significance of a good (English) education for Hugh's Welsh-speaking family, at a surprisingly early stage in the Tudor period.

The Cathedral School's records for the period are too incomplete[273] to support any unambiguous claim that Dafydd in turn sent Hugh to be educated at his old school. There are circumstantial reasons, however, for thinking this could have been the case. Dafydd's own Hereford school experience appears to have confirmed him in his father's conviction that the future lay in an English education, as can be seen from the decision in the 1560s to send at least two of his own sons, Hugh and Owain[274] to Cambridge and Oxford Universities respectively, a commitment requiring substantial outlay in the expectation

273   Hereford Cathedral archivist, personal communication, 14 April 2009.
274   UB Plas Coch 154 & 2993.

of longer-term advantages. Fluency in English, amongst other intellectual accomplishments flowing from the curriculum, would have been a prerequisite. He may well have felt that the grammar school at Hereford could provide for his sons as well as it had for him. At all events, where Hugh at least was concerned, his schooling and intellectual calibre were of sufficient quality that in 1564, he was able to enter Trinity College, Cambridge,[275] at that time still a recent addition to the university. How or why that particular college accepted him is unclear. Of Hugh's Welsh contemporaries to matriculate at Cambridge in the 1560s, most went to either St John's or Christ's, as will be seen below. It has not proved possible to trace any personal connection that inclined Hugh, or Dafydd on his behalf, to prefer Trinity. But whatever the background, he was the first in his family to have attained such heights – a relatively poor (by national standards) Welsh-speaking 16-year-old from distant Anglesey, vaulted into the heart of English intellectual culture, 250 miles from home. At Trinity he would have found himself amongst scions of some of the wealthiest, as well as some of the cleverest, families in the land. It must have been a tumultuous personal experience.

Trinity experience

Trinity College had been founded by Henry VIII in 1546, a mere eighteen years previously, as an amalgam of two previously-existing Cambridge colleges – King's Hall and Michaelhouse. The new entity was considerably richer than either of these, being freshly endowed with assets from dissolved monasteries and private gifts of land from the monarch as one of his last acts.[276] Hugh would have had more reason than some to value these benefactions, since he was a a sizar of the college, the recipient of a bursary in exchange for part-time work as a servitor, waiting on dons or fellow-commoners, the latter being especially privileged undergraduates.[277] This was far from uncommon at the time. One estimate suggests that up to a third of Oxford and Cambridge students in this period were from less well-off families and benefiting from sizarships.[278] The latter would have offset the battels his father Dafydd would otherwise have had to pay in full, amounting at this time to around £20 a year.[279]

He would have been one of only a modest proportion of undergraduates in the college expecting to complete a full degree. In the year of his matriculation (1564), only 80 of the 1200 students in the entire university graduated as Bach-

---

275   Rouse Ball & Venn, *Admissions to Trinity.*

276   www.trin.cam.ac.uk/about/historical-overview

277   Stone, 'The Educational Revolution in England', p.67.

278   J.B.Mullinger, *History of Cambridge University* Vol II (Cambridge, CUP, 1888) p.188.

279   W.P.Griffith, *Learning, Law and Religion*, pp.59-64.

elor of Arts, a pattern which was normal for the period.[280] The reality was that throughout the late sixteenth century, the majority of young men at Cambridge and Oxford were pursuing the elements of a broadly humanistic education through courses inside and outside their colleges with little intention of completing a degree. Increasingly undergraduates were pursuing courses reflecting new civilising ideals of education which had been articulated by such writers as Castiglione and Erasmus, and subsequently, more locally, Sir Thomas Elyot, Roger Ascham and their like. The attributes nurtured during a university education were contributing to the development of a more diversified gentry-based ruling class with new shared cultural values and norms. The academic imprimatur of a degree was of less consequence for many than the social experience at Oxford or Cambridge of developing these gentlemanly virtues and capacities, as a precursor to local leadership or, for some, service to the crown. In general, it was only to the less well-off [281] – in particular intellectually gifted and relatively impecunious outsiders of Hugh's kind – that degrees were important as stepping stones to professions such as the church or the law, with their potential for higher social status in due course.[282] But this was not always the case. His fellow north-west Welshman, (Sir) William Jones of Castellmarch – later a King's Bench judge – matriculated at St Edmund's Hall, Oxford in the early 1580s, but did not take a degree, without penalty to his later ascent in the judiciary.[283]

Hugh himself spent four years at Trinity, Cambridge, graduating as Bachelor of Arts in 1568.[284] No documentation has been traced of his personal experience during this period, but his studies would have been largely within the college, as was customary at the time, under the supervision of a college tutor, shared with perhaps half-a-dozen others. His BA curriculum would have included dialectic (logic), advanced rhetoric, the major classical authors (Virgil, Horace, Cicero, and Aristotle) and natural philosophy (elementary science), with perhaps also briefer instruction in mathematics, geometry and Greek.[285] Trinity at this stage was equipped with no fewer than five lectureships in logic, as well as two in Greek and Latin literature, one in Greek grammar, and a further one in maths.[286]

---

280 Mullinger, *History of Cambridge University*, p.189.

281 Stone, 'Educational Revolution': Tables V & IX show that the split between gentry and non-gentry matriculands at the two universities was approximately 50:50 in this decade.

282 Griffith, *Civility and Reputation*.

283 *ODNB*, Vol 19, pp.659-660.

284 Rouse Ball & Venn, *Admissions to Trinity*.

285 *The Spenser Encyclopaedia* (Toronto, University of Toronto Press, 1990), pp.130-131.

286 Ibid.

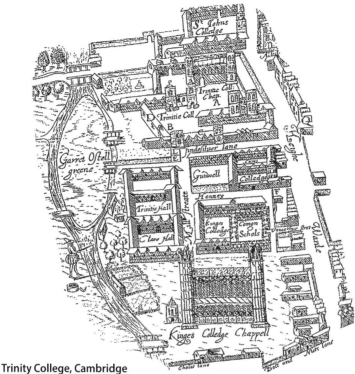

Trinity College, Cambridge

Hugh was a bursary-holder (sizar) at Trinity College, graduating BA in 1568. Trinity had been endowed thirty years previously by Henry VIII whose statue stands above the Great Gate (*below*). The College was expanding even while Hugh was in attendance, as the above plan of 1574 suggests (at top). The young polymath Francis Bacon was one of Hugh's contemporaries at the college.

However, quite apart from these studies, he would have been marked deeply by the Cambridge experience. It is not known whether he had actually arrived in the town by the month of August in 1564, his matriculation year, in time for Queen Elizabeth's spectacular five-day visit to Cambridge that month.[287] If so, he would have experienced the spectacle of this exceptionally extravagant display at first hand. And if not, he would have missed it by only a matter of weeks – close enough to encounter the afterglow of the presence of the royal court, and of the high pageants and festivities that marked the event as so memorable for the university and town alike.[288] Either way, it would have been a heady start for a young student from the remote provinces.

Beyond this, more generally during the 1560s, Cambridge was the intellectual centre of religious controversy of developing national significance. Indeed, with St John's College, Trinity became a particular focus of such debate during the very years Hugh was an undergraduate there. The royal intention in creating the college in the 1540s had been that it should be dedicated primarily to the production of ministers for the newly reformed English church. This helped Trinity to attract fellows from the cream of protestant theological talent. By the 1560s, following the Anglican settlement of 1559,[289] there was a substantial body of influential opinion in the country urging that the church reform process should be carried still further in a Presbyterian direction, not least to combat resurgent post-Council of Trent Catholicism. With protestant theology in continuing international ferment,[290] Cambridge was the magnet for much of the new thinking in England. And under the Masterships of Robert Beaumont and (from 1567) John Whitgift, the future Archbishop, Trinity itself emerged as the radical intellectual hub of new puritan thought. With Thomas Cartwright also a senior fellow of the college – and, after 1566, university preacher and then Lady Margaret professor of divinity – the resultant excitements naturally spilt over into the student body as a whole, of which Hugh was then part. There were student demonstrations, disciplinary measures and intense debates,[291] a foretaste of the wider Parliament-Crown frictions of the 1570s, when puritan discontents about the Elizabethan religious settlement came to preoccupy the political nation at large.

It is impossible to know what were either the immediate or the longer term

---

287   J. Nichols, *The Progresses and Processions of Queen Elizabeth,* Vol I (London 1823), pp.151-189; also Mullinger, *History of Cambridge University*, pp.190-192.

288   Ibid.

289   Act of Uniformity, 1559 (1 Eliz. c.2).

290   D. MacCulloch, *Reformation: Europe's House Divided 1490-1700* (London, Allen Lane, 2003), pp.286-358.

291   J.P.C. Roach, *A History of the County of Cambridge and the Isle of Ely* Volume 3: *The City and University of Cambridge* (Oxford, OUP, 1959), pp.174-176.

effects of Hugh's ringside exposure to these powerful religious and philosophical currents for his personal values and beliefs, nor to ascertain what particular
friends he made inside or outside Trinity during his time there. Immediately
next door to Trinity is St John's College, which in the mid-sixteenth century
was one of the principal honey-pots for Welsh undergraduates at the university.
Two of Hugh's immediate contemporaries at St John's – both of whom matriculated in early 1565, within a few months of Hugh – were Edmund Prys
and William Morgan, the former of whom went on to become a celebrated
bard and translator of The Psalms into Welsh, and the latter, the translator of
the 1588 Bible, to which Prys also contributed. Given that both they and Hugh
were Welsh-speaking natives of north-west Wales,[292] and that their two colleges
were relatively small – St John's having no more than 180 undergraduates in
the mid-1560s[293] and Trinity around 150[294] – it is inconceivable that they would
not have known one another at this formative stage of their lives, and equally
improbable that they would not have shared an interest in the dramatic nationally important doctrinal debates being enacted before their very eyes. On
the other hand, one cannot assume that they became actual friends. Their lives
took sharply different directions after Cambridge, and there is little in Hugh's
papers to signify anything but a conventional attachment to confessional or ecclesiastical matters. There are indications that in the 1550s his grandfather Huw
may have had Catholic sympathies,[295] but that was during Mary's reign, so perhaps can be considered unremarkable. By the time of Hugh's adulthood,
Protestantism was increasingly the norm – and mandatorily so for a crown official such as he became. What is more, as will be seen below, several members
of his wife's family, the Montagus of Northamptonshire, were on the puritan
wing of the Anglican church,[296] a fact which also makes it unlikely Hugh himself was positioned very differently.

---

292 William Morgan was from Penmachno near Betws-y-Coed, Edmund Prys from Maentwrog
      in Merioneth.

293 TNA SP 12/38 fols 104r-105.

294 www.trin.cam.ac.uk/about/historical-overview

295 In Lewis Menai's 'Marwnad Huw ap Llewelyn ab Ifan' 1557 (in Wyn Wiliam (ed), *Menai*,
      p.12), the concluding couplets, …*Am a roes yma i'n rhaid /I wan er mwyn ei enaid /Fry galwai
      Fair o Gwellen /Huw ar law Dduw i'r wlad wen* ('…For what he gave here for our needs /To
      the weak for the sake of his soul /aloft Mary of Cologne called /Huw at God's hand to the
      holy land'), may refer to an endowment or alms left by Huw to a religious house or order, in
      the hope that St Mary of Cologne will intercede for his soul – probably signals of Catholic
      adherence, though this would have been unsurprising during Mary's reign. I am grateful to
      Dr Jerry Hunter for this suggestion.

296 On the Montagus, see pp.73-79. Sir Edward Montagu 3rd, Elizabeth's first cousin and head
      of the family, was noted for puritan sympathies (*ODNB*, Vol 38, p.701), as was his brother
      James, Bishop of Bath and Wells, one of the translators of the King James Bible. (A.Nicholson,
      Jacobean England & the Making of the King James Bible, London, Harper, 2003, p.51).

Hiatus

Following graduation from Cambridge in 1568, there was then a gap of three years before Hugh progressed to the next stage of his education. It was not until mid-1571 that he arrived at the Inns of Court in London to begin the extended training in common law needed for qualification for the bar[297].

The three-year hiatus is puzzling. Perhaps by that stage he had still not decided to commit himself to the law, or perhaps there were passing financial pressures

back home. It was during this period between 1568 and 1571 that his father, Dafydd, completed the construction of the first phase of the new Plas Coch, as indicated by the '1569' inscription over the porch of the front door.

Lincoln's Inn

On 3 May 1571, Hugh was admitted to Lincoln's Inn in London,[298] as a trainee common law barrister. His Anglesey neighbour Thomas Bulkeley had preceded him there by just seven weeks.[299] All of the Inns of Court were expanding at this time, in terms of both attendance and political and social importance. 'A revolution in legal life' [300] was under way in Britain, reflecting the post-Reformation significance of secular law in relation to issues of constitutional and public-administrative significance, quite as much as the escalating numbers of private disputes between citizens. In a period of continuing economic and social upheaval, lawyers were becoming the bearers and articulators of what Bouwsma terms the 'new secular pragmatism'.[301] Their idioms and concepts were reshaping patterns of social and commercial relationship, as well as serving increasingly as media for the expression of general political discourse throughout the second half of the century.[302] One instance of this influence can be seen in fallouts from the general expansion in trade during the period and its associated consolidation of an expanding merchant class closely allied

---

297   *Lincoln's Inn Admissions Register*, 3 May 1571.

298   Ibid.

299   See notes 202 & 203.

300   R.O'Day, *The Professions in Early Modern England 1450-1800: Servants of the Commonweal* (London, Pearson Education, 2000), p.120.

301   Bouwsma, op cit, p.308.

302   C.W.Brooks, *The Law, Politics and Society in Early Modern England* (Cambridge, CUP, 2008), pp.23-59.

to – indeed frequently indistinguishable from – the rising gentry. Steady ex-
pansions of personal liquidity meant that predominantly *commercial* capital was
reshaping what had formerly been an essentially agricultural economy. With
continuing inflation and depreciation of fixed incomes, this fed the growing
market in land, and with it, crucially, an associated pressure for the moderni-
sation of property law, in turn stimulating innovations in relation to the security
of leases and titles.[303] Reflecting such pressures, the common law was being
forced to evolve rapidly, stimulated also by competition from the development
of both equity and statutory law-making in the wake of the statute-based upheavals of the English reformation. The Inns of Court were thus brimming
with self-confidence and intellectual vitality throughout Hugh's period, reflecting their members' sense of themselves as 'in collective possession of the law,
through discussion at the Inns or in what were mainly unpublished learning
aids'.[304] Issues of fundamental constitutional and social importance such as
the relative standing of common and statute law, the proper place of precedent,
the role of judges as interpreters of statute, and the relationships between
judges and policies of the Crown were all being debated and contested
fiercely,[305] with the Inns and their members constituting the veritable intellectual epicentre of such discussions. There was relentless – and doubtless for
lawyers, personally invigorating – pressure to develop and document the common law more systematically, a development which proceeded alongside the
accelerating evolution of educational approaches within the Inns of Court
themselves.

An early glimpse of law
students at Lincoln's Inn in
London – from a stained-
glass window in the Inn's
original hall. Hugh studied at
Lincoln's Inn and was called
to the bar there in the 1570s.
He later became a Bencher
(part of the ruling elite),
rising to Treasurer, the top
office of the Society, in 1602.

---

303 Thorne, *Tudor Social Transformation*, pp.15-21.

304 Brooks, *Law, Politics and Society*, pp.62-63.

305 This discussion reflects J.H.Baker, *An Introduction to English Legal History* (Oxford, OUP,
     2007 edn), pp.41-202; L.A.Knafla, *Law and Politics in Jacobean England* (Cambridge, CUP,
     1989), passim; and O'Day, *Professions*, pp.113-150.

Educating common lawyers

Historically, common law training at the Inns had been conducted through essentially *aural* learning exercises, that is 'readings' or specialist lectures by senior barristers within the particular Inn, and formalised moots, akin to scholastic disputations, for shared discussion of cases and pleadings. There was no personal teaching as such, other than when privately contracted from tutors outside the Inns, nor were text-books used for private study. The focus had thus been predominantly on *techniques* of advocacy, rather than on the substance of the law itself. One result was that the knowledge needed to practice at the bar till the early sixteenth century was acquired by a process of collective quasi-apprenticeship, rather than through personal education in the terms in which it came to be understood subsequently.

By the time Hugh Hughes arrived at Lincoln's Inn, this system was in transition. Readings and moots continued to be central features of a barrister's training, with students required to take part in twelve 'grand' and twenty-four 'petty' moots before being entitled to be called to the bar.[306] However from 1560 onwards a major shift towards the written word, reflecting post-Gutenburg trends then sweeping through wider civil society, was also affecting legal education. Printed legal commentaries were proliferating. A few years earlier, between 1561 and 1569, Thomas Egerton, whose lifelong significance for Hugh Hughes is discussed further below, had also been reading for the bar at Lincoln's Inn.[307] He relied on some of the same texts as would have been recommended to Hugh a decade later.[308] These included Fitzherbert on older common law cases,[309] Phaer on precedents,[310] Littleton on land law,[311] Staunford on the royal prerogative,[312] Rastell on precedents for pleading,[313] and of course Plowden's Commentaries.[314] Also of central importance to Hugh as a trainee barrister would have been the proliferating and increasingly sophisticated law reports, now cataloguing significant pleadings and past court judgements. More than 200 of the 300 such collections to appear between 1485

---

306 P.Raffield, *Images and Cultures of Law in Early Modern England,: Justice and Political Power, 1558-1660* (Cambridge, CUP, 2004), p.21.

307 *ODNB*, Vol 17, pp.1007-1011.

308 L.A.Knafla, 'The Law Studies of an Elizabethan Student', *HLQ* 32 (1969), pp.22-40.

309 Sir Antony Fitzherbert, *La Nouvelle Natura Brevium* (London 1553).

310 Thomas Phaer, *A Boke of Presidentes Exactly Written in Maner of a Register* (London, 1550).

311 Sir Thomas Littleton, *Littleton's Tenures* (London 1557).

312 William Staunford, *An Exposicion of the Kinges Prerogative* (London, 1567).

313 William Rastell, *A Colleccion of Entrees* (London, 1566).

314 Edmund Plowden, *Les Comentaries* (London, 1571).

and 1603 were published between 1570 and 1600.[315]

This developing sense of the common law as a dynamic intellectual discipline, over and above its accessibility through acquired 'craft' skills and practices, naturally put a higher premium on university-based academic training
than had previously been the case. Previously, only civil and canon lawyers had
been subjected to university-level legal training, but now, increasingly, the
rigour of academic discipline was being applied also to the common law. Individuals like Hugh and his colleague (Sir) William Jones were the beneficiaries.
A rising proportion of Inns of Court attendees had first attended Oxford or
Cambridge – from just 13% in 1561, to 42% in 1581 and a striking 49% by
1601.[316] However, by no means all of these were intent on pursuing the law as
a profession. The Inn societies were indeed professional schools for those seeking such a career, but throughout this period they were also serving as, effectively, intellectual finishing schools, 'the nurserie of the greater part of the
gentrie of the realme'.[317] As with the attitude to degrees at the universities,
barely a third of individuals in attendance were intent on completing their studies with the intention of qualifying for the bar. For the majority, the Inns were
cultural academies for young men from predominantly the higher social
classes, at the heart of the capital.

Law as political language

This tendency has tended to be explained by historians of the period as reflecting awareness by growing numbers of gentry heirs of the importance of legal
knowledge in future development of their estates – or more superficially as a
social fashion amongst the aristocracy and gentry.[318] Prest suggests that the
law occupied 'much the same place in the popular mind as economics has enjoyed in the present [*i.e.* twentieth] century' and that therefore passing exposure to its idioms would have been seen as simply a desirable feature of a full
education, rather than necessarily having practical utility.[319] Yet whilst doubtless
true for many, the suggestion needs nuancing. The attractions of attendance
at an Inn also reflected a widening, deeply serious acknowledgement of the
mounting importance of legal and constitutional ideas and concepts, for thinking about and participating in politics and society as a whole, at a time when
many of the axioms of political and constitutional understanding were begin-

---

315   O'Day, *Professions*, p.127.

316   Ibid., p.129.

317   BL MS Lansdowne 155, f.107, cited in W.R.Prest 'Legal Education of the Gentry at the Inns
      of Court, 1560-1640', *Past and Present* (1967) 38, p.23.

318   Russell, *Crisis of the Parliaments*, p.54.

319   Prest, *Inns of Court*, p.37.

ning to be contested in increasingly meaningful fashion. Indeed Hugh's expanding involvements as a senior government law officer and administrator in the 1590s and 1600s[320] point to the likelihood that he personally would have been swimming in intellectual currents of just these kinds amongst his peers in the Inn societies.

Stone observes that, as the gentry cohorts who populated the Inns in the 1580s and '90s (that is to say, the generation immediately following Hugh's) came to reach maturity in the early Stuart decades, the consequences were to prove momentous. The Long Parliament of 1640, says Stone, was 'a remarkably, possibly a uniquely well-educated body',[321] observing of its members that 'it was their [earlier] training at the Inns of Court which gave the squirearchy those dangerous ideas about the limits imposed on sovereignty by the law of the land; it was their training at the university which gave them the sense of responsibility for their own affairs, the confidence in their own powers, the logic and the rhetoric needed to sway their fellow-members, together with the personal contacts which helped them to combine to impose their views upon their kind in 1640.' [322] The trends were clear even in Hugh's time. By 1593, upwards of 36% of Members of Parliament had previously attended an Inn of Court, a proportion which had swollen to 55% by the time of the Long Parliament itself.[323] All of this lay in the future during Hugh's own earlier period as a Lincoln's Inn student in the 1570s, but during his time there seeds were being planted. The intellectual and social chemistry of the Inns was evolving steadily through a distinctive blend of 'amateur' and 'professional' energies, in stimulating proximity to the court and metropolis.

Call to the Bar

It was almost nine years before Hugh was finally called to the bar, rather longer than the average for the period of 7.4 years.[324] The situation back home suggests an explanation for the delay. His father had died in 1574, an event the aftermaths of which almost certainly required time back in Anglesey for months on end, or perhaps longer. He was Dafydd's eldest son and heir, and the evidence is that the two had worked in tandem in Anglesey over the previous ten years. For example, at least two properties in Menai were acquired for the estate in Hugh's rather than Dafydd's name during precisely that period.[325]

---

320 His appointments as successively Attorney General for north Wales, member of the Council in the Marches, and Lord Chief Justice for Ireland, are addressed in detail in Chapters 5 & 6.

321 Stone, 'Educational Revolution', p.78.

322 Ibid.

323 Stone, 'Educational Revolution', p.79.

324 Griffith *Learning, Law and Religion*, p.177.

Moreover, the elegy (*marwnad*) marking Dafydd's death in 1574, composed by Robert ap Ifan, hints at the closeness of the family relationships, including both the promise of and expectations for Hugh himself:

> *Pob abl di-gabl da a gair*
> *o'th fin yn iaith fwyn iawnair*
> *Blaid ewybr yw'r blodeuyn*
> *lain cain sud o Lincon's Inn* [326]

> ' Every fitting and slander-free goodness
>   comes from your mouth in the tender language of the apt word
>   The flower [heir] is of a quick sort
>   a fair blade of Lincoln's Inn '

So the demands on the latter's energy during this period were probably considerable – returning to Anglesey to take over and consolidate the family's affairs and newly constructed mansion, and ensuring the security and comfort of his mother and siblings, whilst at the same time straining not to lose track of a demanding course of study in the capital. If this was indeed the case, it suggests a character with an impressive degree of stamina and steadiness of focus.

Talent-spotted

By now he was in his late twenties, and the indications are that even at this relatively early stage his abilities had won recognition on the island[327] – indeed he had caught the eye of people of influence as a rising talent. In 1577, a full two years before completing his term at Lincoln's Inn, at the young age of 29, Hugh was appointed by the crown as a member of the Anglesey Commission of the Peace. Quite who his sponsors for this appointment as a justice might have been is an intriguing question. One candidate is Sir Richard Bulkeley 3rd, who was Anglesey's *custos rotulorum*[328], and also at that stage influential at court and an intimate of the Earl of Leicester.[329] Though he is by no means the only possibility (as discussed in the next chapter), the appointment would have required his positive endorsement, if not active promotion. No previous member of Hugh's direct family had been made a justice, so the appointment of one of

---

325   UB Plas Coch 83 & 86.

326   Robert ab Ifan, 'Marwnad Dafydd Llwyd ap Huw 1574', in Wyn Wiliam, *Menai*, p.13.

327   Ibid.

328   **Custos rotulorum**: A post created by statute in 1545, the *custos rotulorum* held the records of the county Commission of the Peace and in Wales handled communications with the Council in the Marches and Privy Council, to which all such Commissions were responsible.

329   *ODNB*, Vol 8, pp.575-577.

his years must have been a judgement about personal qualities rather than so-cial position. It may be relevant that, as already noted, Thomas Bulkeley, Sir Richard's nephew, was Hugh's exact contemporary at Lincoln's Inn,[330] having also been a next-door neighbour at Porthaml Uchaf (Porthaml Hall) since childhood. The parallel progress of these two tyros would doubtless have been noted from time to time in Beaumaris. And conceivably, with Sir Richard serv-ing at court throughout most of the 1570s,[331] there may also have been occa-sions for social interaction between the two.

Be that as it may, the significant point is that Hugh's time as a student at Lincoln's Inn was unusually protracted – and part of the explanation, at least for the period between 1577 and 1579, may have been that the demands of day-to-day obligations as a newly appointed Anglesey justice required lengthier spells back home than previously. As will be seen in the next chapter, these ob-ligations were anything but trivial.

A practising Barrister

Hugh's call to the bar had come on 25 November 1579. This meant he would have been equipped with the requisite arts and skills to plead in the English and Welsh common law courts, though it would be a further four years before he was entitled to do so on his own. The indications are however that for much of the decade that followed he was then resident, and highly active, in and around Anglesey. An attempt is made to piece together the evidence for this in the next chapter. Though documentary proof is lacking, the likelihood is that in the first half of the decade he would have worked in tandem with more sen-ior advocates, probably on the North Wales circuits of the Courts of Great Ses-sions, and subsequently as an advocate in his own right, including perhaps in the Council in the Marches and Westminster courts. There are likely parallels here with the marginally later career of William Jones of Castellmarch, who by the end of the 1590s, following a call to the bar at Lincoln's Inn, 'had built up a substantial Clientele among friends and neighbours in north-west Wales, in-cluding the Wynns of Gwydir'.[332] There is evidence, albeit fragmentary, in Hugh's archived papers of involvement as an attorney in suits concerning mort-gage disputes and other land transactions during this period.[333] The connection with Lincoln's Inn as a professional address could have continued alongside an Anglesey domicile, though there is tantalisingly little direct proof of any of his activities as an advocate there till his elevation to the Bench of the Inn in

330 See notes 202 & 203.

331 Jones, *Bulkeleys of Beaumaris*, p.168.

332 *ODNB*, Vol 17, p.659.

333 UB Plas Coch 351, 352, 353.

the following decade, on 29 January 1594.[334] From that moment on there are frequent references to his specific Bencher involvements, as a member of the governing body of the Inn.

During legal terms at Lincoln's Inn, he would now have had immediate first-hand exposure to legal and political controversies of the day. As already mentioned, throughout Elizabeth's later decades the Inns of Court were developing as a sophisticated centre of intellectual and cultural life in the capital, 'the very hub of political gossip' in Dodd's phrase.[335] The combination within the Inns of serious law students and sons of noblemen and gentlemen enrolled 'to acquire a basic knowledge of the law and the social polish of London society' [336] was probably a mix of enlivening and exasperating for the former.

Regardless of the distinction however, both 'professionals' and 'amateurs' at the Inns were exposed, willy nilly, to identical wider political and cultural currents. A stone's throw down the road in Westminster and the Royal palaces were members and former members of the Inns active in every sphere of government – in the law courts, as Palace courtiers, as crown officials, as members of Parliament, or simply as suppliants for office. Though far and away the largest city in the country, London at this stage had a population of little more than 150,000, the size of present-day Norwich or Preston. And the numbers involved at first hand in government and the courts would have been only a fraction of that – perhaps three or four thousand. The sense of personal proximity and attunement to the ebb and flow of events, and to the succession of crises and tensions affecting the body politic throughout these years, would have been unavoidable for individuals like Hugh.

The Egerton connection

To illustrate, one of his Lincoln's Inn colleagues was the redoubtable Thomas Egerton – later Sir Thomas, and subsequently Lord Ellesmere. Egerton was older than Hugh by about six years, and developed into one of the leading jurists of his time. A tough-minded, austere, and dedicated public official, who also built a large fortune on the job, he was one of Lincoln's Inn's shining lights.[337]

Elevated to its Bench in 1579, he quickly gained appointments to progressively more senior Crown legal officerships, rising in 1603 to become James I's Lord Chancellor. As Hugh was being drawn into the Egerton orbit, via

---

334   *LI Black Books,* Vol II (Lincoln's Inn, 1898), p.31.

335   A.H.Dodd, 'The Pattern of Politics in Stuart Wales', *THSC* 1948, p.14.

336   P.Williams, *The Later Tudors: England 1547-1603* (Oxford, OUP, 2002), p.393.

337   Knafla, *Law and Politics; ODNB,* Vol 17, pp.1007-1011.

Sir Thomas Egerton (Lord Ellesmere)
Egerton was a lawyer and Lincoln's
Inn bencher of formidable authority,
who rose to become James 1's Lord
Chancellor. Resident at Tatton in
Cheshire, and always influential in
north Wales, he aided Hugh Hughes's
career, as both patron and intellectual colleague.

the Lincoln's Inn 'club', Egerton became first the Queen's choice for Solicitor
General. This immediately involved him as a key Crown advocate in the succession of spectacular anti-Catholic treason trials of the period 1585-92. Assassination plots against Elizabeth led to intensifying repression of recusant
Catholics, which in turn fed further conspiracies and persistent national anxiety, reflected in the execution of Mary Stuart (Queen of Scots) in February
1587. The state trials of Campion (1581), Throckmorton (1583) Babington
(1586) and others were manifestations of an increasingly pervasive sense of
English embattledness in the face of active Papal and Spanish determination
to bring Elizabeth down and replace her. Moreover, though the defeat of the
Spanish Armada in July 1588 gave a huge boost to national morale, anti-
Catholic paranoia continued thereafter with increasing intensity. As Nicholl
observes, 'it was a time of crisis management, of suspicion and surveillance, of
special powers of investigation to "make windows in men's souls" '.[338]

Egerton's role as a prosecutor in the succession of high-profile state trials,
alongside John Popham as Attorney General, illustrates in stark form the degree to which senior lawyers active in their Inns were simultaneously central
figures in the public-political realm, at a time when the nation as a whole –
and the legal-political establishment in particular – was agitated by pervasive
concerns about national security and social order. Yet strikingly, alongside such
urgent preoccupations, Egerton's commitment to his routine responsibilities
within Lincoln's Inn itself appears to have continued unabated – for example,
as a Reader and then Treasurer (*i.e.* head) of the Inn in 1585.
Throughout the decade, he continued to interact with both students and bench
colleagues on a range of internal matters, both intellectual and administra-

---

338   C.Nicholl, *The Reckoning* (London, Vintage, 2002), p.32.

tive.[339] Moreover, as a relentless network-builder and dispenser of professional patronage, Egerton appears to have sustained a genuine interest in talented younger members of the Inn, participating in moots and discussions of others' readings.[340] For Hugh and others like him, interactions with luminaries like Egerton were probably a familiar feature of life within the Inn, whenever the latter were present during law terms.[341] And through such interactions, the bar students' sense of the law as shaping and bearing directly on the momentous political events of the day, and indeed on the very future of the state, would have been fed continuously.

There are also reasons for believing that Hugh's career specifically may have benefited from Egerton's good offices. The ring worth £5, left by Hugh in 1609 to Egerton, by then Lord Chancellor Ellesmere, under his will, is one obvious pointer, but there are also a number of others. Egerton was from broadly the same part of the kingdom as Hugh – from Cheshire, just across the Flintshire border – and he was thoroughly familiar with the North Wales circuits of the Court of Great Sessions, as well as, from 1586, the Council in the Marches. Moreover, as he rose to ever-greater national influence in the 1590s and 1600s, Egerton's personal interest in those powerful regional entities continued to be close, at precisely the time Hugh himself was becoming a leading presence in them.[342]

Significantly, it was Egerton's son-in-law, Peter Warburton, another Lincoln's Inn colleague and Hugh's predecessor in the afore-mentioned North Wales Attorney Generalship, who appointed Hugh as his Deputy in 1592,[343] a nomination that would have reflected Egerton's endorsement. What is more, Hugh's succession of further prerogative appointments in the 1590s and 1600s – as Sheriff of Anglesey, as *quorum* member of Commissions of the Peace in no fewer than three Welsh shires, and as a member of the Council in the Marches

339   Knafla, *Law and Politics*, pp.13-14.

340   J.H.Baker, *Readers and Readings in the Inns of Court and Chancery* (London, Selden Society, 2000), pp.132, 577.

341   There were four terms: Michaelmas (lasting *c.* seven weeks); Hilary, Easter and Trinity (each three weeks). Attendance fluctuated, according to member's circumstances, in particular his professional geographical sphere. In general, the owners of chambers had to be personally 'in commons' for four months each year or forfeit, unless they held a 'special admission' or had further reasonable excuse for absence (*LI Black Books*, Vol II, pp. 40-41, 78). '[The Inns] operated more like residential clubs or hotels, catering for a fluid, heterogeneous population of semi-permanent guests and short-term transients' (Prest, *Inns of Court*, p.16).

342   Hugh became Attorney General for the North Wales circuits of Great Sessions in 1594, and a member of the Council in the Marches in 1601. These matters are explored in detail in Chapters 4 & 5.

343   UB Plas Coch 150. Also *ODNB*, Vol 59, pp.264-265.

Sir Peter Warburton was part of Hugh Hughes's Lincoln's Inn network — an eminent barrister and judge. He was Hugh's predecessor as north Wales Attorney General in the 1590s, with Hugh initially his Deputy. Hugh bequeathed him *'fyve poundes'* in his 1609 will, a mark of respect and friendship.

from 1601[344] – would all have been vetted by Egerton, amongst others, whether as top crown legal officer, Council in the Marches eminence, or Privy Councillor.

An apparently trivial episode in the domestic politics of Lincoln's Inn, in 1602-05, adds further to the impression that Egerton viewed Hugh positively. The incident concerned the allocation of living and working space, always a charged and sensitive issue within hierarchical institutions. Reflecting powerful standing within the Inn, Egerton held title to many of its chambers, whilst exerting influence over the occupation of yet others. In 1602, Sir John Wynn (of Gwydir) tried to acquire, for his own son John, the chamber of John Panton, a Denbighshire man whose original sponsor (manucaptor) at the Inn had been Egerton himself.[345] The great man blocked the acquisition. Two years later however, he secured the same chamber for William Ravenscroft, a Flintshire man who was one of his own circle, the brother of his (Egerton's) first wife, Elizabeth.[346] At that point, Ravenscroft's own previous room was passed on to Hugh Hughes. The Wynns were left to fume impotently.[347] The story itself proves little other than that Egerton was prepared to act forcefully both on behalf of those he favoured, and against those he did not. Hugh was a beneficiary in this case, and that is significant.

---

344   Chapters 4 & 5 contain more details and full references.

345   *LI Admissions Register*, 29 June 1594.

346   Ravenscroft was in fact brother of Egerton's first wife, Elizabeth (*d.* 1588). (Knafla, *Law and Politics*, pp. 9, 25).

347   This anecdote reflects research summarised in Griffith, *Learning, Law and Religion*, p.154. At this time, the demand for chambers in all of the Inns greatly exceeded supply. (Prest, *Inns of Court*, p.13).

There are plainly speculative elements to claims made for Egerton's support of Hugh, but the essence of the matter can be reduced to syllogistic form: Egerton, as a relentless legal power-broker, was always attentive, both professionally and for reasons of personal interest, to legal and crown-official appointments in the Cheshire / North Wales region. He also became familiar, from continuing collegial interactions, with Hugh's qualities as an accomplished Inn member and rising public lawyer. Hugh flourished across north Wales at precisely the time Egerton's influence was greatest. Ergo, it is reasonable to infer that Egerton was on Hugh's side and assisted his rise.

Indeed, an intriguing, if rather more speculative, convergence may also be suggested. Egerton, with a personal outlook nurtured from childhood in the England-Wales borderlands, was always a keen defender of the value not only of ecclesiastical courts, but also of the relatively autonomous jurisdictions of long-established regional and local authorities – for example, the County Palatine of Cheshire[348] and the Council in the Marches. In the early years of the seventeenth century, he engaged in a celebrated intellectual tussle with Sir Edward Coke over the latter's arguments for getting rid of such bodies, perceived by Coke as loci of prerogative power, by extending the central courts of law – particularly those administering the common law – to encompass their powers.[349] In one sense Coke's campaign was part of the wider struggle against the royal prerogative, feeding tensions that contributed ultimately to the civil war. But for Egerton (by now Lord Ellesmere), a conservative pragmatist less troubled by the prerogative per se, a diversity of jurisdictions was a good in itself, provided they could be made to work equitably.

It is impossible to know with absolute certainty what Hugh's own attitude was to such matters. However, one senses that he would have leaned in Egerton's direction. The crown's influence had been good to Wales, particularly through the Council in the Marches, of which he was appointed a member in 1601.[350] And significantly, as the next chapter will show, he had chosen deliberately to make his career in north Wales, working in courts under a multiplicity of jurisdictions – manorial, shrieval and ecclesiastical, as much as Westminster-based. He appears to have had a broadly sympathetic understanding of each.[351]

---

348 T. Thornton, *Cheshire and the Tudor State 1450-1560* (London, Royal Historical Society / Boydell Press, 2000).

349 *Observacions upon Cookes Reports*, British Library Hargrave manuscript 254 ff 52r-7r – Ellesmere's critiques of Coke's Reports on Fairley's case (1604) & Case of the Isle of Ely (1610). Also, Knafla, *Law and Politics*, Chapter VI 'The Clash of Jurisdictions: Central and Local Authorities, Secular and Ecclesiastical': '[Coke's] reports, together with Ellesmere's critique, represent in the broadest sense a clash of views on the jurisdiction of courts in the English legal system: central and local, secular and ecclesiastical', p.123.

350 Williams, *Council in the Marches*, p.351.

351 Discussed in Chapter 4.

Marriage into the Montagus

Early in 1588, Hugh married Elizabeth Montagu. He was forty. It was an unusually late first marriage for a man of his times and social caste – the median age for first marriages of heirs in the landed squirearchy during this period being just twenty-two.[352] Perhaps he had been too preoccupied with his work and wider family responsibilities to have got round to it earlier. Perhaps he had just not been the marrying kind. It is impossible to know. What is striking is that when he finally made the commitment – and it must surely have been the result of his own personal decision, his father having died some fourteen years previously – it was to an English woman of impressive social credentials, from a family key members of which became important to him for the remainder of his life.

Brigstock Manor near Kettering, Northamptonshire, was Elizabeth Montagu's home until her 1586 marriage to Hugh. She bore him four children, all brought up in Anglesey. The manor's exterior bears some architectural resemblance to that of Plas Coch, suggesting possible influence on Hugh's remodelling of Plas Coch in the 1590s.

---

352 L.Stone, *The Family, Sex and Marriage in England 1500-1800* (London, Pelican, 1979), p.42. Stone cites this figure for 'the *English* squirearchy'. No separate such statistic for Wales has been identified, though there is no reason to suppose it would be different.

The Montagus were a large and closely knit Northamptonshire clan, accomplished landowning England gentry of the late Tudor period – but also considerably more than that.[353] Amongst Elizabeth's close relatives were lawyers and public figures of high distinction. Her grandfather, Sir Edward Montagu 1st (c.1480-1557), had been Chief Justice of both the King's Bench and the Common Pleas under Henry VIII.[354] And a generation later, in the period following the marriage to Hugh, several of her immediate first cousins were to prove similarly accomplished. Henry (1564-1642) was a lawyer who rose to become Lord Chief Justice, Lord Treasurer (1620), and Earl of Manchester.[355] Sidney (1571-1644), also a lawyer, was knighted and made Master of Requests (in 1616).[356] His wife, Paulina Pepys, was aunt of the celebrated diarist.[357] And James (1568-1644) a minister of the church, became Bishop of Bath and Wells and subsequently (also in 1616) of Winchester, as well as being one of the Oxford translators of the King James Bible.[358] All of these individuals had been to either Oxford or Cambridge, and the first two to the Inns of Court.

Sir Edward Montagu
Uncle of Hugh's wife Elizabeth, Sir Edward was head of the Montagu family in the late sixteenth century, with extensive Northamptonshire estates. Hugh's marriage into this family brought him into family networks of high-achieving lawyers and businessmen, one of whom, Sir Edward's brother Roger, played an important role in his Anglesey ventures.

353 This summary draws principally on: E.S.Cope *The Life of a Public Man: Edwards, First Baron Montagu of Boughton 1562-1644* (Philadelphia, American Philosophical Society, 1981); and *Letters of the Montagu Family Vol I – 1537-1643*, Boxes 13/1-6, in the Northamptonshire Records Office. Other more specific sources are detailed below.

354 *ODNB*, Vol. 33, pp.699-700.

355 *ODNB*, Vol. 33, pp.732-736.

356 J. & J.A.Venn, *Alumni Cantabrigienses* (Cambridge, CUP, 1922) Vol 3, p.202.

357 *ODNB* Vol. 43, pp.744-752.

358 *ODNB* Vol. 38 pp.738-740.

Sir Edward Montagu 3rd (1562-1644), the eldest of three brothers, had also attended Oxford and the Middle Temple, and lived most of his life in Northamptonshire, being finally created Baron Montagu of Boughton by James I in 1621. This was a family of high achievers, who within a generation would be one of the most conspicuous and successful clans in the land. When they gathered together at funerals and other family occasions, there must have been an intellectual as well as a political crackle in the air.

At the time Hugh first encountered the family – perhaps in the mid-1580s, though possibly earlier, as is argued below – the head of the family was Sir Edward Montagu 2nd (1530-1602).[359] He presided over the extensive family estates in east Northamptonshire, around Barnwell and Brigstock, with assets substantial enough to allow him to give his two daughters marriage portions of £3,000 each.[360] Sir Edward's next two brothers were Roger and Simon. The former was a prominent businessman in the City of London. The latter was Elizabeth's father, who appears (as will be shown below) to have lived out a comfortable existence as Roger's tenant in the manor house at Brigstock, almost certainly Elizabeth's childhood home.

A question of particular interest here is: how did Hugh meet this family, and Elizabeth in particular? The evidence is patchy, but significant for an understanding of Hugh himself.

None of the male members of the Montagu family had been precise contemporaries of Hugh's at either Cambridge or Lincoln's Inn. But after more than a decade and a half of to-ing and fro-ing in and around the capital, his social networks are likely to have been extensive enough to have brought him into social contact with one or other of the Montagus, whose own Inns of Court connections were multifarious. But beyond this, two specific possible candidates as broker – if not for the marriage itself, then at least for the initial introduction – merit consideration.

First, records of an Exchequer Court suit of 1587 (a year before the marriage), concerning land in south-east Anglesey,[361] show Hugh to have been a co-defendant in an action with one 'Walter Montagu', as a business partner in a matter of land acquisitions. The strong likelihood is that this Walter was the son of that christian name of Sir Edward Montagu 2nd – a first cousin and contemporary of Elizabeth.[362] Walter was born in 1562-3, and was thus at least fifteen years younger than Hugh. By this stage he was married to Jane Morgan

359   Cope, *Life of a Public Man.*

360   Offering, 'Purchasing Power'.

361   This is one of the cases already discussed in Chapter 2 (Jones, *Exchequer Proceedings*, p.13).

362   Walter Montagu (1562/3-1616) was Sir Edward's second son. Knighted in May 1603, he subsequently became Monmouthshire's Sheriff (in 1608) and Member of Parliament (in 1614). (Williams, *Parliamentary History of Wales*, p.78.)

of the Morgans of Tredegar and Pencoed Castle in Monmouthshire.[363] It is plausible to suggest that Hugh could have met him through Welsh gentry networks earlier in the 1580s, and could then have been introduced through him to the Northamptonshire Montagus. But whatever the initial connection, the fact of a personal relationship with Walter prior to 1587 points to Hugh's acquaintance with at least some of the family for a period of years prior to his marriage to Elizabeth.

Roger Montagu's influence

A second possible broker is Elizabeth's uncle Roger Montagu. There are good grounds for believing that Hugh enjoyed an enduring and valued relationship with this individual, both prior to and across the duration of the marriage. In the first place, he chose Roger as the key signatory and 'feofee in trust' of the formal marriage settlement between himself and Elizabeth on 24 February 1588,[364] and at a later stage also chose Roger to act as executor of his will.[365] Beyond this, on occasion Roger lent his name and active engagement to key land dealings of Hugh's in 1591,[366] and even lent him money.[367] Particularly striking in the will is the apparent degree of trust Hugh reposed in him ('my loving uncle') in relation to possible arrangements for Elizabeth's future welfare in the event of her widowhood.[368] A further possible pointer to the personal warmth of the connection is the fact that in 1590 Hugh and Elizabeth chose the name Roger for their only son, a Christian name of which there is no previous trace in any of Hugh's antecedents. Viewed in tandem with the other pointers, it seems less from fanciful to ascribe the choice to respectful appreciation of the uncle's importance to both of them.

It should be added that the signature of Elizabeth's father Simon also appears on both marriage settlement and will. Nevertheless, the impression conveyed by the order of signing is that Roger was the dominant presence for Hugh. This impression is reinforced by fragments of other evidence pointing to the brothers' differences of personal character and circumstance. Roger was a highly successful merchant in the fur and silk trade, a member of the wealthy Skinners Company.[369] By the concluding decades of the century, he had be-

---

363 Ibid.

364 UB Plas Coch 130. Though in the event Roger chose not to undertake this role – see below in Appendix B, 'Hugh Hughes's Will', final sentence.

365 UB Plas Coch 173.

366 UB Plas Coch 144-147, 148.

367 UB Plas Coch 3008.

368 UB Plas Coch 173.

369 R.M. Benbow, *Index of London Citizens Active in City Government 1558-1603* (Centre for

come a leading figure in the City of London, of which he was a common councillor. He was also a hospital governor, and in 1602 was made Master (*i.e.* head)
of the Skinners, a signal honour.[370] Perhaps significantly, this was the same year
in which Hugh was to assume the office of Treasurer of Lincoln's Inn.[371] He
and Roger were probably moving together in high London circles by this stage.

More conspicuously still, Roger was 'silkman' to Queen Elizabeth, in other
words the Crown's supplier of silks.[372] The wealth that his business interests
brought can be gauged by the fact that he was able to carry debts of £1,840 [a
2009 equivalent of £270,000][373] owed by his brother Edward in 1601,[374] and
£2,364 [equivalent to £347,000][375] owed to him by the Crown in 1608.[376] He
also had extensive property of his own in Northamptonshire, in and around
Brigstock. What is striking in the present context is the likelihood that Roger
spent much of his distinguished working life in London, during decades when
Hugh was actively engaged with nearby Lincoln's Inn. It is a reasonable speculation, if no more, that the two became acquainted in London in the years
before 1588, perhaps initially through professional business, and that Roger,
the senior of the two, spotted qualities in this rising and still unmarried barrister and crown official from the provinces suggesting suitability as a potential
partner for his niece, Elizabeth.

Brother and father-in-law

In contrast to Roger's social and entrepreneurial accomplishments, Elizabeth's
father Simon was the older brother's tenant at Brigstock manor,[377] where the
limited available evidence points to his having been content with local gentry
life. He held the associated sinecure of Keeper of Farming Wood close to Brigstock,[378] and, to judge from correspondence between the brothers, looked out
conscientiously for the local interests of his siblings (Roger and Edward), whilst

---

Metropolitan History, IHR) s.v. Roger Montague.

370 Ibid.

371 See p.81.

372 I.W.Archer,'City and Court Connected:The Material Dimensions of Royal Ceremonial
     *ca.*1480-1625' *HLQ*, 70:1 (2008), pp.157-179.

373 Offering, op cit.

374 Cope, op cit, p.28

375 Offering, op cit.

376 M.A.Everett Green (ed) (1857): *Calendar of State Papers Domestic: James I,* Vol 32: 4 May
     1608.

377 *Montagu Letters*, Box 13/6.

378 TNA Index 17334, pp. 378 ff, cited in: P.A.J.Pettit, *The Royal Forests of Northamptonshire, a
     Study in their Economy 1558-1714* (Gateshead, Northumberland Press for
     Northamptonshire Record Society, 1968), p.170.

also safeguarding his own and other less advantaged villagers' long-established rights in the long-settled communities of Rockingham forest. There is a flavour of his having been satisfied with a local manorial role.

The surviving personal letters[379] of the brothers offer a flavour of the family of which Hugh became part through the marriage to Elizabeth. For example, on 19 June 1600, Elizabeth's first cousin Edward (the 3rd) wrote to his mother, that is Elizabeth's grandmother, in anticipation of a visit back home, humorously relishing the prospect of eating the latter's frumenty and cheesecake, longing to help with fruit-picking in the garden, and looking forward to besting his father in games of chess and 'double-handed Irish'.[380] Others, from Roger in London to Edward, express similar delight in the pleasures of life in Northamptonshire and hopes that his brother and family will enjoy his presents of silk and embroidery. The exchanges have a cultured and spontaneous feel, hinting at a literate network of brothers, cousins, and more indirect connections, respectful of one another's interests, and warm and thoughtful in their relations.[381]

Hugh's acceptability to the family as a partner for Elizabeth must surely have reflected recognition – most particularly by Roger, if the speculation above is sound – of his accumulating professional and public accomplishments. In English gentry terms the Plas Coch land holdings at the time would almost certainly have been perceived as those of a modest backwoods squire from the remoter coastal fringes, hardly a satisfactory alliance for a Northamptonshire Montagu in purely social terms. There is no way of knowing precisely what Hugh felt about this passage into a higher social echelon. But it may not be fanciful to find hints of appreciation of the tastes and values of the Montagus in his own choice of redesign for Plas Coch, his family house, during the 1590s. The manor house at Brigstock, where Elizabeth was raised, is still today an example of Flemish-influenced Elizabethan domestic architecture.[382] It was reconstructed by the Montagus some time in the 1550s. One is struck by echoes of some of its features in the recasting chosen and implemented by Hugh for Plas Coch, in the decade following the marriage. This is just one of several small pointers inclining one to sense that Hugh came to feel a degree of identification with the educated and sociable world of the Montagus. A further clue is the choice of Roger, and Elizabeth's cousins, Edward and Henry,[383] rather than any of his many Anglesey kinsmen, as principal signatories for the mar-

---

379   *Montagu Letters*, Boxes 13/1-6.

380   Ibid., 13/2.

381   Ibid.

382   N.Pevsner, *Northamptonshire* (London, Penguin, 1961), p.115

383   UB Plas Coch 408.

riage settlement and administrators of his will. Scarcely less suggestive are the indications of active business collaborations with cousin Walter, as well as with uncle Roger. Hugh seems to have felt easy with a number of members of the family and their ways of doing things.

Thus by the end of the 1580s, whilst unambiguously resident with his new wife at Plas Coch in Anglesey, and living and working much of the time in the heart of Welsh Wales (as will become clear in the following two chapters), he was also now entrenched by family as well as professional connection within the mainstream English governing class. This entrenchment then became all the more conspicuous over the next decade and a half, as he rose to become first a Bencher and then Treasurer of Lincoln's Inn, as well as Anglesey's Knight of the Shire MP in the 1597 Parliament, as is discussed further in chapter five.

Onto the Bench

To be made a Bencher of Lincoln's Inn was to become one of the Society's governing elite. The Benchers met formally and regularly during law terms, minuting their decisions in the Black Books.

Hugh's summons to the Bench came on 29 January 1594.[384] The following year, on 15 May 1595, he was also nominated Autumn Reader,[385] requiring him to give three major lectures, which had as their focus Littleton's *Tenures*.[386] The source is a student's annotated edition of *Tenures*, referring briefly in law French to Hugh's three lectures, as well as to Thomas Egerton's active interventions during the discussions. Complex land-related issues of the kind discussed in Littleton's seminal volume, which had been published originally in 1481 but ran through many subsequent editions, appear to have been Hugh's particular field of expertise. This places him close to the centre of debates surrounding security of contracts and titles to real property which were of such significance in the later decades of the century.[387] Indeed Hugh's intellectual standing in relation to such matters appears to have been reflected in the Society's subsequent invitation to perform again, as a *double* reader, in 1605,[388] an invitation he felt professionally confident enough to turn down, choosing instead to pay the fine of £20.[389] Moreover, his success, like that of his Bencher

---

384 LI Black Books, op cit, p.31.

385 Ibid., p.38

386 British Library Collections, 1379.h.10. The source is a student's annotated edition of *Tenures*, referring briefly in law French to Hugh's three lectures, as well as to Egerton's interventions during the discussions. See also S.J.Baker, *Readers*, pp. 132, 180-181.

387 Thorne, 'Tudor Social Transformations'.

388 LI Black Books, op cit, p.94.

colleague William Jones of Castellmarch, was helping raise the profile of Lincoln's Inn for others from his part of the world. The number of Welsh admissions to the Inn rose substantially between 1570 and 1610, from twelve to forty per annum,[390] with a number of the new entrants attracting the personal guarantees of these two senior figures, as 'manucaptors'.[391]

Being a Bencher meant Hugh also came to play a role in more practical matters within the Inn. Two such assignments are suggestive of how his administrative capacities were regarded by colleagues. One concerned the steady growth in numbers of those being admitted to the Inn, and the resulting pressures on space. Hugh was appointed on three separate occasions in 1599-1600 to new ad hoc sub-committees, examining the possibilities for new building and for reallocations of space already committed.[392] Such investigations would have required political skills in the tactful handling of established residents, as well as a degree of technical acumen about new building and the internal re-design of existing accommodation. He was presumably felt by his colleagues to have such capacities.

Kitchen perks

In a second initiative two years later, Hugh and a fellow Bencher, James Ley,[393] were appointed by their colleagues to get to the bottom of irregularities in the Inn's kitchens. In due course they reported their discovery of a host of abuses by the Society's servants: '... Mr Younge, the minister, claymeth to have weekeley a pounde of candells to cary home to his howse; and the laundres claymeth to have, every tyme she bringeth home the linen of the Howse, twelve loaffes of breadd, at every breakefast a pottell,[394] at every dinner a gallon, and at every supper another gallon of fresh beare; and that the musicians claime to have, after their supper and the revels, two loaffes of bredd a pece to carye home with them; and that the brewers demande to have, every tyme they bringe drinke to the

389   Ibid., p.204.

390   Williams, *Religion, Language and Nationality*, p.175.

391   *LI Admissions Register*, for 1590, 1595, 1596, 1598, 1602, etc. Also Griffith, *Learning, Law and Religion*, p.152.

392   *LI Black Books*, pp. 59, 60, 63 – Benchers council minutes for 25 November 1599, 25 April 1600 & 3 November 1600. 'Individuals and small ad hoc committees were frequently appointed at Lincoln's Inn ... These assignments seem to have been fairly widely distributed, although newly called benchers tended to be given a disproportionate share of the burden, *along with a small group of more senior men who were evidently particularly competent or conscientiou*s' [emphasis added] (Prest, *Inns of Court*, p.86).

393   *LI Black Books*, II, pp.219-220. James Ley (knighted 1603) rose to Attorney General of the Court of Wards, and in 1621 Chief Justice of the King's Bench. In 1626, he became first Earl of Marlborough. (*ODNB*, Vol 33, pp.686-688).

394   A pottell was two quarts.

Howse, two loaffes of bredd for every one of them to cary wth them; and that the panier-man challengeth to have at every meale syx loaves of bredd and a pott of beare of three quarters' – 'wch claymes challenges and demaundes [the Black Book minute adds] are utterly misliked'. They also found that the weights and measures in the kitchens were 'not full weightes' and 'wante measure', and that a range of other malpractices had become routine – for example, 'that the Steward useth to take more of the shillinge for butter than he should doe, and doth cutt his beef at two pence the pounde more than he should doe'.[395] In short, the kitchen perquisites had got thoroughly out of hand. Firm measures were put in place to minimise future leakages.

This two-man investigation had followed a previous, less fruitful inquiry into the kitchens back in 1598, by a committee of nine which had also included Hugh.[396] Possibly it was significant that the second attempt occurred right at the outset of his year as the Inn's Treasurer in 1602.[397] Though the Treasurer's role had not by then achieved quite the rarified personal authority it attained in subsequent centuries, it was nevertheless the top post of the society, its bestowal a recognition by Benchers of the gravitas of the chosen senior member. It may be that it gave Hugh leverage he had coveted to get a firmer grip on the Inn's day-to-day affairs. If so, his colleagues appear to have agreed his weight was needed if the festering malaise in the kitchens was to be sorted out.

Top man — Treasurer of the Inn

The most conspicuous duties of the Treasurer were formal and social. He was an ex officio member of Lincoln's Inn Society's Committee of Auditors, personally responsible for engrossing the annual accounts. As Treasurer, he also benefited financially, being entitled to fees from every student, twenty shillings each in 1606,[398] as well as for a variety of ceremonial functions within and beyond the Inn (including those where he may have interacted with his uncle-by-marriage Roger, as noted earlier). And at the close of his year of office he would have given a dinner for 'the Bench table',[399] a costly affair. All of these were significant but largely formal aspects of the role. Crucially, beyond such specific functions, Hugh as Treasurer would have been *primus inter pares* amongst the Lincoln's Inn governors at a time when the Inns of Court overall were close to the apogee of their independent prestige.

---

395 *LI Black Books*, II, p.72. (22 November 1602).

396 Ibid., 2 February 1598.

397 *LI Black Books*, II, p.74. (29 October 1602).

398 Griffith, *Learning, Law and Religion*, p.163.

399 Ibid., Preface, pp.xvi-xvii.

In a stimulating study of the Inns of Court overall,[400] Paul Raffield has suggested that by the end of the Elizabethan period – which is to say, around the time Hugh was elevated to the top post – they had developed as more than simply societies of professional lawyers gathered into permanent guilds. Beyond that, he argues, they had come to picture themselves as 'a *commonwealth* of lawyers', constituted self-consciously as 'an autonomous state governed by the equitable principles of common law ideology…a microcosm of the ideal English state, in which the ethical subject of law was acknowledged as a constitutional entity and the embryonic social contract between subject and ruler was nourished and enhanced'.[401] In other words, through their own internal practices, organisation and self-presentation, the societies of the Inns were aspiring to illustrate how balanced and benevolent government could and should work. Raffield suggests how this aspiration was manifested not only in the Inns' formal structures of internal governance, but also in the detailed architectural design and decorative ornamentation of their buildings, in patterns of symbolic action within the rituals of 'commons' (dinners) and moots; in sumptuary regulations concerning sobriety of dress; in imagery and dramatic archetypes acted out in the annual revels; and in recurring themes and characterisations of political relationship in masques, frequently performed in the presence of the monarch. Through a proliferation of such didactic signifying devices, Raffield argues, the Inns's members were consciously engaged in a performative 'aesthetics of the law', visibly reinforcing the law's procedural and textual modes of authority – and in the process pointing to an alternative 'Aristotelean' form of polity to that of centralised autocracy, the constantly lurking threat ever since the 1530s reforms of Henry VIII. Thus through the very fabric of the Inns' practices and self-projections, says Raffield, 'the legal profession gave visible shape and proportion to the illusory and fictive rights of the Ancient Constitution' [402] – presenting themselves as constant reminders of the need for a balance between sovereign power and protection of the individual's rights in a 'mixed commonwealth'.

If this picture is close to correct, it would imply that by the end of the Elizabethan period Lincoln's Inn and its fellow societies were nourishing a collective sense of themselves as an intellectually autonomous public sphere, often in tacit philosophical counterpoint to the crown's pretensions – effectively a polite but dynamic critical presence in relation to the constitution of the realm itself.

Raffield's argument relies on assumptions about the psychological and po-

---

400   Raffield, *Images and Cultures*, passim.

401   Ibid., p.1.

402   Ibid., p.263.

litical potency of the symbolic vocabularies the Inns were deploying in these various ways – assumptions which appear credible for a period in which comparable semiological approaches were being used routinely in the self-projection of successive monarchs.[403] It is a thesis which adds a plausible further dimension to the accounts by other historians of the public articulation of political and constitutional interventions by many Inns of Court members of the time. Brooks, for example, has shown how individual lawyers as diverse as William Lambarde, Edmund Plowden, William Fleetwood, Thomas Norton, Sir Henry Yelverton and James Morice gave lengthy public expression to their views on contentious matters of constitutional theory and practice in the later decades of the century.[404] 'The intellectual culture of the time,' says Brooks, 'made it almost second nature for technical legal argument to be merged with more general observations on the nature of the rule of law into modes of general political discourse...' [405] Raffield's stress on semiotics and symbol evident in the physical and behavioural fabric of the Inns themselves goes beyond this; it implies that the Societies' most senior members were routinely enacting a collective sense of themselves as responsible intellectual leaders in the deeper constitutional debates of the period, reaching well beyond any role as mere jurists.

This is important for an understanding of Hugh Hughes's own attitudes. From 1599 till shortly before his death in 1609, he played a prominent role at the highest levels of Lincoln's Inn's governance. As well as becoming Treasurer in 1602-3, he held the senior offices of Keeper of the Black Book, in charge of the records in 1599-1600, and Master of the Walks, in charge of the grounds and gardens between 1605 and 1608. And, as already noted, he was asked to become a double reader in 1605, an honour which had been achieved by only one other Welshman at the Inns during this period – David Williams of the Middle Temple, following promotion to Sergeant-at-Law in 1594.[406] There is thus little doubt that he won recognition as an authoritative figure in the higher reaches of Lincoln's Inn during the concluding decade of his life – and unquestionably this would have nourished in him a sense of being implicated, directly and personally, in the intense and historic constitutional arguments of the time, and the intellectual and political ambiance suggested by Raffield.

From the age of sixteen, his education and subsequent professional and personal networks had thus brought him from Anglesey to a place close to the

---

403   R. Strong, *The Cult of Elizabeth: Elizabethan Portraiture and Pagentry* (London, Thames & Hudson, 1977); K. Sharpe, *Selling the Tudor Monarchy: Authority and Image in Sixteenth-Century England* (Newhaven & London, Yale University Press, 2009).

404   Brooks, *Law Politics and Society*, pp.59-118.

405   Ibid., p.59.

406   Griffith, *Learning, Law and Religion*, p.196.

heart of hierarchical English society. His sense of personal identity must have been profoundly affected. Four years at an elite Cambridge college, rubbing shoulders with contemporaries from backgrounds of previously unimaginable privilege and literacy, followed by the decades-long connection with Lincoln's Inn within a rarefied and disciplined professional culture, would have been formative for a sense of himself as more than simply a Welshman in England, but rather as an active participant in momentous developments that were increasingly 'British' in scope.[407] The marriage into the Montagu family with its web of connections across Protestant intellectual society would have been reinforcing still further a sense of being close to the centre of the polity, whatever any lingering ambivalences he may have retained from his parallel Welsh cultural loyalties.

This chapter has sought to trace some determining features of Hugh's *English* experience – his university education, legal training and marriage, as well as his continuing role at the Inn. It has shown how he rose to eminence in specific English institutions of the time. However, such an account is far from exhaustive of what can be said of him in that connection. Chapter five will focus on three further appointments which were to require his presence beyond the Welsh border – in the House of Commons as Knight of the Shire for Anglesey in 1597, as a member of the Council in the Marches at Ludlow between 1601 and 1609, and as Lord Chief Justice of Ireland-designate in 1609. However, in order to understand how these appointments came about, and what their significance may have been both for him personally and for the developing English-Welsh relationship of the period, it is necessary first to return to the parallel development of his adult career and experience as an Anglesey Welshman in Wales. The next chapter attempts to do this, returning to the story following the final stages of his legal training in the late 1570s.

---

407   The implications of this are considered further in Chapter 6.

4 *Hugh Hughes in North Wales*

DESPITE the clear evidence of his eminence within the Lincoln's Inn society, and hence within the capital's networked community of lawyers and court officials, it is a striking feature of Hugh Hughes's career that, unlike many Welsh lawyer contemporaries such as David Williams of Ystradfellte[408] and the already-mentioned William Jones of Castellmarch,[409] he did not become either a Sergjeant or a Judge in the English courts. Though clearly an accomplished lawyer, as his succession of senior appointments shows, he appears to have chosen to pursue his career from a home base in Anglesey, rather than by ascending the greasy pole of the English judiciary.

It is unlikely he lacked – or had been judged to lack – the ability for such advancement, since late in life, in 1609, he appears to have been appointed Chief Justice for Ireland at a particularly challenging historical moment.[410] As will be argued in chapter five below, Hugh would have taken up this Irish post at precisely the moment the English crown was preparing to enact a radical new colonialist land-redistribution policy – a policy that was to be implemented through the Irish Courts of which Hugh would have been head, as well as being a member of the Governor's executive. This lay well in the future however. It looks as if, by the end of his training at Lincoln's Inn in 1579, he had made an explicit decision to return home to Anglesey. Or perhaps that had always been the intention. Whichever was the case, there are indications that for most of the 1580s and 1590s, he based himself at Plas Coch rather than in London, albeit with visits to the capital during law terms.[411] In this he resembled his younger Lincoln's Inn colleague Sir Peter Mutton,[412] who a decade or so later combined continuing residence at Llanerch, Denbighshire with appointments as Attorney General of Wales and the Marches (from 1609) and Chief Justice of the Anglesey-Caernarfonshire circuit of Great Sessions (between 1622 and 1637).

408 *ODNB*, Vol 59, pp.153-154.

409 *ODNB*, Vol 19, pp.659-660.

410 This appointment and its political implications are considered in Chapter 5.

411 See note 347.

412 *Dictionary of Welsh Biography*, p.1144.

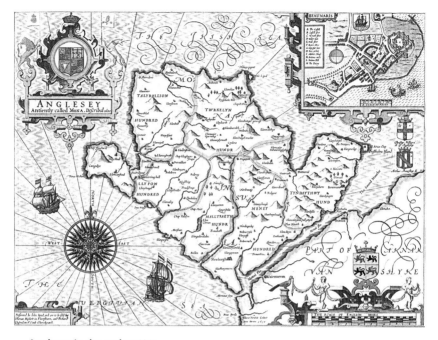

Anglesey in the early 1600s
John Speed's map shows the six administrative divisions (hundreds) of
the shire, of great significance for law enforcement. Hugh Hughes's
multiple local roles as justice of the peace, sheriff, manorial steward and
leading regional crown legal officer involved him in the detail of many
aspects of local and regional governance.

Call of the estate

To be sure, Hugh's position in this regard is less than clear. In a selection of
twenty-seven of his surviving archived documents from these two decades, he
refers to himself as 'Hugh Hughes of Lincoln's Inn' in eighteen,[413] and 'of
Porthaml' in nine[414] – but since the bulk concern contractual legal matters, in
relation to which it was obviously advantageous to stress his professional identity, this provides little basis for conclusions about residency. Equally unhelpful
are the fifteen surviving indentures, leases and articles of agreement[415] identified by the former Bangor University archivist Thomas Richards as having
arisen from Hugh's Lincoln's Inn business over the same period – since, as
W.P. Griffith has commented, '[these] papers reveal business centred on his

---

413   UB Plas Coch 2950, 2956, 2957, 2964, 2965, 29606, 2970, 2971, 2974, 2975, 2976, 2977,
      2981, 2985, 2992, 3002, 3008 & 3019.
414   Ibid., 2946, 2960, 2979, 2983, 2984, 2988, 3004, 3020, 3026 & 3027.
415   Ibid., 340-355.

chambers, the drafting of various legal instruments such as land conveyances, bonds, deeds of title and leases – solicitor's work in other words'.[416] Again, the papers suggest only that Hugh was active at least part of the time at Lincoln's Inn, without conclusive pointers to his place of residence.

The position is made cloudier still by fragmentary evidence that perhaps three of Hugh's brothers – there having been eight in all, as well as two sisters (Elinor and Catharine)[417] – played roles in relation to his properties in Porthaml over the same period. One brother in particular, John ap Dafydd Llwyd, appears to have acted more than once as a surrogate for purchases of land which he subsequently passed back to Hugh.[418] One implication could be that John, and possibly William and Lewis, helped manage the estate during Hugh's absences in London. But yet again, the fragmentary documentary evidence neither confirms nor negates the possibility of Hugh being primarily based anywhere but Plas Coch during the decades in question.

There are also strong further grounds for believing a Plas Coch domicile to have been probable. Not only is there the fact that Hugh extended the Plas Coch (Porthaml Isaf) estate significantly during these decades, but there are also the time-consuming and locally important posts he came to occupy. First, he was active on the Anglesey Commission of the Peace, being appointed a justice in 1577,[419] and continuing to serve actively on this Commission and its *quorum* – as well as, from 1591, on the *quora* of the Caernarfonshire and Merioneth Commissions – for the remainder of his life. He also served as Sheriff of Anglesey in 1581, 1590 and 1600,[420] a post implying obligatory physical presence on the island for each one of those years. At a more local level, he was in addition steward of three separate manorial jurisdictions in the island between 1580 and 1600.[421] And equally he held offices at a higher level within the region, becoming Deputy Attorney General for North Wales in the Court of Great Sessions in 1589,[422] and full Attorney General in 1596,[423] both appointments requiring an active and informed presence close to the home patch. Finally, as has already been shown in chapter two, he was involved in the protracted local land dispute with Rhydderch ap Rhisiart, with several Anglesey hearings, over a period of eight years in the late-1580s and early-1590s – again suggesting a

---

416 Griffith, *Learning, Law and Religion*, p.346

417 Griffith, *Pedigrees*, p.31.

418 UB Plas Coch 2947 (in 1581), 122 (in 1584), 128 & 131 (both in 1588).

419 Phillips, op cit, p.2.

420 Richards, *New Kalendars of Gwynedd*, p.53.

421 See pp. 120-122

422 UB Plas Coch 138.

423 UB Plas Coch 159.

need for a physical presence on the island during all, or at least much, of this period.[424]

These appointments and activities moreover suggest a significant pattern. They point to a progressively deeper professional involvement in the distinctive institutional matrix of government in the Wales of the time. Indeed, when one includes his election as Knight of the Shire for Anglesey in the 1597 Parliament and subsequent appointment to membership of the Council in the Marches in 1601, it will be seen that during the course of his life Hugh played an active role at *every* level of the principality's judicial and administrative system. Quite apart from the interest of this for the understanding of a personal life and career which actively straddled two distinct linguistic cultures, it also makes Hugh something of a prism through which workings of the processes of governance of late-Tudor Wales can be glimpsed.

In what follows in this chapter, the broad political and historical context is first considered, to be then followed by discussion of Hugh's specific involvements in these various institutional tiers.

The new framework for Wales

Dominant historical accounts concur that the 1536/1543 statutes which have come to be known as the 'acts of union' [425] were driven by *raisons d'etat* of the English crown in the wake of Henry VIII's breach with Rome, rather than by any particular interest in or good will towards the Welsh themselves.[426] Behind the new measures lay the monarchy's urgent wish to project more uniform and consistent royal authority into all corners of the kingdom, not least to minimise the mounting risks of invasion by Catholic continental powers in the wake of the breach with Rome. In the case of Wales, this found expression in the innovative administrative and jurisdictional reconfigurations initiated by Thomas Cromwell and completed after his 1540 execution. The measures evolved iteratively; the 1543 Act, which introduced radical changes to the court structure across Wales, as well as Commissions of the Peace, had not in fact been envisaged by Cromwell.[427] And as late as 1540, both the abolition of the Council in the Marches and the creation of a formal Principality for the new Prince Edward under the king's overlordship, were being considered seriously.[428] How-

---

424 This is the dispute examined at length in Chapter 2.

425 27 Hen VIII c.26; and 34 & 35 Hen VIII c.26.

426 Williams, *The Later Tudors*, pp.520-521; Davies, op cit, pp 224-238; Williams, *Recovery*, pp.266-267

427 J.Gwynfor Jones, *Early Modern Wales c.1525-1640* (Basingstoke, St Martin's Press, 1994), pp.77-85.

428 P.R.Roberts, 'A Breviat of the Effectes devised for Wales c.1540-41', *Camden Miscellany XXVI* (1975).

ever this came to nothing – and the final framework had four key elements: Shire government with county Commissions of the Peace across the whole of Wales; the creation of the four circuits of the Courts of Great Sessions and a more powerful and effective Council in the Marches at regional level; and House of Commons representation for the shire and key boroughs of Wales.

Wales after the Union

Circuits of the Great Sessions: *N-W, N-E, S-W, S-E* ▬ ▬ ▬ ▬ ▬ ▬ ▬ ▬

Boundaries of the Shires -

Boundaries of the Hundreds ···

In important respects the new institutional framework consolidated social and administrative trends and practices that had been crystallising over the previous half-century or more.[429] It built on a number of established templates – such as the former King's Sessions in the shires of the old principality, and many of the previous official roles from medieval English law. But nevertheless it was novel in fundamental respects. First, it brought into being an *integrated* hierarchy of institutions run increasingly by Welshmen themselves, articulated in the main through the 1543 statute. And second, it embodied features previously unknown to Wales – the office of justice of the peace, the right to members of Parliament, and equal citizenship under the common law, with English as the formal language of law and administration.

Though in immediate realpolitic terms the primary drivers behind the new dispensation were political priorities of the English crown, nevertheless Welsh attitudes and sensibilities were also of central importance in bringing the changes about. In the first place, the political climate which had permitted their uncontroversial introduction[430] was itself a byproduct of deeprooted Welsh loyalty to the Tudor dynasty. The good will flowing from Henry VII's *mab darogan*[431] status, and the bards' associated belief that the true (brythonic) Britons now ruled, fed widespread ideological acceptance of the arrangements.[432] Moreover, the late-medieval decline of Welsh magnates through escheats and wastage, and the consequent crown acquisitions of the majority of Marcher patrimonies, particularly the Mortimer lands in 1461, had created a favourable context for reform. Unlike the position in Ireland, these developments meant that the decks had effectively been cleared to create a platform for *uchelwr* or local gentry dominance, as 'residuary legatees of the leadership role' across Wales.[433] Increasing numbers of the latter had been chafing against continuing legal discrimination from the preceding colonialist era, particularly measures relating to exclusion from key offices and restrictions on Welsh rights of inheritance through primogeniture – so the prospect of equal participation in English 'privileges and liberties' was highly attractive. This is confirmed by the welter of peti-

---

429   Gwynfor Jones, *Early Modern Wales*, p.85.

430   Glanmor Williams notes the lack of criticism within Wales in the immediate wake of the statutory changes – as well as the many paeans of praise for the arrangements by many educated Welshmen over subsequent decades. (Williams, *Recovery*, p.275).

431   *Mab darogan*: 'Son of the prophecies'.

432   G.A. Williams, 'The Bardic Road to Bosworth: a Welsh View of Henry Tudor', *THSC* (1986), pp.7-31.

433   B. Bradshaw, 'The Tudor Reformation and Revolution in Wales and Ireland: the Origins of the British Problem', in B. Bradshaw & J. Morrill, *The British Problem c.1534-1707: State Formation in the Atlantic Archipelago* (London, Macmillan, 1996), p.72

tions and other representations from groups and influential individuals in Wales in the years immediately preceding the acts of union – in 1536 for example from inhabitants of Montgomery,[434] and from Sir Richard Herbert, Sir John Price and others,[435] in both cases pressing for the same 'laws and privileges' as English subjects. The more secure legal status – in particular the formalisation of primogeniture – and improved economic and political opportunities for those native Welsh 'with the wit, enterprise or luck to seize them' [436] meant that the legislation as a whole was seen by many from the outset in a predominantly positive light.[437]

Federation, not fusion

The framework in its completed form gave tacit recognition to Wales as appropriately a unified institutional whole.[438] This raises a further interpretative consideration. Recent studies[439] suggest that the supposedly unequivocal Tudor drives towards a standardising *unification* of the kingdom, as suggested by Elton and others, may have been overstated. For example, using a case study of the Cheshire Palatinate, Tim Thornton has shown that a far greater degree of local institutional autonomy and resilience was permitted to survive within that particular jurisdiction throughout the sixteenth century than had previously been assumed. Nor was this unintended on the part of the crown and Westminster officials, Thornton suggests: Thomas Cromwell and successors such as William Cecil had always recognised, in their sixteenth-century circumstances, that a kingdom was 'an association of varied and particularist elements',[440] notwithstanding any theoretical aspiration to versions of 'absolute sovereignty' consistent with the Justinian Code. Moreover, not only the Palatinate, but also the Isle of Man, the Durham Palatinate, the Channel Islands, Cornwall, Ireland and Wales, each had their own deep-rooted cultural and institutional peculiarities – and it was accepted by Cromwell, Cecil and others that crown authority had to work with the grain of such strikingly different jurisdictional arrangements, rather than seek crudely to press for a one-size-fits-all uniformity. There are echoes here of the later intense exchanges concerning the constitutional appropriateness of multiple jurisdictions between Sir Edward Coke and Lord Ellesmere

---

434   W.L.Williams, 'The Union of England and Wales' *THSC* (1907-8), pp.54-56.

435   W.Rees, 'The Union of England and Wales', *THSC* (1937), p.50.

436   Williams, *Religion*, p.152.

437   Gwynfor Jones, *Early Modern Wales*, pp.87-88.

438   J.G.Edwards, *The Principality of Wales, 1267-1907* (Caernarfon, Caernarvonshire Historical Society, 1969).

439   *e.g.* Thornton, *Cheshire and the Tudor State*.

440   Ibid., p.242.

(formerly Thomas Egerton) in the first two decades of the next century.[441]

Such a perspective assists understanding of some of the underlying English assumptions which may have informed the rapid succession of initiatives for Wales embodied in the 1536 and 1543 statutes, shaping their subsequent implementation and development. The aim appears to have been greater integration and effectiveness of government, but harmonising as appropriate with locally valued customs and patterns of authority. Indeed, the much-discussed language provisions of the 1536 Act[442] may usefully be understood in this light – less as a contemptuous assault on the language, than as reflecting a bureaucratising drive towards standardisation across 'Britain' of official records, without serious detriment to the continued routine use of local vernaculars in the courts.[443] The pragmatism with which the issue of a Welsh translation of the Bible was treated later in the century – for example in the discussions around the 1563 Act[444] – points in the direction of a similar inclination to work with the grain of cultural difference. All of which adds weight to Dodd's suggestion that what was at stake in the statutory union of Wales with England may best be understood as a process 'not of *fusion* but of *federation*' [445] – if hardly federation between equals. The new integrated hierarchy of Welsh legal institutions was the machinery through which this reconfigured relationship was to be implemented. And from the 1540s onwards, and in particular during Elizabeth's reign, new political and social contingencies bore in on each one of the new bodies brought into being under these arrangements, developing their roles as well as their inter-relationships, both with one another and with the Privy Council and Westminster courts. By the later decades of the century, as the discussion below of Hugh Hughes's particular experience suggests, this complex of interdependent courts and councils had more or less seamlessly produced a smooth-running machinery of government for the principality, whilst in the process preserving much that was distinctively Welsh.

It should be emphasised that the institutions in question – the Council in the Marches, the Courts of Great Sessions, the Commissions of the Peace, and the multiplicity of associated local officials such as coroners, constables, bailiffs, and of course sheriffs – existed to play more than simply 'judicial' or 'law en-

---

441   See p.72.

442   S.18 of 27 Hen VIII, c 26.

443   P.R.Roberts, 'The Welsh Language, English Law and Tudor Legislation', *THSC* (1989), pp.19-25, and 'Tudor Legislation and the Political Status of "the British tongue" '. Also, Gwynfor Jones, *Law, Order and Government in Caernarfonshire*, pp.66-70. For practical reasons in a largely monoglot region, widespread continuing use of Welsh throughout the courts system continued to be the rule. (Dyfnallt Owen, *James I*, pp.39-40)

444   2 Eliz c.28.

445   Dodd, 'The Pattern of Politics', p.8.

forcement' roles. In late-Tudor Wales, they acted also as key instruments of what today would be regarded as public policy and local public administration. To be sure, much of the work involved overtly legal forms and processes. But this reflects the particular stage in the development of the modern state in which their development was occurring.[446] As pressing new social needs developed under the pressures of population growth, land price inflation and periodic agricultural dearth, so the formal roles of the various bodies expanded, as will be shown below. To cite just one example, by the time Hugh Hughes began to become personally involved in the late 1570s and early 1580s, county Commissions of the Peace were being given increasing statutory responsibilities for the welfare of 'the impotent and deserving poor', particularly at times of food scarcity.[447] And the execution of their multiplying responsibilities was being coordinated and monitored by both the Great Sessions judges and the Council in the Marches in its quasi-Privy Council role.[448]

Integrated tiers of authority

This in turn anticipates an especially significant feature of the overall system vis a vis Hugh's own position within it – the integrated nature of the different tiers of institution. As will become clear, his personal experience at each one of the various institutional levels would have shaped his understanding of the roles and workings of the rest – as well as his internalised sense of the system as a whole. His public, and indeed personal (*e.g.* estate), responsibilities appear to have been mutually reinforcing, with positive implications for his value as a professionally informed presence – as well as, crucially, a Welsh-speaking Welshman – within any single one of the bodies.

It is appropriate to consider in greater detail the individual entities in which Hugh played a role, and their interactions within the system overall. However, in discussing these bodies, the researcher faces significant constraints, for there are major gaps in the documentary record. For instance, as already noted, no papers from the Anglesey Commissions of the Peace in the sixteenth or seventeenth centuries have survived – and indeed for the whole of Wales only those for the Caernarfonshire Commission are still in existence. Moreover, even the latter have important gaps, including the years 1589-1608, which cover not only most of Hugh's period as an Anglesey justice, but also virtually the whole of his term on the *quorum* of the Caernarfonshire Commission. Similarly, the surviving records of the Courts of Great Sessions for the two North Wales circuits

---

446   As discussed in the Preface, p.xvii .

447   *e.g.* 14 Eliz, c5 (1576); 18 Eliz, c3 (1576); 29 Eliz, c5 (1587).

448   P.Williams, *The Council in the Marches of England and Wales in the Reign of Elizabeth I* (Cardiff, UWP, 1958), Chapter 5.

for the relevant years are patchy in the extreme.[449] Nevertheless, an attempt can be made.

Anglesey's Commission of the Peace

Views of justices of the peace of the late-Elizabethan period tend toward caricature. Shakespeare's Justice Shallow – provincial, self-important, mildly corrupt – is hard to escape.[450] Equally, the picture of those same JPs in *administrative* guise tends to arrive through the distorting lens of Henry Fielding's Squire Western and later representations of *de haut en bas* gentry dominance of the countryside. Though such caricatures contain a measure of truth, they obscure more than they reveal about the nature and role of Commissions of the Peace of the kind on which Hugh Hughes served between 1577 and 1609. These were in fact key institutions of day-to-day county government by this period, across Wales as much as England. The regular three-monthly Courts of Quarter Sessions at Beaumaris were important judicial and administrative events for Anglesey, and, in a society where daily life was fundamentally *local*, served as recurrent rituals for the continuing reinforcement of social order and hierarchy. The text of a 1552 Caernarfonshire proclamation, giving the required fifteen days notice of the holding of a quarter sessions, states the purpose of the justices as being 'to keep the peace and determine divers felonies, trespasses and other misdemeanours perpetrated in the same county'.[451]

But these duties extended well beyond those of a court of law narrowly defined. Not only trials, but also a multiplying range of local government functions were administered through the justices (*i.e.* the Commission), using criminal judicial procedures. In Caernarfonshire the quarterly Sessions also required the presence of 'twenty four free and lawful men from each hundred, tithing, wapentake and each borough' as well as 'all stewards, constables, subconstables and bailiffs within hundreds and of the boroughs aforesaid'.[452] Almost certainly, the position in Anglesey was identical to that immediately across the Strait – implying that the Quarter Sessions required the mandatory presence in Beaumaris,[453] four times a year, of *two or three hundred* men of both gentry and 'middling sort' from all corners of the county. A succession of presentments from the hundred representatives would be heard, reporting on the

---

449 Parry, *Great Sessions Records*, pp. xlii-xlix & 130-135.

450 *Henry IV Part II*. Also J.Bate, *Soul of the Age: the Life, Mind and World of William Shakespeare* (London, Penguin, 2008), pp. 313-318.

451 Williams, *Calendar of the Caernarvonshire Quarter Sessions*, pp.93-94.

452 Ibid.

453 In fact in mid-century there was jockeying between Newborough and Beaumaris for the right to host the quarter sessions. By the 1580s, Sir Richard Bulkeley 3rd's influence had secured Beaumaris's position as the exclusive location.

state of roads and bridges in each bailiwick, leading in cases of failure or in-
efficiency to indictments by juries, followed by prosecutions and punishments.
This was in addition to the hearing of criminal cases in relation to which the
justices heard presentments and indictments from the grand jury and could
impose a graded range of punishments, up to and including hanging. The most
serious offences were then referred upwards to the Court of Great Sessions,
through the justices' own bills of indictment.

Multiple levels

A striking, if little remarked feature of these arrangements is the evident depth
of what might anachronistically be pictured as *democratic* – or at least vertically
distributed – involvement in Elizabethan county government. The regular
mandatory gatherings of upwards of two hundred part-time citizen-officials
from all corners of the island for the Quarter Sessions were by no means the
only local official occasions at which such personal attendances were routinely
required during any given year. There were also the monthly Sheriff's county
courts (discussed below[454]), at which all free-holders of the county were
obliged, nominally at least, to be physically present as suitors and potential ju-
rors – as well as, at hundred level, the 'sute' or 'dadlau' courts[455] and, increasingly, parish-level vestry gatherings entailing a further diversity of local
'middling sort' responsibilities.[456] Indeed, to contemplate these multiple obligations is to be bewildered by the continuing levels of personal engagement in
local affairs required of individual citizens of different social degrees. The opportunities for bribes to sheriffs, under-sheriffs and their underlings, to turn a
blind eye to non-attendances or other evasions of obligation, must have been
extensive – as were the fees and fines to which they were legally entitled

   As the second half of the century advanced, the balance between the justices' judicial and local administrative roles was shifting increasingly towards
the latter,[457] as their formal responsibilities, extended repeatedly by statute,
reached ever deeper into economic, social and defence spheres[458] – processes
driven in part by ever-increasing privy council concern for social stability and
order in the face of economic dislocations and mounting levels of poverty and
distress. Indeed, by the time Hugh became a justice in the late 1570s, the
strictly judicial dimensions of the quarter sessions were a diminishing propor-

---

454   See p.115.

455   See pp. 115-119.

456   S.Hindle, *The State and Social Change in Early Modern England, 1550-1640* (Basingstoke,
      Palgrave, 2002), pp.208-215.

457   T.Skyrme, *History of the Justices of the Peace* (Chichester, Barry Rose, 1991), pp.138-168.

458   Gwynfor Jones, *Caernarfonshire*, pp.112-147.

tion of a justice's work. Three-weekly petty sessions, first permitted under a 1545 Act[459] but increasingly resorted to as the pressure of business grew, involved one of two justices acting still more locally in their 'divisions', exercising considerable personal discretion.[460]

Anglesey Justices in 1584. This spread of homes of Anglesey Justices of the Peace at the end of the sixteenth century reveals the majority as resident on the more prosperous and fertile eastern and southern sides of the island.

Early recognition for Hugh

As already mentioned, Hugh was young, probably 29 and still in his bar training, when he was appointed to the Anglesey Commission in 1577.[461] His appointment would have been made under the seal of the Great Sessions Justices, on the recommendation of the Council in the Marches. The most locally powerful presences already on the Commission in the year he joined[462] were

---

459   37 Hen. VIII, c 7 (1545).

460   'Whether such (petty sessions) proceedings were formal or informal, it is clear they gave *rise to opportunities for favouritism, bullying and corruption.*' J.Hurstfield, *Freedom, Corruption and Government in Elizabethan England: County Government – Wiltshire c.1530-1660* (London, Jonathan Cape, 1973), p.262.

461   Phillips, *Justices*, p.2.

462   Phillips, *Justices*, p.2. Also Gwynne Jones, 'Some Notes', pp.63-64.

William Lewis, Lewis ab Owen ap Meyrick, Owen Wood and Sir Richard Bulkeley 3rd. The first three of these can be pictured as effectively the native Welsh power axis in the county. Thus William Lewis (1526-1603), living at his ancestral site of Presaddfed near Bodedern, was the second richest man in the county after Sir Richard Bulkeley, as shown by the Subsidy assessments of 1581 and 1597,[463] and had been MP for Anglesey in 1553 (a rare contested election) and 1555,[464] as well as Sheriff in 1549, 1557 and 1572.[465] Owen Wood of Hendregadog was his son-in-law and in 1577 the serving Sheriff,[466] his father, William Wood of Rhosmor, having been Inquisitor of Confiscations for North Wales in 1576, as well as possibly an agent of the Earl of Leicester.[467] As to Lewis ab Owen, he was Owen Wood's uncle, chosen twice as MP for Anglesey, in 1553 and 1572,[468] as well as serving as Sheriff in 1556 and 1572. His service in the Commission of the Peace lasted more than thirty years between 1555 and 1587. This was a tightly knit and powerful group – and at the time of Hugh's appointment, an intense rivalry was brewing between them and Sir Richard Bulkeley of Beaumaris (c.1540-1621),[469] the other contending political presence on the island.

Sir Richard, already the richest man on Anglesey,[470] was building on his antecedents' accumulations of land and power, and on the way to becoming the island's dominant presence. In the 1580s his rivalry with the other three turned into a naked power struggle which boiled over as the decade ended, with calamitous results for Owen Wood and Lewis ab Owen.[471] At this stage however Sir Richard was only a summer presence in Anglesey, being largely resident in London as a Gentleman Pensioner at the court of Queen Elizabeth between 1568 and the early 1580s. But this did not prevent his being the Commission's *custos rotulorum*.[472]

There were 43 members of the Anglesey Commission in all. Only half of these were Anglesey residents, the remainder being *ex officio* and from outside the county, playing little if any direct role in the routine business of quarter

---

463   TNA 179 291/17 & TNA 179 219/17 (a).

464   Richards, *New Kalendars*, p.153.

465   Ibid., p.52.

466   Ibid.

467   Griffith, *Learning, Law & Religion*, p.132.

468   Richards, *New Kalendars*, pp.153-154.

469   *ODNB*, Vol 3, pp.575-577.

470   TNA 179 291/17 & TNA 179 219/17 (a).

471   The controversy is discussed further at pp.101-105.

472   R.Flenley, *A Calendar of the Register of the Queen's Majesty's Council in the Dominion and Principality of Wales and the Marches of the Same (1569-1591)* (London, Hon Soc of Cymmrodorion, 1916), p.133 (fo 48). See also note 328.

and petty sessions. Hugh's close neighbours, Rowland Bulkeley of Porthaml (Hall),[473] Maurice Griffith of Llwyn y Moel (Plas Newydd),[474] and Rowland Meredith of Bodowyr,[475] all of them living within a mile or so of Plas Coch, would have been especially familiar local faces, though the likelihood is that the Lewis (of Presaddfed) / Owen Wood / Lewis ap Owen axis was the dominant internal faction over the few years immediately following Hugh's appointment. One indication of this is that it was Lewis ap Owen in person who is recorded as having handed in an Anglesey justices' petition on defence-related matters to the Privy Council in Westminster in mid-1586[476] – at much the same time Owen Wood was lodging a Bill of Complaint in the Star Chamber about Sir Richard Bulkeley's attempts to brow-beat fellow justices at the Quarter Sessions in July of that year.[477]

In the absence of surviving papers it is impossible to be certain precisely which of the individual justices bore the brunt of daily work. J. Gwynfor Jones suggests [478] that in Caernarfonshire between 1608 and 1624 an average of sixteen out of thirty-two working justices[479] were active attenders at Quarter Sessions, but he notes also that this was 'a much larger group than in the 1560s and 1570s'. In fact the overall membership of the Caernarfonshire Commission in those earlier decades was sometimes as low as seventeen,[480] implying an active attendance reaching barely double figures during that period. Joel Hurstfield's study of the parallel Wiltshire Commission points to Quarter Sessions in that county attended by as few as two or three justices out of thirty or forty[481] during the same two decades. There is little reason to suppose things would have been greatly different in the Anglesey Commission during the early years of Hugh Hughes's appointment.

---

473   Rowland Bulkeley was Hugh's next-door neighbour at Porthamel Hall. He had been MP for Beaumaris in 1554, and Sheriff in 1568. A copy of his will, dated 13 October 1592, appears in the Plas Coch papers (UB Plas Coch 149).

474   Maurice Griffith of Llwyn y Moel (Plas Newydd), another close neighbour, had been Sheriff in 1561, and served subsequently as Hugh's Deputy-Sheriff (in 1581). Probably Hugh's senior by twenty years or more, he also sold the latter lands in Porthamel (UB Plas Coch 131, 3026, 3029), following personal financial difficulties (B.E.Howells (ed), *A Calendar of Letters Relating to North Wales* [Cardiff, UWP, 1967], pp.5-8).

475   Rowland Meredith had been MP for Anglesey in the 1558 and 1559 Parliaments. He was Hugh Hughes's close neighbour at Bodowyr, and the families overlapped on a variety of property and arbitration matters. (*e.g.* UB Plas Coch 80, 83, 137).

476   TNA SP 12/195, item 92.

477   Jones, *Bulkeleys of Baron Hill*, p.204.

478   Gwynfor Jones, *Law, Order and Government in Caernarfonshire*, pp.108-109.

479   Ibid.

480   Phillips, *Justices*, pp.10-11.

481   Hurstfield, *Freedom, Corruption and Government*, pp.253-258.

Expectations

Having almost certainly been appointed for his energy and legal promise, the expectation would have been that he would be an active member of the Commission, at a time when the justices' duties overall were becoming ever more complex and demanding. Indeed by the concluding decades of the century the general responsibilities of justices of the peace had come to encompass oversight or direct administration of a ramifying range of facets of local social and economic life – including the maintenance of gaols, houses of correction, highways and bridges; trading standards; liquor licensing; wage rates and conditions of employment; the safeguarding of grain stocks and food distribution in times of dearth; enforcement of religious conformity; control of vagrancy; and, in particular, poor relief and local defence. Increasingly by this time, the established reliance on quasi-criminal procedures of presentment and indictment, as means of enforcement, was being diluted in favour of day-to-day discretionary activity by justices, individually and in petty sessions as well as quarter sessions, accountable collectively to the Council in the Marches.

That said, a surviving manuscript in the drafting of which Hugh himself may well have had a hand in his role as a *quorum* member of the Merioneth Commission – the Merioneth Wage Assessment of 23 May 1601[482] – illustrates graphically the continuing centrality of *personal* accountability and punishment for ensuring the execution of routine local duties in the community interest. The document appears to have been drawn up for distribution to the high and petty constables across the county, though it is addressed specifically to the Constable of Edeyrnion. Signed by three justices ('Humfrey Hughe, Gruf Nanney, and Robert Morgan'), it nevertheless has a sophisticated lawyer's hand to it, reflected in the preamble's summary of the national statutory framework – for which the *quorum*, advised by Hugh,[483] would almost certainly have been responsible.

The document's specific instructions illustrate the machinery of personal accountability by which the justices controlled the lower-level appointed officials in accordance with the Highways Act 1555. Thus for example, 'Constables and church wardens of every parish must yerelie in Ester weeke call together the parishioners and appoint overseers of the highe wayes wch if he neglecte or if suche overseers refuce their chardge they *shall forfect* xxd [twenty pence] *for such offence'* [emphasis added]. These overseers were then responsible for

---

482   NLW MSS, 1610, F II – reproduced in 'A Merioneth Wage Assessment' in *Journal of Merioneth Historical & Record Society* (1955), pp.204-208.

483   By this date Hugh would already have been a member of the Merioneth justices' *quorum* for about nine years.

the designation of six days in the year for the repairing of roads 'leadinge from one market towne to another', and for ensuring the active presence of all parishioners, subject to a fine of 'xij*d* for every such daies absence'. Similarly they were required to report any such absences to a local justice within a month, again 'upon payne of x*d* for eche default'. And finally the bailiffs and constables in their turn were to collect any such fines from the overseers 'upon payne of xd for eche default' and to ensure the proceeds were then used for further road repairs.

The Merioneth document is rare amongst records of early-modern Welsh justices in having survived – and is of particular interest here because of Hugh Hughes's likely role. It offers a glimpse of the punitive practical means by which local government under the justices was being effected during the period, across a proliferating range of statutory responsibilities. Matters would have been the same in Anglesey, and there too Hugh's role, as an increasingly authoritative lawyer and *quorum* member, would have been an influential one.

By the later years of the century, the justices' roles as public administrators were being extended remorselessly by Privy Council instructions and Acts of Parliament. In Anglesey's case, the spheres of defence and poor relief offer vivid illustrations of how this worked, over a period when personal rivalries between key individual justices continued to be potent.

National security and local rivalry

As regards defence, Anglesey's justices increasingly shared with the sheriff a general responsibility for military matters across the island, subject to instructions from the Council in the Marches (which after 1586 were transmitted through the island's newly created Deputy Lieutenant, Sir Richard Bulkeley 3rd, as *custos rotulorum*). Very particular circumstances prevailed within the island in this connection. Throughout the second half of the sixteenth century, Anglesey's exposed geographical situation gave rise to persistent concern about possible invasion – by the French and Scots between 1539 and 1560, and most especially by the Spanish between 1585 and 1601.[484] This meant that for much of Hugh's period of office, he and his fellow justices found themselves having to balance the obligation to ensure a supply of impressed local men for national military service, especially for the nearby Irish wars of the 1590s, against the more immediate priority of defence preparedness for the island itself. Hugh can be assumed to have endorsed petitions by leading Anglesey gentlemen to the Privy Council and Council in the Marches in 1586 ('Consideracons whie the Isle and countie of Anglesey should be by the Lls [*i.e.* Lords] provided for &c')[485] and 1595,[486] involving pleas for exemption from conscription for the

---

484   E.Gwynne Jones, 'Anglesey and Invasion 1539-1603', *TAAS* (1947), pp.26-37.

island's male population, on the grounds that all local men were needed for home defence protection against invasion. That this latter possibility was real is confirmed by the fact that the Privy Council twice granted such exemptions, in 1581[487] and 1598,[488] despite an urgent national need for more troops. The fervid security climate in the region in the late 1580s and 1590s is confirmed by contemporary papers in the Wynn archives relating to Caernarfonshire, with their repeated references to invasion scares,[489] local recruitment and desertion problems,[490] suspected fifth-column recusant activities,[491] and difficulties associated with adequate musters and deployment of weaponry. [492] The limited evidence available suggests that similar preoccupations consumed much of the time and energy of Anglesey's justices over the period.[493]

Indeed deep tensions between the most powerful of the island's justices came to a head in the late 1580s precisely through the medium of such national security concerns. The long-running power struggle between Sir Richard Bulkeley and the rival Anglesey landowner axis of William Lewis of Presaddfed, Lewis ab Owen ap Meyrick of Llanidan, and Owen Wood of Hendregadog[494] peaked during these years of greatest Spanish invasion threat, particularly following the former's appointment to the county's Deputy-Lieutenancy in December 1587. Whilst there is no evidence that Hugh himself was a partisan in the poisonous personal contentions between these individuals, the fact that all of them were justices and that the hostilities found open expression at Quarter Sessions meetings means he would have been unavoidably involved.

485 TNA SP 12/195. Item 92.

486 NLW, *Calendar of Wynn Papers 1515-1690* (Cardiff, UWP, 1925), p.178.

487 *Acts of the Privy Council* (J.R.Dasent, ed), 12 (London, HMSO, 1896), p.364.

488 Ibid., 28, p.223.

489 NLW, *Calendar of Wynn Papers*, 123.

490 Ibid., 110, 114, 153, 160.

491 Ibid., 107, 110, 241, 123.

492 Ibid., 156, 201, 254.

493 Gwynne Jones, 'Anglesey and Invasion', pp 31-36; J.J.W.McGurk, 'A Survey of the Demands made on the Welsh shires to supply soldiers for the Irish wars 1594-1602', *THSC* (1983), pp.56-67.

494 See p.97.

Centres of Bulkeley power in Beaumaris

Hen Blas (*above*) was the Bulkeley seat within the town boundaries of Beaumaris, until its replacement in the 1620s by Baron Hill (*below*), built by Sir Richard Bulkeley 3rd to overlook the town. Sir Richard was both *custos rotulorum* of the county, and in control of its two parliamentary seats. With his backing, Hugh was elected Anglesey's 'Knight of the Shire' (county MP) for the 1597 Parliament.

According to a Star Chamber suit in 1589, Owen Wood was physically as-
saulted by Bulkeley during a Quarter Sessions meeting in Beaumaris on 28
July 1586, as part of the latter's alleged pattern of intimidation and brow-beat-
ing of fellow justices in the face of challenge to his decisions.[495] The resulting
atmosphere in the justices' routine meetings would have been profoundly unsettling for everyone, particularly as the antagonisms affected their defence obligations. Early in 1588 – with the Armada looming – Lewis ab Owen ap
Meyrick complained directly to the Privy Council about the allegedly discrim-
inatory ways in which Sir Richard, as Deputy Lieutenant, had been supervising
the collection of arms and other resources for the island's defence, favouring
friends and targeting his enemies with excessive assessments.[496] Within a few
months, tensions had run so high that Lewis ab Owen himself was indicted
and gaoled by the Council in the Marches for refusing to hand over 'the common armour' to Sir Richard,[497] and no sooner had a Commission been set up
to investigate the matter than Lewis ab Owen raised the stakes still higher with
allegations implying treason on Bulkeley's part, relating to the Babington plot
and personal endorsement of piracy.[498] Though quickly cleared of these charges
by the Privy Council,[499] the stain on Sir Richard's reputation led him then to
be bent on revenge. Though Lewis ab Owen appears to have died later that
same year, there were further episodes in mid-1588 – in particular, a ferocious
physical attack by Bulkeley's men on Richard Gwynn, the Anglesey muster-
master and a small landowner who was probably also an ally of Sir Richard's
rivals.[500] The proximate trigger for the violence was probably a disagreement
about firearms training, Gwynn's speciality, but the underlying issue was the
same more fundamental power struggle.[501] It remained for Owen Wood to
make one last attempt to topple Sir Richard. In the autumn of 1589, he presented a final sweeping Star Chamber Complaint against the latter, but after a
lengthy hearing Sir Richard received only mild censure (and a short detention
in prison), and was returned to the island on the Privy Council's instruction,
to resume his defence leadership as Deputy Lieutenant.[502] Bulkeley then
rubbed in this vindication by successfully suing Wood for slander,[503] and having

---

495 TNA *STAC* 6/6/W4.

496 *Acts of the Privy Council*, 15, p.375.

497 Ibid.

498 Ibid., 15, p.409.

499 Ibid., 16, p.23.

500 Ibid., 16, p.118.

501 Jones, *Bulkeleys of Baron Hill*, p.216.

502 Ibid., 21, p.137.

503 TNA *STAC* 6/6/W.4

him deposed humiliatingly from the Commission of the Peace.

Thus ended a rivalry between the two factions which went back to at least the early 1550s – when, not long after his defeat by William Lewis in the controversial 1553 Anglesey parliamentary election,[504] Sir Richard Bulkeley 2nd, as Mayor of Beaumaris, had filed a Star Chamber complaint against Lewis ab Owen Meyrick and William Wood (Owen Wood's father), together with Hugh's neighbour, Rowland Meredith of Bodowyr,[505] concerning the holding of a Quarter Sessions at Newborough rather than at Beaumaris.[506] These various events were early stages in the same continuing struggle by prominent inter-linked *uchelwr* families, themselves all justices of the peace, to limit the Bulke-leys' escalating dominance, which was aided by influential marriage connections with the Griffiths of Penrhyn, across the island.[507] The decade-long absence from Anglesey of Sir Richard Bulkeley 3rd at court, following his father's death in 1572, had provided an opening for the Lewis-Wood faction to begin to rebuild its earlier dominance, and it was during this period, specifically in 1577, that Hugh himself was nominated a justice, albeit there is uncertainty about where his key support was actually coming from at this juncture. Indeed, it is possible he had gained the patronage of both William Lewis *and* Sir Richard.[508] Be that as it may, when Sir Richard returned to take up residence in the island in *c.*1585, the factional battle was rejoined in earnest – at precisely the moment when issues of local and national defence were at their most pressing, with the Anglesey justices required to play a full and active role.

Hugh would have been close to all of these disruptive struggles between the commission's most prominent members, even whilst the range of justices' duties – and in particular Westminster's and Ludlow's expectations of efficient local administration in times of escalating official anxiety about social order generally – was increasing year on year. Routine duties had to be performed – and, whatever the upheavals, the Anglesey Commission of the Peace somehow fulfilled its front-line role in wider defence and security matters, over and above the proliferating range of wider social and economic priorities.[509] Indeed their role in this regard underlines the importance of the late-Tudor justices, in Wales as much as England, as de facto instruments of central government, over and above their local judicial and public order roles. Not only were Hugh and fellow

---

504   P.J.Bullock, 'An Early Election Contest in Anglesey', *TAAS* (1976-77), pp.25-35.

505   Gwynfor Jones, *Law, Order and Government in Caernarfonshire*, pp.108-109.

506   TNA *STAC* 4/4/57.

507   Jones, *Bulkeleys of Baron Hill*, Chapters 3-5.

508   See pp. 66-67.

509   See p.99.

magistrates required to act as government agents for the recruitment and organisation of aspects of national defence within the county, but in practice they
were helping also to actively *shape* that policy, drawing attention (for example
through the petitions mentioned above) to specific local contingencies on the
ground where modifications were needed.

Poverty and social order

The same was true of a second major field of national concern, the issue of
poverty and its relief, which developed as a consuming preoccupation for the
Anglesey Commission throughout Hugh's years as justice. The later decades
of Elizabeth's reign saw a succession of innovations in social policy, aimed at
mitigating the calamitous effects for the least well-off of destabilising economic
and social forces throughout England and Wales. The combination of inexorable population increase, accelerating price inflation, tightening land markets, and periodic harvest failures, particularly during the late 1580s and 1590s,
acted to intensify hardship for those in the lower reaches of the economic scale
– resulting in escalating suffering and deprivation, as well as chronic ruling-
class anxieties about the potential for popular disorder and even rebellion.[510]
It was within certain English cities that these tensions were initially most no-
ticeable, as well as most disturbing to the Privy Council[511] – but the symptoms
were being experienced across the nation as a whole.

In Wales there were additional factors, including those arising indirectly
from the former inheritance system of *cyfran*. The accumulated fragmentation
of land holdings under pre-union inheritance practices meant that many farm
units, already barely large enough to sustain a living,[512] were rendered increasingly unviable as the owners were exposed to mounting inflationary pressures.
Conversely, the post-union abolition of *cyfran* in favour of primogeniture meant
that younger sons no longer had entitlement to a share, however modest, in
their ancestors' land.[513] Factors like these contributed to the growing numbers
of landless individuals and families, at best dependent on constantly depreci-
ating wages, at worst reduced to penury and starvation.

---

510   J.Walter & K.Wrightson, 'Dearth and the Social Order in Early Modern England', in *Past &
       Present*, 71 (1976), pp.22-42.

511   Williams, *The Later Tudors*, pp.222-223.

512   Williams, *Tudor Gwynedd*, p.40.

513   N.M.W.Powell, 'Crime and Community in Denbighshire during the 1590s: the Evidence of
       the Records of the Court of Great Sessions', in J.Gwynfor Jones (ed), *Class, Community and
       Culture in Tudor Wales* (Cardiff, UWP, 1989), p.283.

Poor Law innovations

From the 1560s onwards, a succession of statutory measures initiated by the Privy Council through complementary proclamations sought to mitigate the worst consequences of such developments. A distinction was developed, and built upon, between the 'impotent poor' and 'rogues and vagabonds' – in other words, the 'deserving' and 'undeserving', the former to be assisted with a modicum of relief and work opportunities, the latter supposedly to be punished out of existence. In a series of incremental steps, poor rates were established,[514] local houses of correction built, and work materials provided for the able-bodied[515] – in fact, a progressive system of rudimentary social support had begun to develop, subsequently consolidated and codified by the historic 1598[516] and 1601[517] Poor Law Acts. As it happens, Hugh Hughes was Anglesey's Knight of the Shire in the 1597-98 Parliament and may even have participated in the committee debates on that bill (a matter discussed below).

The personal demands implied for local justices like Hugh by such growing social provision were extensive. Not only were they required to set and ensure the collection of local rates to contribute to the costs of poor relief, but they also had to oversee the recruitment, payment and supervision of local officers – notably, constables and overseers – to administer the system at both hundred and parish levels. More straightforwardly, and equally onerous, they had to execute a parallel obligation to prosecute and punish 'rogues and vagabonds'. The 1601 Merioneth Assessment discussed above[518] includes a section titled 'For Relief of the poore and punishment of rogues', which details the ways in which the duties devolved to the local overseers were enforced. Failures to contribute to the poor meant harsh fines if 'rogues' escaped, or poor relief went un-administered.

Few sixteenth-century records have survived documenting the conduct of the Anglesey justices in relation to these matters specifically, but it is clear from studies of other counties[519] that the system evolved iteratively, with small sub-regional variations. Nevertheless it is hard to determine how effectively the requirements to provide poor relief were actually being implemented in Anglesey at this juncture. Hindle has shown that there were considerable variations in enforcement of poor law provisions across Eng-

514 5 Eliz c.3 (1563); 14 Eliz c.5 (1572).

515 18 Eliz c.3 (1576).

516 39 Eliz c.3.

517 43 Eliz c.2.

518 See pp. 99-100.

519 Gwynfor Jones, *Caernarfonshire*; Hurstfield, *Freedom, Corruption & Government*.

land and Wales in the 1590s, with much of Kent, Essex and other southern counties relatively strong performers, and northern counties such as Lancashire and Cheshire considerably less so.[520] The gap between 'the bombast of magistrates and the resistance of taxpayers' was a continuing problem in many areas, quite apart from the fact the operation of the system was dependent overwhelmingly on the abilities and commitment of lower tier overseers and constables, at the coal face so to speak.[521]

The already noted absence of relevant Quarter Sessions records for Anglesey and Caernarfonshire frustrates detailed further analysis of the position in those counties, though later indications may hint at a relatively satisfactory situation – for example the low returns from Welsh JPs in response to Privy Council inquiries about problems with poor law administration in the early decades of the seventeenth century.[522] It could also be that the distinctive oversight role of the Great Sessions judges in relation to Welsh county Commissions of the Peace (discussed below at pages 127-128) was contributing at this time to a discouragement of laxity in implementation, though again the patchiness of relevant court records for the period makes this difficult to confirm.

By the 1590s, the necessarily local nature of poor relief, vagabond persecution and rate collection processes was feeding further the requirement for justices to work individually or in pairs in their local 'divisions', exercising personal discretion outside formal quarter or petty sessions. In Anglesey, there appear to have been just two such divisions at this stage, one embracing the hundreds of Twrcelyn, Dindaethwy and Menai, the other Malltraeth, Llifon, and Talybolion.[523] Steve Hindle has pointed to the way in which growing reliance on the parish as the key unit for administration of poor relief in this period was helping to reshape the social depth of 'democratic' involvement in processes of local governance, drawing previously unengaged 'middling sort' individuals at vestry level into involvement in the late-Tudor political nation – processes which in turn had the side-effect of helping entrench long-lasting ideological distinctions between 'deserving' and 'undeserving' poor.[524]

In the absence of surviving records, it may be assumed that Hugh Hughes, having been appointed to the Commission at a young age, contributed personally as a justice to the workings of all of these processes during much of the

---

520   Hindle, *State and Social Change*, pp.153-162.

521   Ibid.

522   Williams, *Tudor Gwynedd*, p.54

523   'Submission by John Bulckley [sic], Beaumaris, 28 June 1575', (Bulckley was Clerk to the Anglesey Commission of the Peace), in Flenley, *Calendar of Council in the Marches*, op cit, pp.133-134. The divisions in question are stated to have been 'for the execution of the statutes concerning Labourers and Servants', rather than poor law administration per se.

524   Hindle, *State and Social Change*, pp.228-231.

late 1570s and 1580s. There is confirmation that he did so effectively in the fact that he went on to be appointed not only to the *quorum* of the Anglesey Commission in 1591, but also to those of the Caernarfonshire and Merionethshire Commissions the following year,[525] whilst also being appointed Deputy Attorney General for the two North Wales Great Sessions circuits in 1589[526] – all of them unambiguous pointers to the regard in which his legal judgement and professional commitment had by then come to be held by key figures in the Council in the Marches and Great Sessions judiciary.

Sheriff of the county

In November 1580, after just three years service as a justice,[527] Hugh was appointed the island's sheriff for the first time. To serve in this role in late-Tudor Wales had become something of a rite of passage for a leading man of the county – indeed, most of his fellow Anglesey-resident members of the 1578 Commission of the Peace held the post at some point or other.[528] Though no longer commanding many of the direct powers that had attached to it in the shires of the principality before the acts of union – when these territories had effectively been crown feudal lordships, and the sheriff the 'enforcer', just below the chamberlain and the justiciar – the shrievalty continued to be a highly significant post, in terms of both duties and local prestige. In the words of George Owen of Henllys, he was 'the chief officer of trust and credit in the sheere',[529] a key crown representative within the county, albeit since the 1536 Act subordinate to the justices in crucial respects. Appointment to the office for the standard one-year term was felt to be a mark of personal distinction, as recurrent bardic references affirm. In practical terms, the holder was the crown's executive officer, the formal passage-point for crown writs and proclamations relating to the shire, as well as having responsibility for conduct of Parliamentary elections; the empanelling of juries at assize, quarter session, county and hundred levels; keeping the county gaol; carrying out sentences on those convicted by the justices; and jointly organising military musters. All of these were weighty, sometimes controversial, functions of government locally. Quite as important, it was the sheriff who was responsible for the collection of crown rents across the island, and for rendering accounts to the regional Auditor.

---

525   P.W. Hasler, *The House of Commons 1558-1603,* Vol 2 (Members), p.351; Phillips, *Justices*, pp. 12, 21.

526   UB Plas Coch 138.

527   Richards, *New Kalendars*, p.53.

528   For example, William Lewis had been Anglesey's Sheriff in 1548 & 1557, Lewis ap Owen ap Meyrick in 1570, Owen Wood in 1576, Richard ap Owen in 1572, Rowland Bulkeley in 1568 and Maurice Griffith in 1561. (Richards, *New Kalendars,* pp.52-53).

529   George Owen, *Dialogue of the Government of Wales*, p.67.

Finally, not the least of the sheriff's responsibilities was the regular holding of his own county and hundreds courts, as well as the twice-yearly tourn. It was the county court, to which all forty-shilling freeholders paid suit, that was responsible for the election of the county's Member of Parliament, or 'Knight of the Shire'. And the hundreds or local *dadlau* courts also played significant roles. Such bodies have tended collectively to be pictured as faded carry-overs from pre-union days, largely superseded by the justices' quarter and petty sessions, but there are in fact grounds for suggesting that by Hugh's time these courts had evolved to carry a distinctive *cultural* significance, deriving from the overwhelmingly Welsh-monoglot circumstances of rural Anglesey. The evidence is limited, but the possibility is considered later in this section.

Writ to the Sheriff recalling members of the 1581 Parliament.
As Anglesey's Sheriff in 1580-81, Hugh Hughes was responsible for implementing this writ, recalling Anglesey's MPs to Parliament in January 1581, in response to a perceived new Catholic threat.

Personal setback — and recovery

Immediate documentary traces from Hugh's first term as sheriff in 1580-81 are few. Of the scarce surviving papers, the most striking hints at a major upset of some kind. This is a summons, backed by a mandatory £40 bond, to appear in person before two Privy Councillors – Lord Burleigh, the Lord High Treasurer and Sir Walter Mildmay, the Chancellor of Exchequer – 'to answer a charge of contempt in disobeying certain precepts addressed from the courts of Exchequer'. It is dated 31 January 1581/2, a few months after the completion of his term,[530] and covers not only Hugh, but also his brother-in-law, Richard Griffith,[531] and the latter's brother, Maurice Griffith, named as Hugh's under-sheriff.[532] But there the trail goes cold. The calendar of Privy Council papers contains no reference to the case, which may or may not mean that it was resolved before a hearing took place. Nevertheless, the fact of a Privy Council summons suggests a major irregularity of some kind, possibly relating to the sheriff's end-of-year accounting for crown rents collected by local subordinates. If that was indeed the case, Hugh as sheriff would have been liable personally to make good the sum to the crown Auditor. Conrad Russell has suggested that 'being summoned before the [Privy] Council was one of the most alarming experiences which might befall a Tudor gentleman'.[533] The episode would certainly have shaken Hugh, though the fact that it appears not to have had negative impacts on his subsequent career suggests that blame for the incident may have come to rest on his underlings rather than himself. He went on to be appointed the island's High Sheriff on two further occasions (for the years 1591-2 and 1599-1600), as well as accumulating additional official posts later in the 1580s.

Hungry bailiffs

But there are grounds nevertheless for believing that the upset may have had important and continuing reverberations. To help carry out his functions, the sheriff had not only to appoint a working deputy (the under-sheriff) and a county gaoler, but also bailiffs for each of the county's six hundreds. There are numerous recorded instances of sheriffs in other Welsh counties at this period – for example, Edward Kemys of Glamorgan[534] and David Lloyd Jones of Car-

530 UB Plas Coch 2950.

531 Richard Griffith, younger son of Rowland Griffith of Llwyn y Moel, was married to Hugh's sister, Elinor. (UB Plas Coch 69).

532 Phillips, *Justices*, pp.10-11.

533 Russell, *Crisis of Parliaments*, p.49.

534 TNA, *STAC* 8/197/29.

marthenshire[535] – lining their pockets with sales of bailiff posts and other sinecures to friends or close relatives, for sums of £10 or more. Indeed, G. Dyfnallt Owen suggests that, amongst sheriffs, 'there were few places in Wales where a brisk market in private deals for jobs and situations did not flourish'.[536] George Owen of Henllys noted that the going rate was '£10 or £20' for a hundred bailiff. 'There is every yeare a hungrye baylyff placed who thinketh to fill him self by fleecing others ere the yeare go about, and by that time his powling is ended theare succeedeth hym an other as needy as he', he observed.[537] Whilst there is no documentary evidence that Hugh demanded such payments, there is equally no reason to suppose that he did not follow the widespread contemporary practice.

However, this aside, the papers for his three terms as sheriff suggest a more complex situation in Anglesey. Specifically there are indications of steps taken by Hugh to cut off the potential for leakage to the bailiffs of crown revenue (and by extension, *in extremis*, of his own personal resources, as compensation to the crown for losses) under his watch. Thus a document dated 19 January 1591/92, during the second of his shrieval terms, records the posting of a bond of £100, underwritten by four named householders on behalf of Thomas ap John ap Llewelyn, as a condition of the latter's taking on the responsibilities of sheriff's bailiff for the Talybolion hundred of the shire.[538] This is the sole surviving manuscript from Hugh's second term in the shrievalty. The high sum required (£100), to be paid the Sheriff should the bailiff fail in his duties, is especially interesting. It appears to suggest that – probably as a fallout from the Privy Council knuckle-rapping at the end of his first shrieval term – Hugh had now decided on a substantially higher degree of insurance against possible bailiff misbehaviour than the routine payment noted by George Owen as normal. Moreover, by the time of his third term, in 1599-1600, there had been a still sharper escalation, suggesting that his levels of concern about the discretion vested in such individuals, with their substantial opportunities for financial sleight of hand, graft and worse, had continued to grow. Thus indentures amongst his surviving papers show that the levels of bond required of his 1600 appointees had ratcheted even higher than in 1591: In February and March 1600, the putative bailiffs of Dindaethwy, Twrcelyn, Talybolion and Llifon hundreds – respectively, Rheinallt ap William Thomas,[539] John Fletcher of Boda-

---

535   TNA, *STAC*, 8/215/20.

536   Dyfnallt Owen, *Wales in the Reign of James I*, p.129.

537   Owen, *Dialogue of the Government in Wales*, p.82.

538   UB Plas Coch 2989.

539   UB Plas Coch 163.

fon,[540] Hugh ap Rees ap Griffith of Llanbabo,[541] and Edmund Meyrick of Tre-fdraeth[542] – each entered into bonds of a remarkable £500, again co-signed in each case by four associates, for their respective posts – an equivalent of £73,000 in 2009 values,[543] a strikingly high sum for a single deep rural Angle-sey hundred.

Insurance and quality control

What was going on here? Whilst it seems plausible in narrow terms to suggest that Hugh was seeking simply to insure himself against repetitions of the unidentified mishap that had occurred at the end of his first term, the levels of cash increase for the second- and third-term bonds are remarkable, even over a period of continuing inflation. Perhaps therefore there was more to it than simple prudence. In the first place, the sequence needs to be interpreted against the background of Hugh's wider career preoccupations at the time. From June 1589 onwards, that is, from two years before his second term as Anglesey's sheriff, he was also Deputy Attorney General for North Wales, at-tached to the two North Wales circuits of the Great Sessions. In May 1596, he became the full Attorney General for the region.[544] In other words, across the period of his second and third terms as Anglesey's sheriff, Hugh was also the crown's senior (or second) legal official in north Wales. Furthermore, this was at a time of persistent Privy Council and Council in the Marches agitation aimed at securing greater probity and reliability of county justices, sheriffs and other lesser local officials – as reflected in the stream of instructions to this ef-fect issuing from Westminster and Ludlow throughout the later decades of the century.[545] Against this background, escalating levels of bailiffs' bond of the kind initiated by Hugh could well have been part of a wider policy initiated by Ludlow and/or Westminster, aimed at improving the quality of local officials in Anglesey, as elsewhere. Sharp escalations in the level of bond guaranteed by propertied associates of a prospective bailiff would make it more likely that only more 'reliable' individuals would choose to apply for such posts,

In other words, the measures were probably aimed at reducing the un-scrupulous 'pollynge and pyllynge' of the kind referred to in 1576 by Judge David Lewis[546] – and with every prospect of success. The evidence of the

---

540 UB Plas Coch 164.

541 UB Plas Coch 3013.

542 UB Plas Coch 3015.

543 Offering, 'Purchasing Power'.

544 UB Plas Coch 159.

545 *e.g.* Flenley, *Calendar*, pp. 98-9, 132, 148-9, 198-9, 212.

546 In his report to Secretary of State Walsingham, cited in D. Lewis, 'The Court of the President

bailiffs' bonds of 1600 is that there was no shortage of takers, even at £500. So, perhaps it is reasonable to picture the sequence of escalating bonds as having been crafted explicitly as a reform measure reflecting, characteristically for the time, lawyerly energy and imagination aimed at improved social norms underpinned by legal sanctions. If this suggestion is plausible, it would point to a style Hugh may have brought to other of his public roles also, combining knowledge of the low politics of hundred-level Welsh social life, with experience of court and crown administrative behaviours at multiple levels of governance.

This account also suggests how it may have been that Hugh was able to avoid any lingering damage to his reputation in the wake of the 1582 Privy Council incident. Perhaps, as a high-flying Cambridge-educated young lawyer-landowner at the time, he had been able on that occasion to win the confidence of Burleigh and Mildmay, or their Privy Council colleagues, that he was capable of being a 'sound' reforming presence in the crown's service in north Wales, if given another chance. Certainly, that would be consistent with the way in which his career developed over the following decades, as will become apparent.

Underlings

Such speculations, significant as they may be, risk becoming a digression from the analysis of Hugh's first-hand experience of the shrievalty. To return to the particular role of the bailiffs – it is striking that, in the case of Fletcher, the indenture accompanying the bond includes a recital of the bailiff's duties. Crown rent collection duties are presented as central, but there are also prescriptions that serve as reminders of the hard-man dimensions of the role – to 'doe noe extorc[i]on to any of the Queene's ma[jes]ties subjects by color of his sayd office', and still more strikingly – in the event of sentence of death being passed on any person for 'treason, murder of felony' (within the bailiwick/hundred presumably) – to personally 'execute or finde an executioner to execute the sayd felones or felones att such tymes and as often as need shall require.'[547] Such requirements, as much as the financial aspects of the bonds, bring home the stark practical significance of the sheriff's role, with his bailiffs, as key executive agents in late-Elizabethan government, as well as the routinely harsh and acquisitive temper of the times.

In parallel with the £500 commitments made by the putative bailiffs, on 3 March 1600 William Griffith of Coedana gent, also with four co-signatories,

---

and Council of Wales and the Marches from 1478 to 1575', *Y Cymmrodor* 2 (1891), p.62.

547   UB Plas Coch 164. Fletcher signed the document with an '*X*', presumably indicating non-literacy. The first of the four co-signers was William Griffith, the brother of the new under-sheriff (Phillips, *Justices*, pp.10-11)

entered into a bond of still higher value – £1,000 – to act as Hugh's under-sheriff.[548] Again, the high values point to the sheer quantities of hard cash that appear to have been involved in crown rent collection duties.

As regards the post of county gaoler, the terms of a further indenture signed by Hugh as sheriff and dated 1 April 1600[549] also illustrate the scope of farming for individual gain. Rowland Harrison, a 'tanner of Beaumaris', having sought the post at his own 'earnest suit and special request', undertook to carry out all the gaoler's duties at his own 'proper cost and charges', including 'sav[ing] the sheriff harmless from any consequences arising from the escape of prison-ers…maintain[ing] the prisoners with sufficient meals and drinks, and remov-ing them at the request of the authorities to any place or places in the county as required'. The implication is obvious: 'Within the precincts of their prisons, [gaolers] were an undisputed law unto themselves. They were not paid for their services but were allowed to extract what remuneration they could from the exploitation of their prisoners.' [550] Though the indenture itself includes no di-rect reference to a bond or other material *quid pro quo*, this piece of patronage probably also involved financial gain to Hugh himself. In the devolved, priva-tised system of local administration characteristic of the period, public service and private benefit ran hand in hand as a matter of routine.

As the crown's senior law officer in the shire, the sheriff executed writs for a variety of purposes, including on behalf of courts in other counties. The sparse documents from Hugh's first term include reference to an investigation of Richard Meyrick of Bodorgan in mid-1581, in response to a writ *Ad Inquiren-dum*, resulting in an Inquisition at 'Gwindy' on 9 September, at which he re-ported Meyrick as having 'no property in my bailiwick',[551] which on the face of it is puzzling, as this Richard Meyrick appears to have been a major landowner in Bodorgan. A possible explanation is that the sheriff was exercising 'discretion' in return for a payment, or in order to help a friend – an illustration of the extent to which central authority at the time was routinely dependent on local agents in Hugh's position for the execution, and indeed the interpre-tation, of its wishes.

---

548   UB Plas Coch 3012.

549   UB Plas Coch 165.

550   Dyfnallt Owen, *Elizabethan Wales*, pp.194-195.

551   UB Plas Coch 101-103.

Dadleys and sute courts

However, such delegated local power involved time-consuming obligations, in-cluding the operations of the regular sheriff's courts. The twice-yearly county 'tourn', at which attendance by the county's forty-shilling free-holders was re-quired, was run personally by the sheriff,[552] as were, in theory at least, the monthly county courts and still more frequent hundreds courts. Quite how these various bodies worked, and how consistently Hugh as sheriff in practice appeared at them – as opposed to the under-sheriff or his deputies, for whom the participants' fees and douceurs were routine sources of personal revenue – is obscure, since few direct records survive.[553] However, it is clear they were very well used. George Owen noted that ' …in most partes of Wales as I trav-elled, I have seene great assemblies of people together, and it hath been all-wayes towld me that it was the sheriffs hundred howlden there'.[554] Moreover, 'I have been present at a hundred courte, wheare I often resort to see theyr fashions, and wheare I have heard 140 actions of debt and trepass called in on[e] courte daye'.[555] He added that such courts were 'commonly held in some odd or obscure place or blynd Ale-house in every hundred wheare no man of accompte will resorte'.[556]

In Anglesey, these hundreds courts were known locally as 'sute' or 'dadley' (*dadlau*) courts, held regularly in taverns and other public places around the island. Robert Bulkeley of Dronwy's diary, written at his Llanfachraeth home a generation later in the 1630s,[557] refers to them frequently. For example: 'I June 1631 – vespi I went with Rowland ap Richard [his brother-in-law] to ye dadley and there fell a drinking with Owen Foulke, John Thomas O and Ed-mund Gruffydd ye undersheriffe & we dranke all night'; [558] or again, '27 June 1632 – I went to the court & paid for the sherife's dinner & mine owne. I took my man Owen's part against Huw Lewis & dafydd ap Powell…' [559] There are further entries of a similar kind. In the present context, what is especially strik-ing is the reference in these passages to occasional attendance of the sheriff himself at such occasions, in the case of *cwmwd* Talybolion at Dafydd ab

552   Williams, *Tudor Gwynedd*, p.26.

553   Ibid.

554   Owen, *Dialogue of the Government in Wales*, p.71.

555   Ibid.

556   Ibid.

557   H.Owen (ed), 'The Diary of Bulkeley of Dronwy, Anglesey, 1630-36', *TAAS* (1937), pp.26-172.

558   Ibid., p.46.

559   Ibid., p.74.

MARE HIBER

NI:

CUM

SIUE

VERGIUIUM

PARS

ANGLESEY
Comitatus, olim MONA
INSULA Druidum
sedes, Britannice Tir Mon

Inys Moylrionad

Llanbaderte   Hilary poynt
Llanvoch
Llanvehill   Greiger flu   Llanelian
Llanvaier   Llanveullome
Llanfluen   Tryfenni
                 mons   Cap Ilton
Llanrithlad   Dulas
Mathannan flu: Llanvaier   Llanyhauglepentre
Rodinad   Llandonrodok Bodanhill   Llanallhgo
Llanmathly   Llandbah   Ugwradog
Groninit Llanvaygil Llanct flu   Llanhangle treatber Llangrado   Llandona
     Llanyddsan   Llanarghyneath Llanuayer   Roww Hhab hill
Llanvorog   Llanarnissent   in hanerugfythay
Cap ylt nghwt   Llanuaghreth Cap Lleaghgunserwye   Llanbedor   Llanyhaugle
Holy head Llaneeghadhu Preeraddurt Llandrogarne Tregayon   Llanthufnam   Llangordayn
Caerguby B   Bedederre Bodefeg   Llangoythleg   Penmoneth
Llansanfride Pontrhpont Llanvaier in aybut Kirghiog   Hardrana Llanffynnan   Llansadwrne
Dmas vorthon Llanyhangle Llaghbullet Hanglo Kenay flu   Penmoneth Llanrodenell Llandronaye
cap   Tieualghmay   Llanyhongle   Llandyssho
Inys weall   Llanalong   Llaubulane Llan gyneirin   Gynt Au Predgint
                Llangristol   Llanthrenychuaab
        Cap tallalyne Cap maier   Brranth Llanyaieryupull
Aberfraw   Llyn corras: Henedregadog   Gingle place
        Treuerdath   Llangaffo Bodowervssa Llandewyn   BANGOR
Llandewisen Llangadwaladr   Bodow ercha
        Llouerton   Llanvaier Llangayn Llanedan
Boddon   vroinde   um Truerthin
        Newburgh
        Lanthgorinwyn
   Malthrath
   Abermenar ferye Nenai flu
VERGIUIUM   Cairnaruan

Septruho
Orient
Occidens

Chrisopherus Saxton descripsit

45

Owen's tavern in the parish of nearby Llanfigael, alongside the more usual presence of an under-sheriff. If this was true in the 1630s, it was almost certainly also true during Hugh's terms in the 1580s and '90s, suggesting that routine interaction with grass-roots vernacular disputes through this court system may have been part of the experience of the sheriff himself as much as that of his deputies. The key formal functions of these 'base' [560] bodies were to examine allegations of local trespass (endemic in the still-prevalent open-field agricultural circumstances of the period), and, most crucially, to arbitrate the constant civil disputes around routine low-level debts of less than forty shillings which were oiling the wheels of a liquidity-scarce, seasonal rural economy. [561] Tensions around transactions of this kind would have been especially significant in periods of rising inflation like the 1580s and '90s, albeit their regulation at base court level goes largely unmentioned in the surviving records of Welsh quarter and petty sessions. [562]

All of which may in turn have implications for how the role of sheriff was coming to be seen in late-sixteenth century Anglesey. As already indicated, the post-1536 Commissions of the Peace had come to replace the shrieval courts, formally at least, as primary sources of justice and public authority in individual shires – both as tribunals of first instance for misdemeanours and felonies, and increasingly as organs of active public administration. Furthermore, the parish vestry was fast becoming a further lower tier of local government, prompted by the statute-driven priorities of poor relief. [563] From the perspective of Westminster and Ludlow, it would have been these bodies which were now the crucial elements of county governance in Anglesey as elsewhere in Wales, subject to statute and common law, as institutional cogs in the post-union constitutional machinery. Moreover the official language of record and office-holding for such bodies was English – albeit there had to be wide margins of acceptance granted to monoglot Welsh speakers at Great Sessions, [564] and even more so *vis a vis* both suitors and officials at quarter and petty sessions. [565] But even so,

◀ **Anglesey, based on Christopher Saxton's survey and first published in 1579.**
The two boroughs of 'Bewmaris' (Beaumaris) and 'Newburgh' (Newborough) are the sole substantial settlements highlighted.

560 George Owen used the term 'Base courts' to encompass the range of county and hundreds courts.

561 Owen, *Dialogue of the Government in Wales*, pp.83-85.

562 Williams, *Tudor Gwynedd*, p.29.

563 Hindle, *State and Social Change*, pp.207-230.

564 W.O.Williams, 'The Survival of the Welsh Language after the union of England and Wales: the first phase, 1536-1642', *WHR* 2 (1964-5), pp.71-73.

565 Gwynfor Jones, *Caernarfonshire*, pp.66-71.

there is scope for wondering how comprehensively the reformed institutional matrix would by this period have replaced local Welsh-speaking people's long-established cultural identification with the negotiative processes of the local hundred or dadley courts to which they were suitors. These had after all a long cultural history, with origins probably lying in the commotal courts of pre-conquest Gwynedd.[566] Jones-Pierce observes that such courts had 'cognizance of the usages surrounding partible inheritance and native forms of mortgage [which] lingered on in the folk life of parts of Wales ... and until the end of the seventeenth century it would appear that such matters were the subject of extracurial arbitration in *unofficial assemblies which are described in contemporary diaries as dadlau, the term used in medieval law books for the old modes in which legal issues had been determined*' [emphasis added].[567] This likelihood, coupled to the convivial flavour of Robert Bulkeley's diary references to dadleys, sug-gests that by this period the latter were persisting as occasions for Welsh social interaction and vernacular negotiation of differences between neighbours and community members, beyond any strictly 'judicial' role.[568] Indeed the diary confirms that tourn, dadley and sute continued to have popular significance across the island until well into the seventeenth (or even the eighteenth[569]) cen-tury, with the sheriff and his deputies central figures in their operation.

The significance of this 'base' level of local government in late-sixteenth century north Wales appears so far to have been largely unexplored by histori-ans of the period. The emphasis vis a vis local government has tended to be on the post-union county quarter and petty sessions. Against this background, the fresh interpretative observations offered in the paragraphs above may be claimed as an addition to historical and even political understanding. They point to the reality that amongst the overwhelmingly monoglot rural yeomanry and peasantry of Anglesey, these lower tiers of institutionalised arbitration pro-vided a vigorous continuing complement to the work of the county-level Com-missions of the Peace.

This in turn points to an intriguing irony – that, in the particular circum-stances of late-sixteenth century Anglesey (and other Welsh-speaking shires), the sheriff's role may have been developing in two rather contrary directions. On the one hand, he continued to be the embodiment of English-speaking crown legal authority within the county, not only symbolically but still also, in significant respects, in practice. On the other, his supposedly increasingly mar-

---

566   Williams, *Tudor Gwynedd*, p.26.

567   T. Jones-Pierce 'Landlords in Wales', in Finsberg HPR (ed), *The Agrarian History of England and Wales* Vol 5 (Cambridge, CUP, 1969), p.369.

568   N. Evans, *Religion and Politics in Eighteenth-Century Anglesey* (Cardiff, UWP 1937), Appendix 2.

569   The still later diary of William Bulkeley of Brynddu notes, on 27 October 1737, the holding of 'a grand tourn' in Llanfechell. (Evans, *Religion and Politics*, p.122).

ginalised courts had come to act, by default, as residual harbours of local cultural continuity, such that the sheriff, himself bilingual, was now a kind of involuntary *de facto* patron of local Welsh social interaction and negotiation at the vernacular level. To what extent Hugh was personally engaged at day-to-day grass roots level is impossible to determine, given the sparseness of surviving records, but at the very least he would have been attuned to such developments through routine monitoring of his network of surrogates – deputy-sheriffs, bailiffs and the like.

Such aspects of the shrievalty are reminders of the organic character of local institutional development in early modern Wales. Whilst, as has been shown, statutory changes such as the 1536 and 1543 acts of union and the succession of poverty alleviation measures emanating from Elizabethan parliaments had specifiable and direct consequences for institutions at the various levels of government, nevertheless deeper continuities were also in play. Posts like that of sheriff did not disappear, rather they changed their meanings as needs and circumstances altered. And in Anglesey, a bilingual *uchelwr* like Hugh Hughes would have been able to mediate quite naturally across any cultural divides. The fresh interpretation presented in this section suggests that figures like Hugh, with their ability to straddle the cultural divides between crown-legal and Welsh-customary institutions at local level, would have been crucial to the frictionless meshing of the two tiers.

Hugh as Manorial Steward. The patent and royal seal signifying Hugh's appointment in 1580 as Steward of the crown manor of Rhosfair (Rhosyr) in the south-east of the island, one of several Anglesey sinecures to come his way in his professional prime.

Manorial courts

A further set of local governance institutions that were undergoing change in Elizabeth's later decades were the courts of Anglesey's long-standing royal and ecclesiastical manors. Hugh became a key figure in three of these, being appointed steward or deputy-steward to the crown manor of Rhosyr ('Rhosfair') in 1580; [570] the erstwhile Abbot of Aberconwy's Anglesey manors of Celleiniog, Cornwy, Penmynydd and Bodegwedd (Bodegwaith) in 1586; [571] and the Bishop of Bangor's 'manors and lands' in 1595.[572] Strictly speaking these were English-style manors only by analogy, their origins being as *maenolau*.[573] For example the Celleiniog, Cornwy, Penmynydd and Bodegwedd lands, dispersed around the island, had accumulated to Aberconwy Abbey through pre-Conquest grants of granges by Gruffydd ap Cynan ap Owain Gwynedd in *c.*1188-99, Llewelyn ap Iorwerth in *c.*1200,[574] and subsequently Edward I in 1284.[575] By contrast, the Rhosyr manor was a consolidated crown holding deriving from the Princes' former *maenol* in the south-east corner of Menai commote, albeit much diminished in extent over the centuries. And the Bishop of Bangor's lands, concentrated largely along the Menai Strait though extending also into Twrcelyn and Talybolion, were by 1535 in the long-term tenancy of Sir Richard and William Bulkeley.[576]

Hence each of the manors was different in history and structure, but the three were alike in each still having an independent infrastructure of steward and bailiffs[577] to run and regulate its court leet. As with the shrievalty however, by the late sixteenth century the justices of the peace had come to assume many of the manorial courts' historic judicial functions – leaving apparently only the handling of pleas involving sums of less than forty shillings, and minor disputes arising amongst the tenants. Indeed, as Christopher Brooks points out, manorial courts were one of the few jurisdictions in which the numbers of actions declined during the second half of the century.[578] Nevertheless, the

---

570   UB Plas Coch 99 & 172.

571   UB Plas Coch 125 & 171.

572   UB Plas Coch 3002.

573   Carr, *Medieval Anglesey*, p.110.

574   C.Gresham, 'The Aberconwy Charter', in *Arch.Camb.* XCIV (1939), pp.124-144.

575   *Cal. Chanc. R. Vac.*, cited in Carr, *Medieval Anglesey*, p.215.

576   UB Baron Hill 1956.

577   Wiliam ap John ap Gwilym posted a £60 bond as bailiff of the Bishop of Bangor's lands under Hugh's deputy-stewardship, on 14 May 1592. (UB Plas Coch 3007).

578   C.W.Brooks, *Pettifoggers and Vipers of the Commonwealth: the 'Lower Branch' of the Legal Profession in Early Modern England* (Cambridge, CUP, 1986), p.96.

attractions of the post of steward to a rising lawyer of Hugh's stripe would have
been considerable. Quite apart from the fees, fines and amercements arising
from the routine case-work, the steward's role as legal adviser to some of the
island's largest landowners would have brought with it enhanced prestige and
contacts, as well as opportunities for land-related intelligence of potential personal significance. It is striking for example that one of the Plas Coch estate's
prize acquisitions in the period following Hugh's 1586 appointment as steward
for the Aberconwy Abbey properties (which, as elsewhere, had passed into
Crown ownership following the dissolution) was the former township of Nantcall near Clynnog in Caernarfonshire, part of the former Abbey's estate.[579] The
papers are incomplete, but they show that by 1590 he had acquired an initial
lease in Nantcall,[580] on nearby crown land recently controlled by the Earl of
Leicester,[581] and by 1595 was in receipt of rents.[582] By 1606 he was well on the
way to taking over the ex-Abbey-owned remainder of the Nantcall houses and
lands[583] – much of which in the late 1580s[584] had been the focus of a dispute
within the then-leaseholders' family, a dispute of which Hugh would have had
inside knowledge as a key official of the estate. There is no direct evidence to
suggest anything underhand on Hugh's part, but the coincidence of dates may
well be significant. Whatever the professional value he was able to give the
Abbey's manor as steward – at a time when his own specialist professional interest in recent developments in land tenure[585] was of growing significance for
the management of manorial jurisdictions[586] – he may also have gained intelligence of direct personal benefit.

The real significance of manorial stewardships in the context of this chapter's argument is that they underline again the means by which Hugh was able
to stay embedded in the routine grass-roots social and administrative life of
the island, even whilst maintaining an ascent on the regional and wider national
scene. Just as conduct of Anglesey's sheriff's courts would have kept him alert
to grass-roots concerns, so local manorial experience of tensions surrounding

---

579   UB Plas Coch 374-393.

580   Ibid., 378.

581   C.Gresham, *Eifionydd: a Study in Landownership from the Medieval Period to the Present Day*
      (Cardiff, UWP, 1973), p.303.

582   UB Plas Coch 379.

583   Ibid., 381-384.

584   Ibid., 377.

585   Baker, *Readers and Readings*, p.132.

586   Brooks, *Pettifoggers and Vipers*, p.199-201. Brooks suggests that during the last two decades
      of Elizabeth's reign, there was mounting activity by common lawyers such as Kitchin,
      Calthorpe and Coke, aimed at integrating manorial customs and tenures into forms
      assimilable by the Westminster common law courts.

land tenure and management would have fed personal attunement to the social and economic pressures affecting late-Elizabethan and early-Jacobean north Wales. And it was pressures of these kinds which were manifesting themselves both in the civil suits and felonies tried at the Courts of Great Sessions, and in the 'public policy' preoccupations of the Council in the Marches (as well as the 1597 House of Commons), over the period in which Hugh now also became centrally involved in these very bodies. The next section turns to this matter.

A royal appointment
A fragment of the official document confirming Hugh's 1596 crown appointment as Attorney General (chief crown legal officer) for the North Wales circuits of the Courts of Great Sessions.

Attorney General for North Wales

The Courts of Great Sessions were arguably the most distinctive elements of the Tudor settlement for Wales. Whilst the 1536 and 1543 Acts' provisions for county magistrates, with their Quarter and (subsequently) Petty Sessions, were designed explicitly to align Welsh practice with that in England, the creation of the four judicial circuits of Great Sessions was an innovation peculiar to Wales, albeit the circuits themselves followed the geographical boundaries of the circuits prior to 1536. The Great Sessions courts, whose duties were set out in the 1543 'Ordinances',[587] were given extensive powers, equivalent to those of both King's Bench and Common Pleas in England – as well as a substantial equity jurisdiction, though for the purpose of initiating proceedings in this connection they were linked to four local chanceries, rather than the main Chancery court in Westminster. Geographical location within Wales made them relatively inexpensive for local suitors, and from the outset they appear to have been widely respected. Initially there was a single judge for each circuit, but within a decade and half of their inception, the courts' popularity and the resultant pressure of business led to a second judge being added in each case, consistent with William Gerard's urging in his 1576 Discourse to Walsingham.[588] Most of these judges and many senior court officials were in fact English, but that did not detract from the widespread sense that Welsh distinctiveness was being maintained and respected. Indeed, that is why Gerard at least urged the creation of specifically Welsh-speaking judges.[589] As Richard Suggett observes of these courts, 'Behind the English and Latin legal record there was a concealed world of arbitration, settlement and compromise in the Welsh language'.[590]

Hugh Hughes rose to become the first Welsh-speaking Attorney General attached to the Great Sessions, in his case to the two North Wales circuits of Anglesey / Caernarfonshire / Merioneth ('the Anglesey circuit') and Denbighshire / Flintshire / Montgomeryshire ('the Chester circuit'). The respect this appointment attracted within Wales is implied in a 1604 *cywydd* by the Anglesey poet Huw Pennant:

> *Benser a Reder odiaeth*
> *Yn Lincoln's Inn uwch hyn aeth*
> *Hwyroedd gael Cymro iddi*

---

587 33/4 Hen VIII c.26.

588 18 Eliz c. 8. See also Thomas, *Further Notes on the Court of the Marches*, pp.161-163.

589 Ibid.

590 Suggett, 'Welsh Language and Court of Great Sessions', in Jenkins, *The Welsh Language*, pp.153-180.

Ngwynnedd wych hedd ond chwi...[591]

> ' As a Lincoln's Inn Bencher and fine Reader
> Went even further than this.
> It was high time that Gwynedd should have a Welshman like you
> Bringing fair peace to Gwynedd ... '

The last two of these lines allude to Hugh's path-breaking significance as a Welsh senior lawyer-administrator. His distinctiveness as a native Welshman in the role is consistent with the apparent Englishness of the recorded names of the other sixteenth-century Welsh regional Attorneys General.[592] His initial appointment was on 20 June 1589,[593] as the Deputy to Attorney General Ralph Barton, an elderly and highly experienced Gray's Inn Bencher from Lancashire.[594] Barton had been a member of the Council in the Marches since 1570 and was a brother-in-law of William Gerard, who was the Council's vice-president at the time. He would have interacted closely with Sir Thomas Egerton in the same context in the late 1580s – a possible chain of influence relevant to Hugh's appointment.

Criminal prosecutions

The terms of the 1589 deed show that Hugh was appointed Barton's immediate subordinate, in what was a demanding post. As number two to the Crown's top legal official in the region, his key responsibilities included confirming and signing all indictments before their submission to the assize Grand Juries, and personally conducting criminal prosecutions of prisoners in court.[595] He was also obliged to appear in person for the crown in every case in which the crown's name appeared. Hugh agreed to 'discharge the duties of the office and save [Barton] harmless from any untowardness incident to its execution', as well as allowing the latter 'to have, receive and take' the annual fee arising from the office.[596] In addition, if Barton happened to appear in person to perform the duties, Hugh was automatically to give way. Though it has not been possible to trace any records of specific trial activities, it may be assumed that a great deal of expert judgement and personal hard work was involved, both during the Courts' twice-yearly assizes in each of the six counties, every summer and autumn – a total of twenty-four sessions a year, each lasting six days – in inter-

---

591 Wyn Wiliam (ed), *Menai*, p.17.

592 W.R.Williams, *The History of Great Sessions in Wales 1542-1830* (Brecknock 1899), pp.79-81.

593 UB Plas Coch 138.

594 Hasler, *Members 1558-1603*, p.387.

595 W.R.Williams, 'The King's Court of Great Sessions in Wales', *Y Cymmrodor*, XXVI (1916), pp. 79-80, 120.

596 UB Plas Coch 138.

action with officials of the judges and the Council of the Marches, and in preparatory and crown-advisory work behind the scenes.

Within less than three years, Ralph Barton died.[597] His successor as Attorney General, from 19 May 1592,[598] was Peter Warburton, a Lincoln's Inn Bencher since 1582, who was also a contemporary and close Cheshire associate of Sir Thomas Egerton.[599] Within eight days of this appointment, Warburton confirmed Hugh, who he must also have known well as a colleague and probably friend at the Inn (as is argued below), as his Deputy.[600] This arrangement continued for almost four years, till Warburton resigned the senior post because of pressures arising from an accumulation of further appointments.[601] At that point, on 8 May 1596, Hugh was raised to full Attorney General for the North Wales circuits in his own right.[602] The connection with Warburton, who finished his career as a much-respected senior judge, persisted however.

Authority and the gallows

As an institution, the late-Elizabethan Great Sessions was more than simply a trial court in eyre, it was a regional manifestation of government. The cyclical arrival of the Assizes carried symbolic and ceremonial significance for county towns, as an emblematic embodiment of law and constitutional order – a locally visible representation of national hierarchy and authority, backed by the gallows, compelling attention and even awe. As already noted, the 1580s and '90s were a period of fierce judicial enforcement of behavioural norms,[603] and popular dread of the assizes played a crucial psychological role as 'social theatre', over and above the courts' more specifically judicial functions.[604] The Attorney General and his Deputy would have been key actors in such 'dignified' [605] dimensions of the courts' political role. Though few accounts have survived of the actual routines of the North Wales Great Sessions during the period, Hugh can be expected to have featured consistently, in person, in

597   On 18 March 1592 – see note 592.

598   Williams, *History of Great Sessions*, p.80.

599   *ODNB*, Vol 17, p.264.

600   Williams, op cit, p.150.

601   *ODNB*, Vol 57, p.264.

602   UB Plas Coch 159.

603   Hindle, *State and Social Change*, pp.116-121.

604   J.S. Cockburn, *A History of English Assizes, 1558-1714* (Cambridge, CUP, 1972), p.3.

605   'Dignified' in Bagehot's sense, in his 1867 work, *The English Constitution* (Oxford, OUP, 2011 edn), contrasting the *dignified* ('that part which is symbolic') with the *efficient* ('the way things actually work and get done') elements of the constitution.

the ceremonials as well as the actual judicial processes.

The most explicit articulation of this connection between the Great Sessions and wider issues of constitutional government and citizens' obligations would have been through the judges' 'charges', or introductory speeches, to the grand jury at the commencement of particular sessions.[606] Such charges were evolving across England and Wales throughout the Elizabethan period as important media for public communication of both legal-political principles and recent statutory developments from the centre to localities,[607] and whilst Attorneys General were technically independent of the judges, the formers' well-informed views would have helped influence selection of the issues highlighted by the judges as relevant to particular local circumstances. So Hugh may well have played a significant contributory role in these processes too.

Networks, and the transmission of policy

It is important in addition to keep in mind that, over and above the range of his Great Sessions responsibilities, Hugh had now also been a specifically Anglesey justice for nearly twenty years by this stage – across a period when, as has been shown, the duties attaching to that role were becoming steadily more demanding of time, energy and powers of judgement. Indeed, as has already been shown,[608] at some point in 1590-91 he was elevated to the *quora* of not only the Anglesey Commission of the Peace, but also to those of Caernarfonshire and Merioneth. This meant that, at this level, he would have been operating close to the centre of the affairs of all three sets of county justices – active at many of their Quarter Sessions, whilst also being available for Petty Sessions and less formal single-or-combined justice activities within his own Anglesey division. As has already been noted, the role of a senior lawyer within a *quorum* was to ensure informed and up-to-date local implementation of the fast-changing policy and legal framework by his fellow justices, acting collectively. So on top of his higher Attorney General responsibilities, operating in this way, in both languages, in three geographically extensive counties would have involved Hugh in an enormous personal workload. Indeed the fact of a simultaneous personal presence on three *quora* from the early 1590s onwards suggests physical and intellectual stamina, as well as negotiating and advocacy skills across linguistic and cultural divides, which must have been recognised as valuable by the key members of the Council in the Marches and circuit court justices who had appointed him.[609] His Great Sessions activities – whether as crown

---

606   Brooks, *Law, Politics and Society*, pp.22-23.

607   Ibid., pp.87-92.

608   See p.16.

609   As argued Chapter 3, Sir Thomas Egerton, a weighty legal presence at the Council in the

advocate in court, or as authoritative back-stage adviser – can be expected to have had the effect of thickening an already rich understanding of the social and political circumstances of communities across north Wales.

It is relevant in this connection that the period witnessed continuing *inter-actions* between the two levels of local government: county Quarter Sessions and regional Great Sessions. Hugh's first-hand familiarity with what was going on at both levels would have put him in an influential position in relation to a wide range of governance issues. The issue of what today would be called 'sentencing tariffs' offers an illustrative example. Nia Powell has pointed to the degree of 'sympathy and compassion' reflected in some of the levels of sentence imposed at the Denbighshire assizes in cases of theft by individually poor and needy individuals, during the dearths and local famines of the mid-1590s, when Hugh was the crown's representative on that circuit.[610] Such observations complement Thomas Lewis's parallel argument that, at shire level, justices of the peace at this time were often deliberately undervaluing stolen goods in order to enable offences to be graded as petty rather than grand larcenies, thus avoiding the possibility of a death sentence attracted by the latter category, by ensuring that the indictments need not be referred to the higher court.[611] Given that Hugh was playing a leading role at both levels, the signals he would have given – either in advising his fellow Anglesey, Caernarfonshire or Merioneth justices, or in prosecuting particular cases before the assize judges – would have commanded particular attention. The authority of his position would appear to have been such that he was in a position to interpret and nuance crown policy on these matters – effectively, a political role in circumstances requiring social sensitivity, rather than simply a legal one. Moreover his experience of local circumstances through repeated service as sheriff (his second term was in 1591-2, it will be recalled) and as manorial steward would also have been able to inform his advice.

Furthermore, as Lewis notes,[612] a key significance of officers of the Great Sessions courts in relation to local justices lay in the fact that, since the former were operating across several shires (in Hugh's case, six of them), they were in a position to evaluate and communicate experience of other counties' interpretations of both their legal and their administrative obligations. The latter – proliferating over the ever-widening range of social and economic matters from poverty relief to trading standards – are especially likely to have benefited from

---

Marches and on the move from Crown Solicitor General to Attorney General in 1592, was almost certainly one of his key sponsors at this stage.

610   Powell, 'Crime and Community in Denbighshire', pp.286-287.

611   T.H.Lewis, 'The administration of justice in the Welsh county in its relation to the organs of justice, higher and lower', *THSC* (1966), pp.158-159.

612   Ibid., p.161.

the higher courts' comparative perspective. This perspective would have been evident in more than just the Charge at the opening of each Great Sessions. It would also have arisen in relation to particular indictments where there had been administrative dereliction, for example vis a vis neglect of roads and bridges, or failure to provide facilities for the indigent. Given that Elizabethan local government operated through criminal judicial procedures, such cases were the bread and butter of the Great as well as the Quarter Sessions. It seems unlikely that a regional Attorney General, with his finger on the pulse of crown policy and priorities, could have avoided being drawn into disputes about substantive fields which today would be regarded as matters of public administration and social policy.

Skilled bilingual lawyer

This chapter has sought to piece together the fragmentary traces of Hugh Hughes's public life in Anglesey and other north Wales counties during the later decades of the sixteenth century. Having apparently taken the decision in his mid-twenties to pursue a career from the family's expanding establishment at Plas Coch at Llanedwen, the same talents which had attracted success at Cambridge and Lincoln's Inn won him early recognition as a coming man on the island, as a local justice, as sheriff, and as a skilled common law advocate. A combination of Welsh family pedigree, English establishment networks flowing from his education (and reinforced by his Montagu marriage), and senior judicial patrons, possibly aided by fallout from the chance mishap during his first term as sheriff, attracted growing official recognition as a skilled bilingual lawyer and official in the Privy Council's interest. There are even signs – in the bailiffs' bond sequence[613] – that he may have become an actively reforming presence in the region, vis a vis higher standards of local government probity. Overall, these simultaneous involvements in the various interlocking tiers of legal-administrative institution in north Wales, coupled to sustained interaction with Lincoln's Inn during an intellectually dynamic phase of the Inns of Court's existence, appear to have led to growing standing within the governing class of the region, reflected most strikingly in the appointments as Deputy and then full Attorney General of the North Wales Great Sessions or Assize circuits. It should be added that his value as a respected Welsh lawyer-administrator would have been especially great for the Privy Council and Council in the Marches[614] during the 1590s, when north Wales, like other parts of the country, was plagued by national security concerns about possible Spanish invasion, political conspiracy, and conscription tensions related to the Irish wars

---

613   See pp. 110-114.

614   His appointment to the Council in the Marches in 1601 is considered in the next chapter.

– as well as persistent concerns about food shortages, social order and the relief of poverty, all of which were felt to require ever more active – not to say, draconian – juridical intervention.

Hugh's feel for the social realities of Anglesey Welsh life, discussed above in chapters one and two, would also have been a significant asset. Historiographically, the present chapter has been able to cast fresh light on the extent to which communal Welsh social and institutional life at hundred level was continuing in this period to be negotiated and regulated in the vernacular, through the sheriff's long-existing 'sute' and 'dadlau' courts, notwithstanding the emphasis laid by recent historians on the latters' apparent supersession by the post-union commissions of the peace. This is a matter that could repay further research, not least for the light it could cast on the pervasive linguistic tolerance that continued to prevail in local official life notwithstanding the 'language clauses' of the 1536 and 1543 acts.

In sum, despite a tantalising paucity of direct documentary evidence relating to Hugh's north Wales career, it has been possible here to suggest how what must have been an unusual combination of local knowledge, sophisticated Welsh-English cross-cultural understanding, and up-to-date public policy attunement and legal expertise were building him a distinctive and respected presence in the region. This combination of skills appears to have enabled him to apply up-to-date legal and administrative understanding at the vernacular local level, quite as effectively as in the higher courts. Such aptitudes then went on to win him recognition on a wider national canvas, as the next chapter shows.

Hugh Hughes was Anglesey's county MP ('Knight of the Shire') in the 1597 Parliament. The House of Commons of which he was a member met in St Stephen's Chapel, Westminster, shown here in session several decades later in 1640. It was during Hugh's 1597 term that the landmark Elizabethan Poor Law was passed, a significant step in social reform through national legislation.

5 *Hugh Hughes and the national scene*

BY THE MID-1590s Hugh was a public figure across north Wales. Almost certainly the reconstruction of Plas Coch was under way, adapting the earlier mansion which had been built by his father in the 1560s on the family's historic Porthaml Isaf site – and he and his wife Elizabeth now had a growing family, including a male heir, Roger their eldest child. A Bencher at Lincoln's Inn since January 1594,[615] his promotion in May 1596 to Attorney General for the North Wales circuits would have reflected Privy Council recognition of both legal and political weight. It was an appointment which entailed a strong personal identification with the crown. Increasingly he was becoming part of the institutional fabric of the new 'imagined community' [616] of *Britain*.

Anglesey's MP — Knight of the Shire

All of this is consistent with the reality that in Anglesey his preoccupations were increasingly in harmony with those of Sir Richard Bulkeley 3rd, beyond question by this stage the dominant political presence on the island. Sir Richard's prestige, national as well as local, had been confirmed by the speed with which earlier in the decade he had been quickly reinstated as the county's Deputy Lieutenant and, 'by the Queen's command', overseer of Anglesey's defence, following the embarrassment of a formal censure and brief imprisonment in 1590-91, as a result of Owen Wood's Star Chamber suit against him.[617] Such rapid official rehabilitation so soon after a conspicuous public disgrace points to the favour Sir Richard continued to enjoy at court and within the Privy Council, ever since his service at court as a Gentleman Pensioner in the 1560s and '70s.[618]

This high Bulkeley standing appears to have worked in Hugh's favour also. As already suggested, Sir Richard had probably assisted the latter's rise locally,

---

615   *LI Black Books*, II, p.31.

616   Anderson, *Imagined Communities*, pp.37-46.

617   See pp.101-105.

618   Jones, *Bulkeleys of Beaumaris*, p.193.

first as justice and then as sheriff on the island. Now, the Bulkeley hand can also be detected in Hugh's election on 3 October 1597[619] as Anglesey's Knight of the Shire for the 1597-98 Parliament. This was possible because control of the county seat, like that for the borough of Beaumaris, had rested with Sir Richard for at least fifteen years up to this point. As D.C. Jones has shown,[620] each one of the county MPs for Anglesey in the four immediately preceding parliaments – those for 1584, 1586, 1589 and 1593 – had been a Bulkeley relative or protégé, as was also true of the county's representative in the subsequent 1601 parliament.[621] Moreover the 1597 election, like the others just mentioned, appears to have been uncontested, suggesting that – whether as a reflection of the power of Sir Richard's backing, or perceptions of Hugh's own merits, or both – there was no overt opposition to his election from the island's other landowners and forty-shilling freeholders. This is noteworthy because such consensus over parliamentary candidacies was by no means automatic at the time in Wales. Both the Denbighshire elections of 1588 and 1601,[622] and the Montgomeryshire election of 1588,[623] were bitterly contested by rival gentry factions within those counties. And in Merioneth, allegations of corrupt practices during the 1597 election resulted in Star Chamber action against the two Deputy Lieutenants.[624] However in Anglesey no such challenges appear to have arisen with respect to Hugh that September. In any event, the sheriff in charge of the island's 1597 election was a Bulkeley relative, William Glynn of Glynllifon, Caernarfonshire, Sir Richard's son-in-law, who had himself been Anglesey's Knight of the Shire in the previous (1593) parliament.[625] The wheels of patronage appear to have been organised to turn smoothly on Hugh's behalf.

Settling in

So what role might he have played, following his arrival at Westminster for the opening of Parliament on 24 October 1597? Hayward Townsend, another neophyte member of the 1597 Parliament, kept a journal recording his first-hand experience, probably identical to Hugh's, of the state opening, swearings-in, and other key events of the session. Townsend was a member of Lincoln's Inn,

619   Richards, *New Kalendars*, p.87.

620   Jones, *Bulkeleys of Beaumaris*. pp.261-264.

621   1584: Owen Holland of Berw, Sir Richard's brother-in-law. 1586: Sir Henry Bagnall of Plas Newydd, cousin by marriage. 1589: Richard Bulkeley of Porthamel, cousin. 1593: William Glyn of Glyllifon, son-in-law. 1601: Thomas Holland, nephew. (Richards, op cit, p.154).

622   J.E.Neale, *The Elizabethan House of Commons* (London, Jonathan Cape, 1949), pp.111-128.

623   Ibid., pp.99-110.

624   Edwards, *Star Chamber Proceedings*, p.90.

625   Richards, *New Kalendars*, pp. 53, 154.

and would certainly have known Hugh.[626] Moreover there would have been many other familiar faces, from Welsh gentry, Inns of Court and Montagu family connections. However, more substantively, a sense of the broader context is first appropriate, as there is continuing historiographical debate about the nature and role of the late-Elizabethan Parliament itself. Sir John Neale's path-breaking but in retrospect rather Whiggish contention that the period witnessed a progressive crystallisation of Commons' opposition to Crown priorities, with a nascent puritan 'party' in the vanguard,[627] has met convincing challenge in recent years – in particular from those, following Elton,[628] who argue that during the late sixteenth century the Commons continued to be, like the Lords, overwhelmingly an instrument of royal government, for advice and law-making,[629] rather than an even embryonic arena of political struggle against the crown. So it is probably more accurate to picture it as an essentially unified, if opinionated, assembly at the service of the crown at this stage than as an arena nourishing political challenges on matters of state.[630] On this account the most conspicuous conflicts to surface in the late-Elizabethan Commons and Lords – those concerning for example the fate of Mary Queen of Scots, the issue of the Queen's marriage, the succession, and the increasingly sensitive matter of crown monopolies – were reflections of vertical differences of view within the court and privy council transferred into the two Houses, rather than, *pace* Neale, concerted horizontal movements of challenge to crown policy from organised groups of MPs.[631] This being so, the crown's central preoccupation within the Commons during this period – Elton,[632] Graves[633] and others have argued – was to negotiate the passage of nationally significant legislation and taxation through effective management of otherwise rather fragmented bodies of members. Michael Graves in particular has illustrated the key role of parliamentary 'men of business' – individual members whose skills of argument, drafting and political judgement made them Commons' leaders by example – in ensuring the effective implementation of crown legislative priorities.[634]

---

626 T.E.Hartley (ed) *Proceedings of the Parliaments of Elizabeth I* Vol III, 1593-1601 (Leicester, Leicester University Press, 1995), pp.225 et seq.

627 J.E.Neale, *Elizabeth and Her Parliaments* Vols I & II (London, Jonathan Cape, 1957).

628 G.R.Elton, 'Parliament in the Reign of Elizabeth I' in C.Haigh (ed), *The Reign of Elizabeth I* (Athens, Georgia, 1985).

629 G.Seel & D.Smith, *Crown and Parliaments 1558-1689* (Cambridge, CUP, 2001).

630 Ibid.

631 D.Smith, *The Stuart Parliaments 1603-89* (London, Hodder, 1999), esp Introduction. pp.7-9.

632 Elton, 'Parliament in the Reign of Elizabeth I'.

633 M.A.R.Graves, *Elizabethan Parliaments, 1559-1601* (Harlow, 1996)

634 M.A.R.Graves, 'Thomas Norton the Parliament Man: An Elizabethan MP, 1559-1581' in *The Historical Journal* 23, 1 (1980) pp.17-23.

Given the interests and evident sympathies of both Hugh Hughes and Sir Richard Bulkeley, it seems likely that in the 1597 Parliament the former would have been unambiguously aligned with the crown's interests in the Commons – though how actively is tantalisingly difficult to determine. The evidence already adduced of his associations with such significant Privy Council figures as Lord Ellesmere (the former Thomas Egerton),[635] at this stage Lord Keeper and Speaker in the House of Lords, and Sir Robert Cecil, then the Queen's Secretary, is suggestive. It was Cecil who was to propose Hugh's nomination to the Council in the Marches in 1601.[636] As a county member, Hugh would have been entitled to serve on a number of specific bill committees in the parliament, on matters to which his north Wales administrative experience had equipped him to contribute. Apart from the all-important issue of the triple crown subsidy agreed by the Commons, the key preoccupations of the 1597 Parliament reflected the catalogue of misfortune the country had been experiencing in the middle years of the decade, compounding the social impacts of continuing inflation.[637] Following the 1592-3 plague, in which more than 10,000 Londoners lost their lives,[638] there had been four successive years of failed harvests and ensuing dearths, leading to chronic deprivation and sporadic food riots up and down the country.[639] As chapter four has suggested, these were social conditions of which Hugh had been having direct experience through his role at the Great Sessions in Denbighshire and elsewhere. It is conceivable he could have contributed specific details from this experience to the committee discussions on both subsidy bills and poverty alleviation measures in the session. But if so, there is no record of such interventions.

The persistent national social and economic strains of the time were also being exacerbated for many by ever-increasing demands for impressed men for the armies in Ireland and the Netherlands.[640] Indeed by this stage the country had already experienced more than a dozen successive years of sustained warfare, aggravating the social and law-enforcement pressures at home, in relation to which Hugh himself, as a *quorum* member of Anglesey as well as of Caernarfonshire and Merioneth, would have developed his own personal concerns. The scale of the tensions confronting crown and Commons alike is worth emphasising: Over 100,000 men were conscripted for military service overseas

---

635   See pp. 68-72.

636   Hasler, *House of Commons Members 1558-1603*, p.35.

637   Russell, *Crisis of the Parliaments*, pp.4-11.

638   D.M.Palliser, *The Age of Elizabeth: England under the Later Tudors, 1547-1603* (London, Longman, 1983), pp.189-201.

639   J.Sharpe, 'Social strain and dislocation, 1585-1603' in J.Guy (ed), *The Reign of Elizabeth I: Court and culture in the last decade* (Cambridge, CUP, 1995).

640   See pp. 100-101.

between 1585 and 1603, for wars costing a total of c.£4.5 million, at a time when the revenues of the crown from its own resources were no more than £300k a year.[641] Such strains help explain not only the scale of the crown's multiple subsidy requests in the session, but also the fraught and anxious domestic political climate in which the Commons chose to initiate the social and poverty relief measures for which this particular parliament is best remembered – most notably the landmark Elizabethan Poor Law of 1598.

Welsh Commons caucus

The Commons' initiative on this matter reflected the queen's well-established distinction between 'matters of state', on which parliamentary discussion could only, and exceptionally, be initiated with explicit crown permission, and matters of 'commonwealth', in relation to which members' freedom of debate and innovation were relatively unfettered.[642] The issues with which the 1598 Poor Law was concerned were in the second category, matters of what today would be called social policy, albeit driven importantly by ruling class anxieties about corrosions of public order. The measure was the culminating stage in the succession of relatively progressive measures by Elizabethan parliaments aimed at relieving social distress and deprivation in society's lower reaches, whilst also persecuting 'rogues and vagabonds', with the aim not least of reducing the prospect of further social disorder. Again, Hugh was entitled to have been a member of the bill's committee during its Commons stages, and would have been able to draw on personal experience of the issues both at grass roots level and in the courts, though no specific record of this has survived.

In a survey of the general performance of Welsh elected members in the Elizabethan and early Stuart parliaments, A.H. Dodd suggests the period 1567-1603 saw the clear evolution of a 'Welsh interest' in the Commons, manifested especially in a developing bloc participation on private bill committees concerned with bridges, ports and county boundaries within the principality.[643] Neither makes specific reference to Hugh, but he would have been part of this congerie, which in the 1597 parliament included such local familiars as William Maurice of Clennenau (MP for Caernarvonshire) and William Jones of Castellmarch (MP for the borough of Beaumaris). However Dodd's emphasis on the primacy of Welsh links feels a trifle forced in Hugh's case. It seems unlikely that by this stage he would have thought of himself as exclusively a 'provincial' within the Commons.

641   C.Haigh 'Politics in an age of peace and war, 1570-1630', in J.Morrill (ed), *The Oxford Illustrated History of Tudor and Stuart England* (Oxford, OUP, 1996), p.338.

642   Elton, *Tudor Constitution*, p.256.

643   A.H.Dodd, 'Wales's Parliamentary Apprenticeship, 1536-1625' in *THSC* (1942) pp.12-13.

Sir William Jones
Like Hugh, the Welsh-speaking Sir William of Castellmarch (Caernarfonshire) was a 1597 MP and Lincoln's Inn Bencher. The two of them collaborated in encouraging a flow of aspiring law students from north-west Wales to come to Lincoln's Inn in the closing decades of the sixteenth century. Sir William subsequently became Chief Justice for Ireland, a post to which Hugh had previously been appointed just before his sudden death in 1609.

At a personal level, he is equally likely to have identified with the educated family networks of his wife's well-established Northamptonshire family – two of his wife's Montagu cousins, Sir Edward and Henry were fellow MPs in this session, for Tavistock and Higham Ferrers respectively[644] – and the large number of successful Inns of Court colleagues numbered amongst the 1597 MPs, quite as much as with fellow Welsh landowners. Indeed, many of the latter would also have shared cultural outlooks and social networks with their English equivalents, having been through the mill of similar processes of higher education. Throughout the Elizabethan period there had been a steady rise in the proportion of members who had attended the universities of Oxford and Cambridge or the Inns of Court, or in many cases both. For example, in the 1563 Parliament, of 420 MPs 139 (33%) had attended university and/or the Inns of Court, whereas by 1593, the figure had risen to 252 out of 460 (55%).[645] The equivalent figure for the 1597 Parliament was still higher. So more than half of Commons members, whether English or Welsh by origin, were by this time products of essentially the same demanding higher educational experience, with the spin-offs of increasingly shared cultural outlooks, networks of the like-minded, and enduring friendships transcending differences of regional origin. It is worth underlining the resulting intellectual confidence and vigour amongst Hugh's parliamentary peers, at a time when the tensions and security challenges of the 1590s were also acting as forcing agents for the freshness and originality of thought and expression manifesting itself in the theatre and preaching of the time.[646] What was emerging was a new and increasingly inde-

644   *ODNB*, Vol. 33, pp. 699, 733.

645   J.P. Sommerville, *Royalists and Patriots: Politics and Idealogy in England, 1603-1640* (London, Longman, 1999), p. 34.

646   See p. 168.

pendent-minded social and intellectual elite – and through its multiple inter-actions, the crystallisation of something akin to an embryonic 'public sphere' in civil society.[647]

This in turn was all part of a progressive unifying of national life in post-Reformation England and Wales. In an increasingly educated though still pow-erfully hierarchical society, London was becoming unequivocally the hub, politically, culturally, and economically, for Wales as much as England. Yet even though Hugh had been an active participant in the dynamic life of the capital for some years previously through Lincoln's Inn and the Westminster courts, to journey there as a member of parliament would have been a distinctive kind of experience. A meeting of parliament in late-Elizabethan London, says Neale, 'was the season of seasons',[648] a gathering of immense prestige for those in-volved. 'A matchless attraction it was to be in London at this time,' he contin-ues, 'To be "of the parliament"; to move on the fringe of the court, marvelling at its fashions and splendours; to see and hear the Queen; perchance to kiss her hand; to be at the heart of politics, and listen to famous men speaking in the House; to gather news from all quarters of the kingdom and the world. Such a one stood on tip-toe among his neighbours on his return home...' [649]

Such hyperbole reflects the truth that 'until 1640 the selection of knights of the shire for Parliament was essentially a process of social recognition, the ac-knowledgement of status.' [650] Indeed Hugh's sense of himself as both a region-ally significant presence and a now-equal participant in national matters of state would have been powerfully reinforced by election to and participation in the 1597 assembly. All of this paralleled continuing progress as a senior crown legal officer, whilst his involvement in the internal affairs of Lincoln's Inn during term times was also intensifying. Not only was he an increasingly active Bencher in the Society's administration (as already shown[651]), but in 1599 he was appointed Keeper of the Black Book, the guardian of the Inn's records,[652] the first of his succession of top jobs amongst the society's Benchers, as already discussed in chapter three.[653]

---

647 *cp* J.Habermas, *The Structural Transformation of the Public Sphere* (trans. T.Burger & F.Lawrence, Cambridge Mass, MIT Press, 1991), in which the later, eighteenth-century 'public sphere' is seen as a citizen-based 'site for the production of discourses that can in principle be critical of the state' (p.57).

648 Neale, *Elizabethan House of Commons*, p.150.

649 Ibid.

650 K.Thomas, *The Ends of Life: Roads to Fulfilment in Early Modern England* (Oxford, OUP, 2009), p.152.

651 See pp. 79-83.

652 *LI Black Books*, II, p.59.

653 See p.83.

Council in the Marches — another first

Back in Wales, Hugh's appointment to the Council in the Marches in 1601, on Robert Cecil's nomination,[654] was a further signal of recognition. He was one of a select batch of new Welsh gentry members of the Council appointed that year, the others being Sir William Herbert, Sir Thomas Mansell (Glamorganshire), Richard Price (Cardiganshire), Roger Puleston (Flintshire) and Sir Richard Trevor (Denbighshire),[655] all weighty figures both within their counties and further afield. The latter two were known as especially forceful and overbearing, both having faced corruption charges in Star Chamber suits arising from the stormy 1588 and 1601 Denbighshire parliamentary elections.[656] Collectively this fresh Welsh intake had the effect of tilting the numerical balance within the Council somewhat away from the long-established Marcher members' dominance – a development which appears to have fed the always lurking sense of grievance about the Council's territorial jurisdiction felt by many English border gentry in counties such as Shropshire, Herefordshire, Gloucestershire and Worcestershire. Indeed, as will emerge below, Hugh's appointment coincided with an increasingly rancorous phase in the Council's long existence.

Ludlow Castle, Shropshire. In the sixteenth and early seventeenth centuries the castle was headquarters of the Council in the Marches of Wales, which acted as a quasi-Privy Council for the principality. In 1602, Hugh became one of the first native Welsh-speakers to be appointed a full member of the Council. Travelling there from Anglesey on horseback, via Conwy and Chester, would have required two or three tough days on the road.

---

654   See note 637.

655   Williams, *Council of the Marches*, pp. 350-359.

656   *Dictionary of Welsh Biography*, pp. 816, 981. See also p. 132 above.

Robert Cecil, Earl of Salisbury
As James 1's Secretary and key adviser, Cecil nominated Hugh Hughes for the post of Irish Chief Justice in 1609. However, Hugh died in London, probably of the plague, before being able to take up the post.

Created originally in 1473[657] to advise the Prince of Wales, the Council in the Marches had developed in the mid- and late-Tudor period to become a key government institution for Wales, its initial prerogative powers having been extended and consolidated in the 'act of union' statute of 1543.[658] By Elizabeth's time, the Council was based at the imposing Ludlow castle, and was Wales's over-arching government agency, a quasi-Privy Council for the region, with – in theory at least – full judicial and executive powers to supervise law and order. In Penry Williams' words, it was 'part of that remarkable Tudor policy of creating centralised regional administrations within England and Wales'.[659] The Council's president was also Lord Lieutenant for Wales, as well as having the dominant influence over appointments to shrievalties and Commissions of the Peace throughout the principality, above and beyond the judicial, defence and law-enforcement duties. The role also had an important ceremonial dimension of a vice-regal kind; Court occasions at Ludlow Castle became glittering social gatherings for the actual and aspiring governing classes of Wales.[660] However, the Council's record of performance was mixed. Its glory days, following the rumbustious presidency of Bishop Rowland Lee in the late 1530s, had been between 1560 and 1590, under the presidencies of Sir Henry Sidney and the Earl of Pembroke. But by 1601 it was entering a problematic

---

657   Skeel, *Council in the Marches in Wales*, p.22.

658   s. 34-35 Hen VIII.

659   Williams, *Council of the Marches*, p.3.

660   A.H.Dodd, 'The Lost Capital', in A.H.Dodd, *Studies in Stuart Wales* (Cardiff, UWP, 1952), pp.50-52

phase. After a protracted illness, Pembroke died in January of that year, and as a consequence the Presidency was vacant for a number of months immediately following Hugh's appointment. However, in June 1602, after predictable court-factional jockeying, Robert Cecil prevailed[661] and the new crown appointee to the post turned out to be Lord Zouch, a very English and somewhat high-handed nobleman[662] who was in fact an uncle of Hugh's wife,[663] and could well have known Hugh previously through the Montagu family networks.

Internal tensions at Ludlow

In the late-1590s, there had been mounting tensions between the ailing Pembroke and his senior lawyers, led by the Chief Justice of Chester, Sir Richard Shuttle-worth, about issues such as the pace and nature of procedural reform and the location of real authority within the Council.[664] Absenteeism by both members and senior officials had reached disturbing levels, and internally there were mounting concerns about declining fee income from the court processes overall. Thus despite the praise the Council continued to attract well into the 1590s from contemporary commentators such as George Owen[665] concerning the success of its law and order role in Wales, it was facing challenges on a number of fronts by the time of Hugh's – and indeed Lord Zouch's – appointment. Two of these disruptions, closely related, were especially significant from 1602 onwards.

The first was the rumbling controversy about the Council's increasingly pressurised income. There was a wider context to this difficulty. As the Inns of Court turned out more and more lawyers in the late sixteenth century,[666] the latters' availability for the Westminster common law courts led them to search with increasing opportunism for work previously handled by other more local or prerogative jurisdictions. The Council in the Marches was an obvious in-stance.[667] In reaction to these incursions, as the lawyer-members within the Council gained the upper hand in the years leading up to Pembroke's death, they mobilised the Council to resist the threat to their incomes from profes-sional rivals in Westminster, whilst simultaneously maximising fines and fees locally. This had a further consequence. Because of their relative proximity to Ludlow, it was the high proportion of the Council's litigants from the four bor-

---

661 Williams, *Council of the Marches*, pp.298-299.

662 Ibid. Also, *ODNB*, Vol 60, pp.1008-1010.

663 Cope, *Life of a Public Man*, p.42.

664 Skeel, *Council in the Marches*, pp.120-128.

665 Owen, *Dialogue of the Government of Wales*, pp.21-24.

666 See pages 63-65.

667 P.Williams, 'The Attack on the Council of the Marches, 1603-1642', *THSC* (Pt II, 1961), pp.10-14.

der counties who felt the increasing levels of charge most immediately – and this in turn fed the festering local gentry resentments, particularly in Herefordshire and Worcestershire, counties which were under-represented numerically on the Council itself.[668] This set the stage for a growing convergence of interest between these border gentry and key actors in the Westminster courts, including Sir Edward Coke.

It is difficult to determine where Hugh personally would have stood on the issue. As himself a common lawyer, professionally attuned to the dynamic development of that body of law and the associated growth of the profession, he would have recognised and understood the pressures from London. However he is likely also to have identified closely with the prestigious Council of which he had recently been made a member with Cecil's patronage, and would have been reluctant to see it weakened. He appears not have been one of the quorum of four salaried lawyers – the 'councillors attendant', all of them judges – whose posts were given greater formal standing by Pembroke in 1600, to ensure greater efficiency and consistency of attendance at Ludlow during law terms. In this context, he was a Welsh gentry member as much as a legal eminence.

Penry Williams has suggested that amongst the groups of members who acted obstructively towards the new president's (*i.e.* Zouch's) attempts to wrest back control of the Council's procedures and appointment from the now-dominant lawyers was a faction of lawyer-members led by Egerton, including Puleston and Trevor (both of whom had Inns of Court experience).[669] Was Hugh a member of this group, given his respect for Egerton? Or did he align himself with Zouch (his uncle by marriage), who was backed consistently throughout the dispute by Robert Cecil (Hugh's own sponsor)? Unfortunately, the surviving records for the Council's internal debates are too patchy to provide any kind of an answer. Moreover, as in the case of many of Hugh's roles in public bodies, he is conspicuous in the documents that survive only by omission – a state of affairs which in this case might be interpreted as reflecting either crafty office-political manouvering in the face of awkwardly conflicting loyalties, or simply his relative unimportance to the key players.

The Four Shires controversy

A similar difficulty arises in relation to a second, related strategic issue that came to preoccupy the Council during much of Hugh's period of office (indeed extending beyond his death in 1609). This was the Fairley case, a minor legal dispute which blossomed into the long-running political struggle better known as the Four Shires controversy. In late 1602, one John Fairley (or Farley) had

---

668   Ibid.

669   Williams, *Council of the Marches*, pp.304-306.

been sued in the Council by 'a poore widdow' to hand over a copyhold cottage she claimed was rightly hers. Lord Zouch, sitting as judge, ruled in her favour, and ordered Fairley to hand it over. The latter refused, so he was arrested and imprisoned in Ludlow castle. He then appealed, sideways as it were, to the King's Bench, which in the autumn of 1604 issued a writ of *habeas corpus*, ordering Fairley and his case to be transferred to the Westminster court. Zouch's indignation at this invasion of his jurisdiction precipitated a hearing before the Privy Council, but the outcome was that the senior judges to whom the matter was delegated ordered Fairley's release, having concluded that the four counties did indeed lie outside the Council's proper ambit.[670] This was a victory for the Westminster lawyers, and Sir Edward Coke as Attorney General in particular, in their competition with the ambiguous, part-prerogative part-statutory jurisdiction (and income) of the Ludlow court.[671] It also gave encouragement to the dominant four shires gentry, triggering acts of disobedience towards its edicts by local justices and sheriffs over the next three years.[672]

Yet the king himself had still to be won over to the judges' view. So organised pressure was mobilised in the border shires aimed at winning his endorsement. The leader of this campaign was Sir Herbert Croft, Herefordshire's deputy-lieutenant and county MP in the 1601 and 1604 parliaments, and a member of the Council in the Marches from the same 1601 intake as Hugh.[673] The two would certainly have known one another, though Hugh would probably not have cared for Croft's disdain towards the influential body of which they were now both members. The affair must have given rise to continuing personal discord around the table at gatherings of the Council, not least because of the chronic dislocations to its authority and the undermining of its ability to carry through its responsibilities on the ground. The Welsh members like Hugh, who had experienced the continuing benefits of the Council's supervisory role within the principality,[674] are likely to have shared the frustrations of Zouch in this respect at least. In mid-1605, Croft and his allies made their next move. They drew up and presented a petition to the king, urging royal confirmation that the four shires be exempted from the Council's jurisdiction. But, having obtained an advance copy of the petition, Zouch and the Council's leading lawyers, perhaps including Hugh, drew up a detailed point-by point critique, highlighting the challenge to such an interpretation of James's prerogative. This

---

670   R.E.Ham, 'The Four Shire Controversy', *WHR* (1977) 8, p.390.

671   Williams, *Council of the Marches*, Chapter 13.

672   Dyfnallt Owen, *Wales in the Reign of James 1*, pp.28-35.

673   Williams, *Council of the Marches*, pp.346-347.

674   '[The Council in the Marches] has brought Wales to the civilities and quietness that you now see it, from that wilde and outrageous state that you shall reade of...': Owen, *Dialogue of the Government in Wales*, p.24.

raised the constitutional stakes, touching on a nerve of particular crown sensitivity. It appears to have ensured James's inaction in the short term.[675]

Croft and company immediately switched tack, introducing a parliamentary bill in February 1606 aimed at securing the exemptions. Though this safely negotiated its Commons stages, it was stalled by Cecil (now Salisbury) in the Lords. Croft realised it was unlikely to pass, so, following a personal audience, he then settled for the king's promise of revised Instructions aimed at reining in the Council on at least some of the contentious issues. In July, the Council's jurisdiction over misdemeanours in the four shires was abolished, as were both its jurisdiction (highly profitable) over sexual offences, and its right to inflict torture. These restrictions represented a partial, if temporary, victory for the petitioners. Zouch, humiliated and furious, resigned as Lord President.

Again, there was a gap before a replacement was found. It was not till the summer of the following year (1607) that Ralph, Lord Eure was appointed, a tough and administratively experienced Yorkshire magnate who quickly ensured that Sir Herbert Croft lost not only his seat on the Council, but also the deputy-lieutenancy and Commission of the Peace.[676] There had been a precipitous decline in the Council's income over the previous five years, compounded by the reduced fines resulting from the recently revised Instructions – from £2,311 in 1602-3; to £1,140 in 1604-5; and £683 in 1606-7[677] – and Eure appears to have been determined to redress the position. Throughout his first few months in office, he lobbied Salisbury and other privy councillors intensively for renewed crown support, arguing that the crown's authority was being undermined by the persistence across the four counties of flagrant non-cooperation and disobedience by sheriffs, justices and even the majority of deputy-lieutenants towards the Council's injunctions, under Sir Herbert Croft's continued direction.[678] Eure's contention, almost certainly shared by a Welsh lawyer-administrator like Hugh on the basis of his direct experience as a quorum justice and crown advocate, was that the Council was in fact popular at grass roots level for its success in providing justice in the face of powerful bullying minorities like those now active in the four border shires.

675 Ham, 'Four Shire Controversy', p.392.

676 TNA, *Calendar of State Papers* 14/28/51.

677 Williams, 'Attack on the Council of the Marches', p.5.

678 TNA *Calendar of State Papers* 14/31/30; 14/32/13.

Crown resolution

The result was an historic conference in London on 3 November 1608, attended by the king, the privy councillors and the Westminster judges. James made his position clear. The Council in the Marches was his prerogative court – and 'none doe oppose themselves against the jurisdiccion of the Councell ... but certain higheheaded fellows ... such as Sir Harbert Crofte ... whoe, because they would oppresse the meaner people and beare the whole swaye of theire country without controulment, doe oppose themselves against government and the state of kinges to whom they know not what apperteigneth.' [679] Reportedly, at the conclusion of the speech, the two chief justices and chief baron of the exchequer 'swelled soe with anger that teares fell from them'.[680] This unambiguous support from the monarch secured the Council's territorial authority once again. Despite the Westminster judges, its formal writ was to continue to encompass the four counties. New Instructions were issued the following May, restoring all of the Council's former powers apart from the right to inflict torture – and from that point on, its popularity appears to have begun to grow again, as reflected in the growing number of cases coming before it from October 1609 onwards.[681] The disobedience of local officials gradually diminished – though not Croft's appetite for the struggle, which persisted till the middle of the following decade, before finally petering out.

Hugh lived till June 1609, so he would have been aware of the success of Eure's efforts. However, what role, if any, he had played in assisting the outcome is impossible to determine from the sketchy surviving materials. Indeed, it could well be that one's impression of the overwhelming significance of the Four Shires controversy for the Council between 1604 and 1609 is an historiographical distortion – a reflection of the lack of surviving records detailing its other more routine activities across the period. There are indications that despite the internal tensions during Zouch's and Eure's presidencies, solid progress was being made by Sir Richard Lewknor (Chief Justice of Chester) and his fellow 'councillors attendant' in stabilising the Council's procedures, and that Wales itself was quiet and ordered in the early years of the seventeenth century.[682]

679   *Ellesmere Manuscripts* (Huntington Library) E1, No 1763.

680   Ibid.

681   Ham, 'Four Shire Controversy', Table I.

682   Williams, *Council of the Marches*, Chapter 13.

Undercurrents of Welsh–Marcher tensions

As regional Attorney General and an active quorum member of three Welsh-speaking Commissions of the Peace, Hugh's role on the Council would have been at the interface between national and local initiatives throughout this period. The disruptions and power struggles between the presidency and the bordershire gentry may perhaps have drawn historians' attention disproportionately, when compared with successfully continuing routine activities of the Council across the same period. Certainly Lord Eure claimed to Salisbury in 1610 that 'notwithstanding the great opposition that hath been and the devises to withdraw, and even to terrifie the subjects hence, there hath been out of those 4 English counties more suitors then out of halfe Wales, as may appeare by the records of the Court [of the Marches]'.[683] And the routine administrative and executive roles of the Council as a key organ of government for Wales also continued to be vital. It was in relation to these that Hugh's particular value as a member would have lain. Yet at the same time, as has already been indicated, it is inconceivable he would not have been deeply engaged, emotionally and politically, in the struggles surrounding the Council's jurisdiction and indeed its very survival as a credible entity during his term of office. In chapter four, reference has been made to the likelihood of his identification with Egerton's endorsement of regional and local prerogative jurisdictions in the face of Coke's constant pressure to extend the standardising reach of the central courts of law at the formers' expense.[684] Though, as it happens, on the specifics of the Fairley case Egerton had sympathised with the King's Bench judges in their wish to bring greater consistency to key judicial appointments to the prerogative courts, his principled view was that a diversity of independent jurisdictions like the Council in the Marches was constitutionally desirable. Indeed, he laboured mightily to secure and improve the Council in the Marches' authority in that regard.[685] One senses this would also have been Hugh's inclination, grounded in his own experience in Wales, where many felt themselves to have benefited substantially from the crown prerogative over the previous seventy years – quite apart from his personal sense of himself as a crown official.

However, using a longer historical lens, it is also possible to picture his situation in the Council in the Marches in different, even perhaps more atavistic, terms. Rees Davies has suggested that a key strategic need of English rulers from the fourteenth century onwards, if political stability through 'a broader based polity' was to be achieved, was to generate 'a greater measure of conver-

---

683 TNA, *Calendar of State Papers, Domestic, James 1 1603-10*, vol 57, fol 218, 10 October 1610.

684 See p.72.

685 Knafla, *Law and Politics*, pp.146-154.

gence between the outer parts of the British Isles and the English polity – *in social customs and structure, economic attitudes and practices, laws, land tenure, civic notions and, preferably, language…*' [686] [emphasis added]. On this account, the acts of union of the 1530s and 1540s may be taken as signals that such conditions of convergence were felt to be well advanced in Wales's case,[687] albeit, as observed earlier, the boundaries of tolerance about language were more broadly drawn than has been assumed by some in the past. The Council in the Marches can be understood as an important institutional medium through which these changing norms were being consolidated, and yet at the same time it embraced and continued thereby to foster differences of social and cultural diversity – for example through respect for the Welsh language in its own practices.[688] Indeed the improvement in the ratio of Welsh to Marcher appointees to the Council in the early years of the new century[689] can be interpreted as reflecting the degree to which cultural convergence was occurring – a trend manifested also in a mutual toleration of difference now developing within the emergent ruling class.

Latent ethnic sensitivities?

Hugh himself can be seen to have embodied such perhaps contradictory processes within his own person. Nevertheless it is tempting to suggest that the turbulence within the Council arising from the Four Shires controversy between 1604 and 1609 could have touched latent 'ethnic' sensitivities between its Welsh and English participants. This is not to suggest that such tensions became explicit – evidence for that is lacking – rather that the potential for English and in particular Marcher gentry high-handedness and lack of sensitivity towards the continuing cultural distinctiveness and needs of Wales had a long history, and that Sir Herbert Croft's campaign relied for its local effectiveness on reopening the divide between what was good for the border shires and what was good for, as it were, 'mere' Wales. Whatever the degree to which Hugh may by this stage have become culturally assimilated as part of the new English – or rather 'British' – governing class, he was also still Welsh through and through, and proud of it, as his lineage-consciousness shows. Given an intel-

---

686   Davies, *The First English Empire*, p.199.

687   C.Brady, 'Comparable Histories? Tudor Reform in Wales and England', in S.Ellis & S.Barber (eds), *Conquest and Union: Fashioning a British State 1485-1725* (London, Longman, 1995), pp.65-85.

688   Roberts, 'Welsh Language, English Law & Tudor Legislation', p.39.

689   The five Welsh members appointed in 1601 (of whom Hugh was one), were followed by three further such appointments in 1602: Sir Richard Bulkeley 3rd (Anglesey), Sir Thomas Jones (Carmarthenshire) and Sir Thomas Mostyn (Flintshire). (Williams, *Council of the Marches*, pp.345-352).

lectual commitment to a strong Council in the Marches, now being put in jeopardy by the wrecking tactics of the Marcher gentry in their pursuit of secession, the crisis would have been perhaps an enforced reminder of persistent cultural realities lying beneath the surface of the actual union settlement. It would be understandable if, alongside Hugh's intellectual disagreements, there was not also an element of visceral irritation at those – including his border county friends – who were colluding in a regression to old, corrosive divisions.

The complex question of how to capture the essence of the Welsh-English relationship of this period – and in particular the extent to which it is helpful or otherwise to use the language of 'colonialism' in discussing what was at stake – is considered further in the final chapter, using Hugh and his career as a prism. But whatever else the overall relationship was, it was overwhelmingly a close and trusting one by this stage, particularly when compared with England's escalating difficulties in Ireland. There, the Battle of Kinsale in 1601 was an important punctuation point in a long period of savage intermittent conflict, after which English policy across the Irish Sea became ever-more explicitly colonialist. It is unsurprising, given the evident success of the English-Welsh federation, that that experience was seen by influential crown officials as potentially relevant for a desired new Irish settlement.[690] Nor in this context is it surprising that Hugh's personal experience as a senior common lawyer and crown official may have been viewed as potentially helpful for engaging with the problems faced by the English government in that connection. This is now discussed in the section following.

Chief Justice for Ireland

In 1609 Hugh was appointed Chief Justice of Ireland, the apotheosis of his legal career. Or at least, that appears to have been the case. As A.H. Dodd has pointed out,[691] formal documentary confirmation of the appointment is still lacking – possibly because he died that same year, before being able to take up the appointment. Nevertheless the circumstantial evidence is strong. First, there is the detailed mid-nineteenth century antiquarian record of the Plas Coch genealogy executed for Hugh's direct descendant, the MP William Bulkeley Hughes (1797-1888).[692] This states unambiguously that 'he was appointed by King James I Chief Justice for Ireland, but died before he proceeded to that country' – which at the very least points to a strong family memory of the elevation. And second, building on that memory, there is the inherent plausibility of such an appointment, given Hugh's earlier promotions through patronage

690   Brady, 'Comparable Histories'.

691   In P.W. Hasler, *Members of Parliament*, Vol II, p.352.

692   *Hughes of Plas Coch Pedigree 1865.*

by Cecil (by then, Earl of Salisbury) and Egerton (Lord Chancellor Ellesmere), both of whom would have been decisive in any such arrangement. Reinforcing this is the fact that two of Hugh's close Lincoln's Inn colleagues, the senior judges Sir James Ley (in 1604) and Sir William Jones (in 1617) [693] were both appointed to the post – again hinting at the guiding hand of Ellesmere in advancing high-achieving members of the Inn in that particular theatre. Of course it is conceivable that further research could emerge to suggest that Hugh did *not* achieve this position. But in the mean time, on the basis of the reasoning above, the assumption is made in the discussion that follows that he was indeed appointed to this senior judgeship, but that his sudden death in late 1609 came before the formalities had been completed, as Thomas Richards implies was the case. [694]

His appointment to Chief Justice came at a crucial moment in the development of crown policy for Ireland, and it is not too much to say that, had Hugh been able to fulfil the duties, he would have had a role in seminal developments in Irish history – indeed in the formative stages of western colonialism itself. It is useful to examine the circumstances as he would have encountered them, in order to be in a position to speculate as to what the post might have entailed, and why he might have been considered suitable for it. The wholesale defeat of the Gaelic lords under Hugh O'Neill at the Battle of Kinsale in 1601 was an historic watershed for Ireland. In the immediate wake of this disaster for the Irish, a new and far-reaching English approach began to take shape. The long-term stability of Ireland on English terms was seen as a vital issue of national security. The risks of future Spanish invasion through a Catholic nation on England's flank could not be tolerated. Moreover, the previous century's piecemeal attempts at a stable political settlement had proved inadequate – measures such as 'surrender and re-grant', the attempted plantation of Munster and the like. [695] Hence in the first decade of the sixteenth century, there was a transformation in the crown's policies for Irish pacification and control.

The new approach had two key elements. Native forms of political organisation and land-holding were to be broken up. And Catholicism and its adherents were to be suppressed. Hence English common law was to be extended forthwith to all areas of Ireland, and English statutes against Jesuits and other seminary priests applied rigorously. [696] Hans Pawlisch has shown how the legal underpinnings for such radical extensions of English power were found in the

693   See note 393 & p.136.

694   UB Plas Coch, Vol 1 – Introduction by Thomas Richards.

695   R.E.Foster, *The Oxford History of Ireland* (Oxford, OUP, 2001 edn), pp.97-116;
        N.Canny, *Making Ireland British 1580-1660* (Oxford, OUP, 2001), pp.1-187.

696   Ibid., p.113.

concept of 'conquest right', developed through contemporary Spanish discussion of South America, drawing on both canon and Roman law, concerning the rights and privileges of conquerors and conquered.[697] In the hands of Sir John Davies (1569-1626), the Solicitor General for Ireland during the formative years of 1603-6, this evolving body of jurisprudence provided justification for the suppression of indigenous Irish law and the re-making of property rights through the application of English common law. Gaelic law, which to that point still prevailed in most of Ireland outside the Pale, vested property rights in the extended kin, making individual holdings temporary, as had been the case in medieval Welsh law. As the decade advanced, these and other native land tenure conventions were subjected to root-and-branch change to bring them into line with English principles and practice.[698]

Agents of colonisation

It is the institutional mechanisms employed to achieve such ends that are of particular significance when it comes to considering the possible role Hugh Hughes would have played as Irish Chief Justice in the period from 1609 onwards. The English administration had to overcome two persistent obstacles to its new programme. One arose from the continuing failure of sixteenth-century Irish Parliaments to implement Tudor statutes across the country at large – a situation which had grown ever more problematic in the concluding years of the century with the growth of Old English[699] Catholic opposition to crown policies. There was thus a need both to marginalise the parliament in order to enforce the new dispensation, and subsequently (in 1613) to pack it with a Protestant majority. Similarly, the Irish bench was seen as compromised by its continued predominance of Old-English judges, whom experience in the previous decades had shown to be unsatisfactorily soft on recusants. Hence radical change was needed there too. The solution was to first purge the judiciary, and then pack it with new English lawyers, leaving only a token Old-English representation.[700]

From 1605, under Lord Deputy Sir Arthur Chichester, a sweeping new policy of officially sponsored plantations across the country began to emerge, in parallel with harsh though uneven attempts to suppress catholicism in the face

---

697   H.J.Pawlisch, *Sir John Davies and the Conquest of Ireland: A Study in Legal Imperialism* (Cambridge, CUP, 1985), pp.8-10.

698   R.E.Foster, *Modern Ireland 1600-1972* (London, Allen Lane, 1988), pp.45-52.

699   'Old English' here refers to the Catholic descendants of the original Norman English who settled in parts of southern Ireland during the twelfth and thirteenth centuries. Historians distinguish them from the later, generally Protestant 'New English' (or 'Anglo-Irish') who arrived in the seventeenth century.

700   Pawlisch, *Sir John Davies*, pp.122-141.

of continuing Old-English obduracy. To assist these measures, Pawlisch and Canny concur, the real innovation was the systematic use of *judicial resolutions*, to provide the legitimacy for unimpeded executive action. Formally, these were declarations of law arrived at in difficult cases by processes of 'debate and certification' by a collectivity of senior judges, setting precedents and effectively by-passing conventional parliamentary processes of law-making. Such declarations had the force of statute and Sir John Davies's 1615 Reports,[701] which document Irish legal developments over this period, show that they were central to the imposition of the new crown policies for Ireland from 1607 onwards. To cite just two instances, they were used to void customary patterns of Gaelic land-holding and descent by invalidating native titles standing in the way of the Ulster plantation of 1610, and also to eliminate the claimed corporate autonomy of Munster towns from 1609 onwards.[702] Achieving such ends through judicial resolution required close coordination at the highest level between the English and reconstituted Irish judiciaries, creating a basis for the imposition of a level of centralised executive control which had formerly been impossible. The overall result was a *de facto* redefinition of the terms of English sovereignty across Ireland, creating for the first time what was effectively a colonial administration. It was a precedent which was to be developed, with multiplying refinements, for application in British colonial possessions over the following three centuries. So out of the exigencies of early seventeenth-century Ireland, a template for future imperial practice was emerging.

It is not hard to see that, had Hugh been able to take up the post of Irish Chief Justice in 1609, he would have had a close and continuing role in these developments and their enforcement. He would have been an *ex officio* member of the council of the Lord Deputy, as well as one of the most senior Irish judges involved in declarations of the law – effectively, for Ireland *new* law – by means of judicial resolutions bearing on constitutionally significant cases, during a period of dramatic social and political upheaval across the country. To have been nominated for such a role at such a sensitive moment for English policy in Ireland suggests he must have been seen as having both the legal gravitas and the political toughness to carry it off effectively and loyally.

He would have known what he was getting into. At least two close Anglesey neighbours with whom he had recorded dealings – Sir Henry Bagnall of Plas Newydd[703] and Sir William Herbert of St Julian's[704] – had been deeply involved

---

701   Sir John Davies, *Le Primer Report des Cases in Les Courts del Roy* (Dublin 1615), translated as *A Report of Cases and Matters of Law Resolved and Abridged in the King's Courts in Ireland* (Dublin 1762)

702   Pawlisch, *Sir John Davies*, pp. 57-82, 122-141.

703   UB Plas Coch 1204 & 2960.

704   UB Plas Coch 123, 140, 2964, 2977, 2985 & 2986.

in the front line of matters Irish. Bagnall, a son-in-law of Hugh's associate Maurice Griffith[705] and resident at Plas Newydd in the last few years of his life, had been a long-serving soldier in the Irish campaigns till his death in the Battle of Blackwater in 1598.[706] And Herbert, a landowner in nearby Llanidan though resident in Monmouthshire, was a leading 'undertaker' in the Munster plantation, paying a crown rent of £200 a year for 13,000 acres in County Kerry, on the strength of which experience he wrote copious analyses of English policy there.[707] Through social interactions with these and other enterprising individuals with Irish interests in and around Llanedwen, Hugh can be assumed to have been well-versed in the complex realities of Irish politics and administration – quite apart from his wider range of acquaintance in London and the law. Conceivably he had also come across (Sir) John Davies at an earlier stage, during the latter's time as a student at the Middle Temple in the late 1580s and early '90s, before either of them had become involved directly in Ireland. Twenty years younger than Hugh, the dynamic Davies was yet another protégé of Ellesmere,[708] his practical and theoretical legal accomplishments coming later to be overshadowed by recognition as an accomplished poet and man of letters.

Wales as template

With so much uncertainty surrounding the question of Hugh's preferment to the Irish post, it is hard to judge the extent to which, in London, his specifically Welsh background and experience would have been considered crucial for the problems with which he would be expected to deal, and hence a factor in the appointment. On the face of it, the experience of mediating between two sharply different cultures (albeit ultimately on English terms) could have provided highly relevant insights. From a Westminster perspective, the ways in which the Welsh had come to terms with the English must have constituted something close to an ideal, as evidenced in proposals for different variants of a 'Welsh Policy' for Ireland in the 1560s and '70s by figures including Lord Deputy Sir Henry Sidney, to Sir John Perrot, Sir William Herbert and, most of all, Sir William Gerrard.[709] Shifts from Welsh to English law, from crown fiefdom to regional self-government, from traditional Catholicism to increasingly devout Protestantism, from *cyfran* to primogeniture – all had been accomplished over the two centuries since the Glyndŵr rebellion in largely painless fashion. And the routine operation of regional and local administration

---

705 See note 480.

706 Griffith, *Pedigrees*, p.57.

707 *Dictionary of Welsh Biography*, p.355.

708 Pawlisch, *Sir John Davies*, pp. 25, 30.

709 Brady, 'Comparable Histories', pp.77-86.

through the hierarchy of 'acts of union' institutions also offered a beguiling lesson in harmonious governance across cultural divides. The contrast with Ireland was stark,[710] and from an English strategic perspective the underlying challenge for that island was similar – how to create a stable and acceptable settlement, on terms which would ensure English security. However by the 1590s, any hopes for a reformist approach along Welsh lines had been wrecked on the reefs of 'Old English' intransigence. Yet the subsequently radical change of crown policy in the wake of Kinsale towards a pioneering colonialist settlement did not imply invalidation of the relevance of the Welsh experience. The latter's value as a guide to handling the legal and political challenges continued to be significant. Thus Hugh's long experience in mediating across Celtic-English cultural divides was almost certainly a factor in the pivotal Irish appointment.

However, he died unexpectedly in London in early June 1609[711] – possibly from the plague[712] – and was never able to take up the appointment.

Nevertheless, this last decade of Hugh's life had seen him play roles close to the highest levels of late-Elizabethan and early-Jacobean government, whilst continuing to be engaged in local affairs as a Welsh-speaking Welshman. He

---

710   Ellis, 'Tudor State Formation', pp.56 et seq.

711   The Inventory of his goods and chattels (UB Plas Coch 184) was made on 19 June 1609.

712   There were notably serious plague epidemics in London in the summer of 1609, with 4,240 deaths directly attributable (J.F.D.Shrewsbury, *A History of Bubonic Plague in the British Isles* (Cambridge, CUP, 1970), p.299).

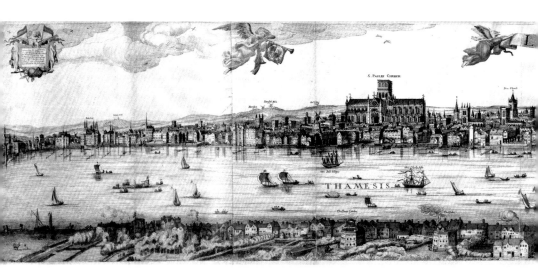

was of course not alone in combining such accomplishments, as examples such as the already-mentioned Simon Thelwall (1526-86) and Sir Peter Mutton (1565-1637), both Welsh-speaking lawyers from Denbighshire, demonstrate. The literate and sophisticated Thelwall,[713] called to the bar at the Middle Temple in 1568, combined lifelong local Welsh-language cultural patronage with service as MP for the borough of Denbigh in 1553 and 1571, membership of the Council in the Marches, and service as a Justice on the Chester circuit in the 1580s – whilst Mutton,[714] following training at Lincoln's Inn, retained a lifelong local Welsh-speaking presence at Llanerch, whilst also rising to Attorney General in Wales and the Marches in 1609 and Chief Justice on the Anglesey circuit in 1622, as well as becoming a member of the Council in the Marches and MP for Denbighshire and Caernarfon, in respectively 1604 and 1624. Such individuals, like Hugh himself, appear to have had little difficulty in reconciling continuing loyalty to their community roots and culture with creative intellectual participation in the evolving institutions of the overarching political entity in which the Welsh now saw themselves as full partners.

713 *Dictionary of Welsh Biography*, pp.932-933.

714 Ibid., p.1144.

The London Hugh Hughes would have known, with Lincoln's Inn Fields and Westminster on the left of this 1616 panorama by Claes Vischer.
Old St Paul's Cathedral had lost its spire by this time. The two theatres in the foreground on the Southwark side of the River Thames are *The Bear Garden* and *The Globe*. The large church in the foreground is St Mary Overie, now Southwark Cathedral.

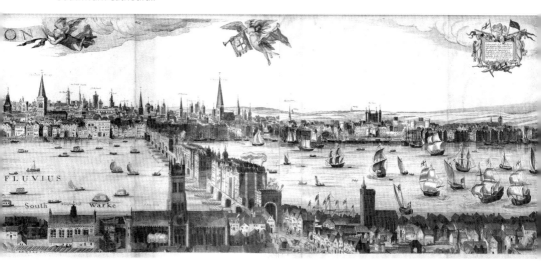

"*History, unlike fiction and physics, never quite gells; it is an armature of rather randomly preserved verbal and physical remains upon which historians slap wads of supposition in hopes of the lumpy statues coming to life. One of the joys of doing original research is to observe how one's predecaessor historians have fudged their way across the very gaps, or fault lines, that one is in turn balked by.*"
— John Updike, *Memories of the Ford Administration*

6 *Was Hugh Hughes 'British'?*

AT THE MOST STRAIGHTFORWARD LEVEL, this study has tried to throw light on some of the ways in which Hugh Hughes rose to regional, even national, eminence in the concluding decades of Elizabeth's reign and the first decade of her successor, and the means by which he came to build up his family's Anglesey estate. In the process it has sought to gain a degree of wider insight into the ways in which Wales was being administered a generation or so after the reforms that later became known as the 'acts of union'. The overall challenge has been to find a way of conceptualising the kind of public actor Hugh was, in the context of his times – in terms of both what he *thought* he was, and of what light his actions and commitments might cast on the emerging Anglo-Welsh polity at this particular stage of historical development. In the background also lurks the more familiar question – recurrent in Welsh historiography and indeed Welsh politics to this day – of whether or not the 'union' was purchased at the expense of Welsh distinctiveness, and the role, allegedly a self-interested one, played by the Welsh 'gentry' in hastening any such erosion. Using Hugh as a prism, it is possible to offer tentative reflections on some of these matters, so crucial for an understanding of early modern Wales.

Motivations

It may be helpful to consider first on what has been learnt from the investigation about Hugh as an individual. The evidence suggests an able and intelligent man, groomed for success by an energetic and enterprising father who had strained every sinew to ensure the best available education for his eldest son and heir. Hugh turned out to be an individual with the determination and staying power to take full advantage of the expanding opportunities offered by Cambridge in the 1560s, and the Inns of Court from the early 1570s onwards, and to convert them into success as a senior crown legal official and public servant, in a period of accelerating political and social development across the kingdom.

◁ Westminster Hall in the early seventeenth century — with the Courts of Chancery and King's Bench in full swing. As a senior common lawyer, Hugh Hughes would have known these courts well, whilst also maintaining an active Anglesey and north Wales presence throughout his life.

To have accomplished this as scion of what, in lowland-English terms, would have been regarded as an modestly endowed Welsh-speaking family points not just to intellectual accomplishment, but also to a high degree of self-confidence and solidity of character, which doubtless flowed in part from a sense of personal rootedness in a secure and distinguished lineage by the criteria of his own culture (as outlined in chapter one). A high flyer from the outset – how else would he have been judged suitable to matriculate at Trinity? – these accomplishments rested on personal qualities quite as much as on patronage.

Keith Thomas notes that whilst prevailing theory in early-modern England was unsympathetic to the general idea of social mobility, individual opportunism was in fact the order of the day, and 'academic proficiency was frankly recognised as a route to advancement in public life'.[715] For talented young Welshmen like Hugh in the late-Tudor period, education was the route into the expanding opportunities offered by English society and its institutions.

It must be admitted that, despite the extensive research reflected in the thesis, Hugh remains a shadowy figure in personal terms. Quite apart from the difficulty of projecting a twenty-first century imagination into the subjective ontological world of a sixteenth-century Welshman, this reflects the fact that documented traces of his personal attitudes and feelings are minimal. The signatures on his will[716] – a more or less identical 'Hugh Hughes' appears in what must be his hand at the bottom right-hand corner of each of the will's five pages – have a clear and free-flowing character, suggesting perhaps a confident and articulate nature, but it would be invidious to place stress on this as firm evidence. For the rest, one is left to read between the lines elsewhere for clues to the colour of his mature personality. For example, the records of the Lincoln's Inn Benchers, referred to in chapter three, show that on several occasions his senior colleagues assigned him administrative roles requiring a combination of personal tact and clear-headed forensic nous – sorting out complex humanly sensitive irregularities in the Inn's kitchens, and untangling the state of the society's all-important buildings and tenancies. He seems to have been regarded as a man who could be relied upon to get things done, grounded, diplomatic and practical.

One also gains the impression of a certain doggedness and tenacity alongside the intelligence. Building and maintaining a growing estate in a period of intense competition over land, as illustrated in the dispute with the Rhydderchs discussed in chapter two, required an active and vigilant presence in Anglesey. But simultaneously he was able also to sustain a multi-faceted public career in London, Ludlow, the North Wales Courts of Great Sessions, and the justices'

---

715 Thomas, *Ends of Life*, pp.29-30.

716   UB Plas Coch 408.

quora of Caernarfonshire, Merioneth and Anglesey itself. Such dedication and physical and intellectual stamina – travelling on horse-back to forensically exacting work-places, up, down and across the country, year on year – were not unusual amongst men of the time working at this level of course. Lincoln's Inn colleagues like William Jones and Thomas Egerton had quite as many strings to their bows. It is difficult of course to know how much he was operating alone in the various tasks; the likelihood is he could rely on deputies, clerks and like in some of them – for example, as discussed in chapter four, as High Sheriff, as North Wales Attorney General, and in managing the family estate. Yet the fact remains that his commitments, private and public, were substantial and unrelenting. Taken in sum, they reflect a deep involvement in the affairs of the day at all levels – local, county, regional and national – reflecting in his own person a growing consistency of outlook and aspiration in English and Welsh public administration of the time.

What drove him on? Keith Thomas suggests that 'in early modern England, the desire to secure the favourable opinion of other people was a primary determinant of human behaviour'.[717] Honour, the esteem of others in a strongly hierarchical society, was one attraction, for Hugh perhaps as much as for other Welsh gentry of the time.[718] In his particular case, there may also have been a competitive element peculiar to the south-east corner of Anglesey and the particular position his direct Porthaml Isaf forebears had occupied relative to some of their previously more notable neighbouring kinsmen down the ages, as discussed in chapter one.[719] Over and above such motivations however, he seems to have been a man of integrity by the rather confusing standards of the time, conscious of his responsibilities to a community which extended not just to Anglesey, but far farther afield. The scale and appearance of Plas Coch mansion, following its 1590s expansion and remodelling, appears to have been an assertion of new, not to say flamboyant, contemporary energy, created in apparent contrast to the more conventional hall-house dwellings of contemporaries at, for example, nearby Plas Porthaml or Plas Berw. Its design suggests a deliberate statement on behalf of his family's standing and aspirations for the future – not just as long-established local *uchelwyr*, but also as actors in a sophisticated wider world.

---

717 Thomas, *Ends of Life*, p.147

718 Gwynfor Jones, *Welsh Gentry*, Chapter 1.

719 See pp. 7-10

Friends and neighbours

Though a praise poem of the 1590s to Hugh and his wife asserts in conventionally fulsome style that he was 'good to the poor and weak / and fair to the
humble ones' (*a da ar ran y gwan gwael / a dwyfal wrth un difalch*),[720] there is
little surviving evidence of such personal charity. The material gulf between
his world and that of the least fortunate in Anglesey would have been growing
ever greater as his career advanced and wealth increased, though at the same
time (as explained in chapter four) his duties as a justice included an obligation
to enforce measures aimed at securing the welfare of the indigent on a continuing basis. Where his own affairs were concerned, he was probably a hard man,
operating to the letter of the law. There are few grounds for believing he showed
any particular thoughtfulness towards the poor inhabitants of Maesoglan and
Bodrida townships, following acquisition of the crown lands on which they had
been long-term tenants (as described in chapter two). After the growing fashion
of the time, what had previously been sub-divided open fields supporting a
number of families were quickly consolidated into relatively large individual
farms,[721] and the erstwhile tenants dispersed, in the process doubtless contributing to the problems of vagrancy and poverty with which Hugh in his role
as justice was having increasingly to deal, as a result of the social legislation
that punctuated the later decades of the century.

On the other hand, he appears to have been engaged in processes of institutional reform, however indirectly. The saga of the sheriff's bailiffs' bonds discussed in chapter four[722] points to his having been involved in adjustments to
the quality of local government in Anglesey during the 1590s, probably reflecting privy council policy of the time. Official fears about potential social chaos
and disorder, as much as the need to maximise crown rental incomes, were
putting a premium on securing more reliable 'bureaucratic' behaviour at local
level. The arguments in chapter four suggest that this is the context in which
the increases in bond levels for bailiffs enforced by Hugh in his successive terms
as Sheriff should be understood.

As to the personal company he kept, again the evidence is frustratingly
slight. There are indications that at least some of his friends may have been
drawn from the (largely English) fraternity of lawyers amongst whom so much
of his life was spent, not least at Lincoln's Inn, as well as from the family and
associated networks of his wife, Elizabeth Montagu. In the last decade of his
life, Hugh served in several key offices of the Lincoln's Inn society, as Bencher,

---

720   Huw Pennant, 'Moliant Huw Huws ac Elizabeth ei wraig' in Wyn Wiliam, *Menai*, p.18.

721   See p.17.

722   See pp. 110-113.

Keeper of the Black Books, Treasurer, and Master of the Walks – an indication
of the personal respect he grew to command amongst largely English colleagues at the Inn. In a long and detailed will,[723] he named his colleague and
fellow Bencher Sir Peter Warburton, later Lord Justice Warburton, as overseer,
and referred specifically to a 'loving friend', Mr John Cekrewe,[724] to whom he
bequeathed a ring of forty shillings value. *Vis a vis* Elizabeth's relatives, two
names in particular recur in the records in such a way as to suggest a degree
of intimacy – Roger Montagu, 'my loving uncle', named as executor and bequeathed a ring of the value of five pounds in the will,[725] and Walter Montagu,
Elizabeth's first cousin, who married into the Morgan family of Tredegar in
Monmouthshire, and made an appearance as a durable business partner during
the legal dispute with Hugh ap Rees Wynn of Maesoglan.[726] But these apart,
there is little evidential basis for confident conclusions about his social life and
personal relationships.

Who did he think he was?

It is reasonable to speculate that the language of the household at Plas Coch
was well on the way to becoming English by the 1590s, if only because Elizabeth herself would have been most comfortable in that language. It is not
known whether she acquired some rudimentary knowledge of vernacular Welsh
to help run the household. Ogwen Williams has noted that 'in the sixteenth
and early seventeenth century, the fact that [many of] the gentry's womenfolk
were Welsh-speaking would have been effective in sustaining their bilingualism
and in maintaining Welsh as the everyday speech of their households'.[727] Elizabeth's Northamptonshire background makes it questionable whether this
could have applied at Plas Coch, which may well mean that the family was one
for whom the native idiom was losing its ascendency relatively early, in comparison with other gentry houses in Anglesey and north-west Wales.[728] However, even if this were the case, it is not to say that Hugh himself would not
have continued to interact routinely with local peers, tenants and other acquaintances in Welsh, quite apart from his constant professional use of the language.[729] One way of picturing this is by analogy with the way in which the

---

723 UB Plas Coch 408.

724 It has not been possible to trace this individual.

725 UB Plas Coch 408.

726 TNA E123/12(a).

727 Williams, 'Survival of the Welsh language', p.84.

728 Ibid., p.85. Williams suggests that in many gentry households, Welsh continued to dominate
     until the late-seventeenth, or even early-eighteenth centuries.

729 His brother Owen, as rector of Llanfachraeth (see Griffith, op.cit, p.30), would have used

eighteenth-century Russian landowning class used French in the drawing room and some professional contexts, and their own vernacular Russian in interactions with familiars and the peasantry.[730]

This in turn brings into focus the question of his personal sense of cultural identity. The discussion in the previous chapters has conveyed the reality that Hugh developed as a novel kind of Welsh-English cultural hybrid. Such a phenomenon is far from unfamiliar in our own time. As Linda Colley has observed in a seminal discussion of 'Britishness', 'identities are not like hats. Human beings can and do put on several at a time',[731] a truth which is now virtually a commonplace in a twenty-first-century context of continuing flows of cross-border immigration and 'multicultural' absorption in countries like Britain.

Such contemporary experience is consistent with the impression that Hugh's Cambridge education and deep professional embeddedness in the English common law, together with the modest extant clues about his marriage and personal friendships, would have produced in him a strong affinity with the dominant English culture's values and individualism[732] – whilst at the same time sustaining a sense of himself as Welsh *au fond*. Most of his adult life was spent working in the distinctively Wales-focused institutions deriving from the acts of union, one by-product of which had been to reify (or even to invent anew) the very idea of a common Welsh identity, reflected for example in the geographical compass of the Council in the Marches.[733] And his resulting stock-in-trade as a mediator and legal translator across the linguistic divides would have had a powerful influence on his personal self-perception. His home and ancestral roots lay in the (from a London perspective) relatively remote island community of Anglesey, giving rise to perhaps his deepest sense of himself. But beyond this, the workings of the language clauses within the 'acts of union' institutions probably meant that, in his public roles, a bilingual figure of Hugh's standing would have found himself in a position of exceptional au-

---

Welsh routinely in his work – indirectly reinforcing the obvious assumption that he and his siblings had been raised as first-language Welsh-speakers.

730 '...French the sphere of thought and sentiment, Russian the sphere of daily life...' – O.Figes, *Natasha's Dance: A Cultural History of Russia* (London, Penguin, 2003), p.103.

731 L.Colley, *Britons: Forging the Nation 1707-1837* (Newhaven, Yale University Press, 1992), p.6.

732 A.Macfarlane, 'The Origins of English Individualism', *Theory and Society* 6 (1978), pp.255-277.

733 Though Colley suggests that, even in the early eighteenth century, 'the degree to which the Welsh were able to see themselves as one people was ... limited by an acute north-south divide, the country's central range of mountains making trade, communications and ordinary human contact between counties in South Wales, like Glamorgan, Carmarthen and Pembroke, and northern counties, such as Flint, Merioneth and Caernarfon, very difficult indeed.' Colley, *Britons*, p.15.

thority and influence, leading to a distinctive, and perhaps to the more parochial majority of his Anglesey acquaintances ambiguous, sense of 'hybrid' identity, alongside any sense of local rootedness.

Welshness in Tudor times

It is significant for the argument being developed here that there was little if any popular prejudice against the Welsh in late-Elizabethan and early-Jacobean England. The general histories of the period concur that they were seen generally in a positive light, unlike the Irish of the time.[734] One confirmation is the way in which the Welsh were being represented in the *public* entertainments of the period. Stock characterisations in late-Tudor drama paint them consistently as good-humoured, brave and trustworthy, if talkative and occasionally hot-tempered.[735] At the very least, in Bartley and Richard's words, they tended to be experienced sympathetically as 'the strangest of provincials and the nearest and most intimate of foreigners'.[736] Shakespeare's well-disposed representations of Fluellen and Glendower[737] probably reflect popular sentiment of the period, with an emphasis on loyalty and good humour in the one, and oddity and wisdom in the other. Moreover if such well-disposed acceptance applied to the Welshman-in-the-street, it would have applied all the more strongly to those like Hugh whose education and professional accomplishment in the highly regarded field of law was a motor of growing social advance.

How then might one conceptualize Hugh's life and career more generally, in the context of recent political-historical and literary debates about the relationships between apparently unequal protagonists like the Welsh and the English in the early modern period? For example, should one understand his role as a lawyer-administrator working within a template of English statute and common law in the 'acts of union' institutions in Wales as that of an agent of 'internal colonialism', as implied by the analysis of Michael Hechter? [738] Others[739] have pointed to the limitations of Hechter's thesis when applied to Wales

---

734 *e.g.* Williams, *Religion*, p.144.

735 E.J.Miller, 'Wales and the Tudor Drama' *THSC* (1948), passim. It appears that this general English goodwill towards the Welsh was wearing thin by the time of the Commonwealth in the next century, possibly reflecting disapproval of widespread Welsh loyalties towards the crown during the civil war. See P.Lord, *Words with Pictures: Welsh Images and Images of Wales in the Popular Press, 1640-1860* (London, Planet, 1995).

736 J.O.Bartley & M.Richards, 'The Welsh Language in English Plays', *Philological Quarterly* 12 (1933).

737 In, respectively, Henry V and Henry IV Part I.

738 M.Hechter, *Internal Colonialism: the Celtic Fringe in British national development, 1536-1966* (London, Routledge & Kegan Paul, 1975).

739 *e.g.* P.J.Madgwick, 'Reviews' in *WHR* (1976-77), pp.241-244; C.Brady, 'Comparable

– in particular the paucity of empirical evidence in support of a model alleging economic exploitation of a 'peripheral' principality by a dominant London-based 'core'. To this might be added a corollary, that in Hugh's case the complexities of his personal loyalties – long-established roots in and manifest identification with Wales alongside an English marriage and English professional training applied within Wales – discourage too confident an ascription of simple subordination to a dominant power as an appropriate explanatory framing. Indeed, such an account begs many questions about the intentions behind the 'Acts of Union' settlement itself, including 'the paradox' noted by John Morrill, that 'the expansion of English institutions and English cultural forms took place for almost all of the early modern period in the context of relative English indifference to any systematic absorption or integration of the outlying kingdoms into an enlarged English state'.[740] That matter is considered further below.

An alternative to Hechter's sociological approach might be to argue that there are insights from contemporary post-colonial theory, for instance in the work of Robert Young[741] and Homi Bhabha,[742] which could help make intelligible the behaviour of an institutional actor like Hugh in late-sixteenth-century Welsh county and regional government. For example, might it be useful to picture him as a 'native agent' acculturated by the dominant power to rule over a culturally 'inferior' and linguistically distinct ('other') native population, in the way suggested by Bhabha as characteristic of the effective imposition of colonialist regimes?[743] Or more specifically, might Hugh not be thought of as one of those early modern 'native gentry and reformed Anglican clergy [who] became the apparatus in Wales for government within an English hegemony', suggested by Griffith in the introductory chapter of his landmark study of nineteenth-century Anglesey local government?[744] Whilst there are important elements of truth in such suggestions – most obviously the incontestable reality that in the late-medieval period Wales had been conquered by the English and the subsequent Glyndŵr rebellion suppressed in unambiguously colonialist fashion, with continuing reverberations of multiple kinds – their explanatory adequacy in relation to the position as it had evolved in Wales for figures like Hugh by the late-sixteenth century is more questionable.

Histories?' in Ellis & Barber, *Conquest and Union*, p.65 et seq. Also, Leighton Andrews AM's letter in *New Welsh Review* 69 (2005), pp.106-107.

740   J.Morrill, 'The Fashioning of Britain' in Ellis & Barber (eds) *Conquest and Union*, p.26.

741   R.Young, *Postcolonialism: An Historical Introduction* (Oxford, OUP, 2001).

742   H.Bhabha, *The Location of Culture* (London, Routledge, 1994).

743   *cp* J.Aaron, 'Postcolonial change' in *New Welsh Review* 67 (2005), pp.32-36.

744   W.P.Griffith, *Power, Politics and County Government in Wales: Anglesey 1780-1914* (Llangefni, Anglesey Antiquarian Society, 2009), p.6.

In chapter three, it has been suggested that a combination of educated Welsh enthusiasm for the union, the fact that the 'language clauses' of the 1536 Act were neither intended nor generally perceived as hostile to the survival of the Welsh language,[745] and the readiness with which Welsh translations of the Bible and Prayer book were given statutory blessing by both Privy Council and parliament[746] all point to growing toleration of cultural 'otherness', in parallel with a significant degree of convergence between Welsh and English aspirations across this period. If such was indeed the case, it implies that by the later years of the century Hugh and his kind would in practice have been embedded in circumstances more subtle and complex than implied by the relatively one-dimensional theorisations of 'internal colonialism' or 'postcolonialism' – albeit the latter, in its associated concepts of 'ambivalence' [747] and 'appropriation',[748] has resources which might be argued to contain useful echoes of aspects of the Welsh-English relationship at later stages.

Identity and 'imagined community'

Nevertheless, it is possible to suggest a richer account, one which dovetails more convincingly with the evidence assembled here. This grants a prominent position to the concepts of 'imagined community' and 'Britain', as well as to the role of personal agency and choice on the part of individuals like Hugh himself. Such an argument has several facets. In the first place, the post-Reformation entrenchment of English as the official language of public administration and law in Wales *as it actually occurred* may be better understood as a product of adventitious historical forces and contingencies than as a calculated act of cultural repression. Reference has already been made to Peter Roberts's analysis of the relevant clauses of the 1536 Act, suggesting that suppression of the language formed a negligible part of the latter's design.[749] Benedict Anderson's seminal study of the emergence of nationalism and the nation state[750] re-

---

745   Roberts 'The Welsh Language, English Law', pp.27-33.

746   Ibid., pp.54-63.

747   'Ambivalence suggests that complicity and resistance exist in a fluctuating relation within the colonial subject. Ambivalence also characterises the way in which colonial discourse relates to the colonised subject, for it may be both exploitative and nurturing, or represent itself as nurturing, at the same time…' – B. Ashcroft, G. Griffiths & H. Tiffin, *Post-Colonial Studies: the Key Concepts* (London, Routledge, 2000), p.10.

748   *Appropriation*: A term used to describe the ways in which post-colonial societies take over aspects of the imperial culture …that may be of use to them in articulating their own social and cultural identities…[and] in which the dominated or colonised culture can use the tools of the dominant discourse to resist its political or cultural control' – Ibid., p.15.

749   See note 443.

750   Anderson, *Imagined Communities*, Chapters 1 & 2.

inforces this understanding. On Anderson's account, the emergence of English in the late-medieval / early-modern period as the dominant 'administrative vernacular' across the island occurred in a 'gradual, unselfconscious, pragmatic, not to say haphazard' fashion,[751] exemplifying general trends across western Europe driven by the need for 'documentary interchangeability' by officialdoms in particular federated polities, for their own inner convenience. At this stage, suggests Anderson, 'there was no idea of systematically imposing a unifying language on the dynasts' various populations' – that particular drive coming much later, on the back of *nationalism* from the late-eighteenth century onwards, he argues. Coupled to inexorable bureaucratic logic, in states where Latin was being superseded as the language of record, it was the rapid development of print-capitalism in the early sixteenth century which made it inevitable that certain 'dialects' (in the present case English) should then prosper through 'market' processes, and subsequently crystallise as dominant languages of administration, whilst others 'lost caste' and became subordinate.[752] In the case of Welsh, the effect was at one level, in Gwyn Williams's words, a 'retreat to the kitchen' and a shrinkage of its cultural role back into local and domestic life.[753] Yet simultaneously, the growing body of religious texts and instruction in Welsh following Morgan's 1588 Bible translation came also to secure the future of the language in more dynamic and 'exalted' form, 'as something more than a spoken language'.[754] Nevertheless the significant point here is, in the sixteenth century it was English that rose to the surface, rather than Welsh that was actively repressed.

The final form of the 1536/1543 statutory framework had the effect of maintaining a substantial degree of Welsh distinctiveness under an English security umbrella and framework of law. It also gave strength to powerful currents already tending towards cultural convergences of new kinds. As discussed in Chapter three, on the Welsh side there was continuing ideological support for the Tudor monarchy – initially a legacy of Henry VII's *mab darogan* status and, as the century went on, a reflection of the multiplying London successes of Welshmen in many fields, not least as crown advisers and court intellectuals.[755]

---

751 Ibid., p.42.

752 Ibid., p.45.

753 G.A. Williams, *When Was Wales?* (London, Black Raven Press, 1985), pp.121-131.

754 Davies, *History of Wales*, p.244. The welter of Welsh-language religious texts in the immediate wake of the 1588 appearance of Morgan's Bible included *Deffynniad Ffydd Eglwys Lloegr* (1594) by Morus Kyffin; the revised *Book of Common Prayer* (1599) by William Morgan; *The Psalms of David* (1603) by Edward Kyffin; *The Psalms* (1603) by William Middleton; *The Homilies* (1606) by Edward Jones, and others. William Salusbury's initial translation of the New Testament (in 1568) had of course preceded all of these.

755 Williams, *When Was Wales?* pp.123-124.

Reinforcing this, the dissolution of the monasteries created lavish opportunities for personal gain across Wales as much as England – 'the greatest upheaval in the land market Britain has yet seen' says Gwyn Williams.[756] One by-product was a nakedly material gentry interest on both sides of the border in securing any such gains, reflected in increasingly concerted resistance to further interference by the Papacy and Catholic continental powers – and as a corollary the ever-greater consolidation of the Elizabethan protestant settlement.

Educated Welsh enthusiasm for such mergings of outlook and interest found further expression in the efforts of intellectuals such as John Dee, Humphrey Llwyd of Denbigh and Sir John Price of Brecon by the 1580s to assert a then highly influential interpretation of Anglo-Welsh history, which pointed towards a shared *British* destiny and empire, through shared Brythonic origins.[757] This was consistent with views expressed by William Cecil (who was of recent Welsh descent[758]) as early as the 1540s,[759] echoed in the later promotion of Elizabeth as 'Britannia' – a British rather than an English queen, endorsing venturers and colonisers in America and the like. Such a 'British' emphasis addressed the continuing ideological need of the Tudor monarchy for a fresh, historically-grounded national identity which would legitimise the breach with Rome.[760] Coming in a period when assassination plots against the monarch were rife and anxieties about Spanish invasion greatest, such developments point to authentic solidarities being generated in the face of a common enemy. As Colley notes of a later period of threat to the home countries from the continent, 'Men and women decide who they are by reference to who and what they are not. Once confronted with an obviously alien *Them*, an otherwise diverse community can become a reassuring or merely desperate *Us*.'[761]

Overall then, it is clear that a cluster of factors – religious, economic, cultural, political, mythological, and, crucially, technological (the print-capitalism phenomenon) – were contributing powerfully in the later sixteenth century towards a dynamic fusion of interests, identities and shared responses amongst at least the land-holding classes of England and Wales. What is more, as chapter two has shown through the prism of Hugh Hughes's extended experience of Cambridge and London, these developments were being reinforced through the exposure of increasing numbers of such (male) individuals from both sides

---

756   Ibid., p.122.

757   P.J.French, *John Dee, the World of an Elizabethan Magus* (London, Routledge, 1979).

758   D.Loades, *The Cecils: Privilege and Power behind the Throne* (London, TNA, 2007), pp.10-11.

759   J.E.A.Dawson, 'William Cecil and the British dimension of Early Elizabethan Foreign Policy', *History* 74 (1989), esp pp.196-200.

760   Williams, *When Was Wales?*, pp.122-125.

761   Colley, *Britons*, p.6.

of Offa's Dyke to common patterns of schooling and higher education at the universities and Inns of Court, a trajectory which continued until well into the early Stuart period. Lawrence Stone speculates, 'it may well be that early seventeenth-century England was at all levels the most literate society the world has ever seen'.[762] Whether or not this was the case, young men of the time attending these elite bodies were exposed to emergent new discourses of politics, culture and national interest in unprecedented fashion, with aspects of Welsh culture understood as 'British' and thus elements in the emerging new collective identity.[763]

Hugh in 'Britain'

Colley's account[764] of the 'forging of the British nation' in the eighteenth and early nineteenth centuries lays stress on the energies released in the wake of the 1707 Act of Union between England and Scotland. She points to the role of a shared Protestantism and the need to defend it against Catholic France as key factors in the crystallisation of a progressively more chauvinistic sense of shared 'Britishness' throughout the populations of England, Scotland and Wales during this period, climaxing in the period of the Napoleonic wars. The analysis is a compelling one. However, viewed from the perspective of Welsh history, it is possible to feel that Colley understates the significance of the parallel, if less comprehensive, processes of creative integration which were occurring between England and Wales in the Elizabethan period. Here too, were developments which transcended previously 'self-evident' ascriptions of national identity. A number of the factors to which she refers as decisive in the eighteenth and nineteenth centuries were also present in the sixteenth, in the decades following the 1536 and 1543 Welsh Acts. These included: a nationally distinctive and defensive Protestantism; a common political-religious enemy (albeit Spain rather than France); increasingly shared patterns of education and acquaintance across borders; growing economic interpenetration; and a London-bound traffic of provincial talent. Such developments may have been patchier and more embryonic than in the period of their full flourishing a century and a half later. But it is surely reasonable to argue that the 'imagined community' which was being brought into being was more than the sum of its parts. In the terms of the time, England and Wales were increasingly united under a self-consciously 'imperial' crown. 'Britain' seems a not inappropriate term to use.

And Hugh Hughes was in the engine room of these processes. The framework of law and legal institutions in which he was such an active participant

762   Stone, 'Educational Revolution'.

763   Colley, *Britons*.

764   Ibid.

was a crucial part of the glue permitting such developments to take place, without obvious dislocation to the layered local identities of any of the participants. The interlocking institutions of local and regional government in Wales – commissions of the peace, Great Sessions courts, Council in the Marches – were different from, whilst mostly paralleling, their English equivalents. All of them were alike in being accountable ultimately to the Westminster common law courts and/or the Privy Council, albeit often mediated through the Council in the Marches. This meant that there was an essentially identical system of law and administration across England and Wales, which, while respecting Welsh distinctiveness in crucial respects, applied common juridical principles and standards across the country as a whole, in a period when the overarching challenges to national security and social order were largely indistinguishable on the two sides of Offa's Dyke. One consequence was to nurture amongst educated Welshmen a growing sense of cultural kinship, a tacit sense of what may appropriately be seen as Britishness, without necessary detriment to their local loyalties. And in Hugh's case, such a perspective would also have been fed by his attunement to the fervid late-sixteenth / early-seventeenth century debates centred on Lincoln's Inn and other Inns of Court, focussing on the evolving role of law in relation to emerging ideas about constitutional monarchy. These intense and serious discussions (as suggested in chapter three) were directed at the very philosophical fabric of what was now a polity in which English and Welsh enjoyed equal status – again, with overarching implications which it is more appropriate to picture as British rather than merely English. What was at stake was how to picture the monarch's contract with the people as a whole on both sides of the border, under law. Hugh's embeddedness in such discussions from the vantage point of the higher reaches of Lincoln's Inn, coupled to hands-on practical engagement as a county justice and regional crown official in north Wales, would have fostered in him in the sense of working on behalf of a single dynamic, if diverse, nation.

Cultural and political turmoils

In considering how Hugh and others were experiencing the turmoils of the time, it is of course important to keep in mind the event-driven, inherently unpredictable nature of political and social developments, then as now. What may appear in hindsight to have been inevitable progressions of policy or institutional development were generally by-products of responses to unanticipated contingencies – security threats, recusant plots, natural disasters, macro-economic surprises (like inflation for which then-current theory had few if any explanatory concepts), tensions surrounding the royal succession, and the like. The late-Elizabethan world was fraught with anxieties about the potential for social chaos and disintegration, reflected in the elevation of Tacitus as a seminal intellectual source for political philosophers of the period.[765] In response to such apprehensions, it was the law that held promise of stable social ordering principles. As Bouwsma observes of the period, lawyers 'reliev[ed] the terrors in this hazardous world by supplying a social foundation on which some sense of order and meaning of life could be reconstructed.' [766]

Of course, the social anxieties in question were also finding reflection, frequently to brilliant effect, in the drama and poetry of the time. By the turn of the century, London's theatres had evolved as veritable public fora in which, despite niggling censorship, every facet of contemporary human experience – personal, political, theological, philosophical – was being explored in language and narratives of startling energy and freshness. It was the era of Thomas Kyd, Kit Marlowe, Ben Jonson, and, above all, William Shakespeare. James Shapiro has shown how 'in the hands of Shakespeare and his fellow playwrights, [the theatre] not only absorbed social energies that had become unmoored in a post-Reformation world, but also explored in the plays it staged the social trauma that had enabled it to thrive, the repercussions of which the culture had not yet fully absorbed'.[767] This was an era in which art and life came to mirror one another with rare intensity. Inns of Court members like Hugh constituted a significant proportion of the audiences not only for the plays,[768] but also for the proliferation of public sermons characteristic of this moment, particularly at St Paul's Cross,[769] occasions which acted as key media for discussion of the burning concerns of the day.

It is thus reasonable to suggest that, in the swirling social environment of the time, the key preoccupation of a highly educated lawyer like Hugh would have been with the security and stability of the realm as a whole, regardless of questions of more regional identity. Rather than representing him and fellow Welsh gentry-lawyers as fundamentally compromised imposers of an alien English hegemony, as might be regarded as the implication of commentaries such as those of Hechter, Griffith, and others,[770] it seems truer to the actual circumstances to picture him as a conscious and committed participant in the evolution of a now-federated English-Welsh state, an embryonic *British* state in fact.[771]

---

765   Bate, *Soul of the Age*, pp.336-337.

766   Bouwsma, 'Lawyers and Early Modern Culture', p.327.

767   J.Shapiro, *1599: A Year in the Life of William Shakespeare* (London, Faber & Faber, 2005), p.171.

768   W.R.Prest, *The Inns of Court 1590-1640* (London, Longman, 1972), pp.155-162.

769   M.Maclure, *The St Paul's Cross Sermons 1534-1642* (Toronto, Univ of Toronto Press, 1989).

770   See pp. 161-162

771   This *British* emphasis gained added strength with the accession of James I, and his drives

A prism for his times

At the same time Hugh can serve as a prism for understanding how the processes of federation were working within Wales itself. The 'acts of union' had ushered in a period in which Wales became routinely governed through a multi-layered matrix of institutions compatible with but distinct from those of England. The evidence of his experience, as offered in this book, is that by the end of the century these institutions – the Council in the Marches, the Great Sessions courts, and the county Commissions of the Peace, together with the longer-established manorial and sheriff's courts at more local levels – were evolving effectively in a web of interlocking relationships. The Council in the Marches was responsible to the Privy Council in London, whilst also relating to the Great Sessions and Quarter Sessions in human as well as supervisory terms; Great Sessions judges were members of the Council, as were, increasingly, a number of county justices, even as the Council was handing down instructions and guidance to the county Commissions of the Peace. Equally there were constant interactions between the Great Sessions and the Quarter Sessions – not only judicial and political (through the judges' Charges[772]) but also of a personal kind through both the membership composition of Great Sessions' grand juries and the required presences of county justices at the regular assizes. And at the next level down, whilst there was no formal provision for appeals from the local sheriffs' courts to the county justices, nevertheless the sheriffs themselves were generally also JPs (though not simultaneously), with the result that there was continuing cross-fertilisation between those tiers also.

Within such a system, in the overwhelmingly monoglot circumstances of most of early modern Wales, bilingual legally skilled individuals like Hugh, grounded in both cultures and in his particular case present at all of the various levels of governance, were coming to carry a distinctive authority. It was they who made the system work. Through the prism of Hugh's experience it is possible to see how by this stage a new cohort of Welsh individuals with real power and influence was emerging within the interstices of the administrative and judicial machinery – actively guiding the English 'centre' on matters concerning the Welsh 'periphery'.

Hugh can serve as a prism also in a second, more general respect. He can be seen to have embodied in his person some of the most significant forces and flows touching Wales and the Welsh at the turn of the seventeenth century – even more so perhaps than alternative representative archetypes such as the cultured antiquarian Humphrey Llwyd, or the self-promoting Sir John Wynn.

towards integration of Scotland into the wider polity.

772   See pages 126-128.

For centuries, through processes of economic and cultural osmosis as much as brute colonialist power, English individualism had been helping erode the former rural communalism of native Welsh society,[773] albeit there are growing indications that the latter's agricultural market economy was more innovative, and at earlier stage, than has hitherto been assumed.[774] By the mid-sixteenth century, convergences of economic circumstance on the two sides of the border were contributing to the widespread Welsh embrace of the 'union'. One finds reflected in Hugh not only the fresh aspirational energies that were unlocked in many Welshmen by equal access to 'English' opportunities, and a positive identification with the Tudor crown and state, but also an active embrace of the dynamic new cultural universe in which post-reformation values and economic forces were reshaping political and social relations, and a commitment to the power and social creativity of the law within a newly emergent type of European state. Of course there were conflicts, and prices to be paid. One also finds reflected in Hugh a tempering, indeed probably a domestication, of his personal manifestations of native Welshness within the new order of things. But despite this, overall his life points to the subtlety and intelligence with which the post-union Welsh were developing their accommodation with the Leviathan that was – and indeed remains – their dominant neighbour.

This book's aim has been to track the personal development of a single individual with a foot firmly in camps on both sides of the ancient English-Welsh border, during a period when processes of political and cultural integration were increasingly real for Wales and at least its more educated inhabitants.

Despite Hugh's many appointments and promotions, the dogs that didn't bark during his life and career may well be as significant for an appreciation of him as those which didn't. Far from translating his position into a massive fortune and extravagant possessions like some of his senior colleagues, the estate he built was a relatively modest one for a public lawyer of his standing at the time. It is striking too that his record of public service attracted no honours or other titular recognition from the crown, unlike some of his north Wales contemporaries. The implication is probably that he should be seen as an accomplished rather than an overpoweringly distinguished individual – in career terms, a safe pair of hands close to the top of the tree, rather than a spectacular or adventurous high achiever.

He is probably best understood simply as an individual who through circumstance found himself applying his talents to the development and operation

---

773   Davies, *First English Empire*;   Macfarlane, *English Individualism*.

774   N.M.W. Powell, 'Near the Margin of Existence'?: Upland Prosperity in Wales during the Early Modern Period', *Studia Celtica* (2007), pp.137-162.

of the legal infrastructure of the then-emergent constitutional entity of 'Britain'. Whether or not he pictured himself as acting literally in such terms is impossible to know. But the evidence is that that was how he chose to spend his life. His primary practical sphere of operation was north Wales, to which he was deeply attached, but he understood himself to be operating also on a larger national canvas – an estimation which would have been reinforced by his final official appointment, as Chief Justice of Ireland.

*   *   *

As a coda, it is worth considering whether the general argument of the book about early modern governance in Wales carries any twenty-first century relevance – for example, for the continuing debates about devolved government in Wales. There are grounds for thinking it may indeed have such relevance.

Significant recent surveys by political scientists[775] have sought to throw light on what might be called the phenomenologies of political identity in the present-day populations of Wales and Scotland. To what extent, these studies asked, did people in the two politically devolved regions now think of themselves as 'Welsh' and 'Scottish' as opposed to 'British'? Though the analyses relied on very different methodologies, their findings are illuminating. The Scottish study concluded that a sense of 'Scottishness' was increasingly the dominant political identity within Scotland, with 'Britishness' receding as ever-less significant, indeed becoming increasingly invisible, in people's self-identification. On the other hand, whilst the Welsh study found that devolution had encouraged growing levels of self-definition as 'Welsh' by people living within Wales, such levels continued to coexist with an unchanged levels of self-proclaimed 'Britishness'.

This is not the context in which to consider these studies in detail, though they invite a variety of questions. For example, the methodological issues raised by the two studies were legion, not least concerning a lack of clarity about how the subjects of either of the surveys actually understood the concept of 'Britishness'. Nevertheless, a general pattern of some interest was apparent: *Present-day Welsh subjects appear to experience less difficulty in thinking of themselves as adhering simultaneously to two 'national' identities — i.e. 'British' as well as 'Welsh' — than do present-day Scottish subjects.*

It is plausible to detect in this finding an echo of the early-modern origins of the Welsh federation with England. If, as has been argued, the legal and cultural marriage of Wales and England implemented by individuals like Hugh

---

775   J.Bradbury & R.Andrews, 'State Devolution and National Identity: Continuity and Change in the Politics of Welshness and Britishness in Wales' and M.Stewart Leith, 'Governance and Identity in a Devolved Scotland' – both in *Parliamentary Affairs* 63 (2010), pp.229-249.

Hughes in the decades following the 'acts of union' was felt and experienced by the educated community of the time as working towards a positively regarded larger whole ('Britain') without significant detriment to local ('Welsh') identity, perhaps a pattern was set which has prevailed down the centuries, regardless of the ebb and flow of very contrary political attitudes and prejudices at particular historical moments, such as the notorious Blue Books of the 1840s and the reactions they provoked.

The state of Welsh language and culture in the twenty-first century can be interpreted in different ways. To concerned cultural nationalists, understandably, the present glass is at least half empty, and the culture is struggling for survival. One often-voiced historiographical corollary is that things have never recovered since the culture was betrayed by Wales's leaders in the sixteenth century.[776] But others might interpret the lively survival of the language and culture into the current century, with its contemporary energy manifested through the far-reaching multi-level Eisteddfod network, the significant proportion of Welsh speakers amongst the young, and other indicators, as evidence rather that the glass is at least half-*full*. Indeed, it could be argued that the present flourishing of this ancient minority language and culture, in the contemporary media-saturated age, geographically cheek-by-jowl with the world-conquering English language and culture, is itself an astonishing triumph of a truly improbable kind. If this view is taken, then it may also be appropriate to look more sympathetically at the seminal role of the sixteenth-century Welsh leadership, given the blame attached to them by the 'half-empty' school. An implication of the arguments in this book is that the Welsh leadership, at shire and Great Sessions levels as well as in the negotiations concerning the Welsh-language Bible, made the new dispensation work so uncontroversially that the issue of repression did not arise, and in this way, unlike in either Scotland or Ireland, the indigenous language and its associated culture survived, to fight another day up to and beyond our own times.

Thus, over and above his role as a lawyer and crown official during his own lifetime, Hugh Hughes, as a mechanic in the machinery of the union in Elizabethan and early-Jacobean times, may be acknowledged as at least a modest contributor to the survival of Welsh language and culture into our own times.

*   *   *

---

776 *e.g.* Evans, *Fight for Welsh Freedom.*

Appendices

Appendix A

Hugh Hughes in historical context

       1485 Battle of Bosworth Field. Henry VII's accession
       1509 Henry VIII's accession
       1536 First Welsh 'act of union'
       1543 Second Welsh 'act of union'
       1547 Edward IV's accession

1548   **Hugh Hughes is born in Llanedwen**

       1553 Mary I's accession
       1558 Elizabeth I's accession

1564   Trinity College, Cambridge
1568   graduates and returns to Anglesey
1571   to Lincoln's Inn, London
1577   appointed Justice in the Anglesey Commission of the Peace

       1577 Sir Francis Drake's circumnavigation of the globe

1579   called to Bar at Lincoln's Inn
1580   Steward of Rhosyr Lands
1580-92 in dispute with the Rhydderchs of Myfyrian
1586   marries Elizabeth Montagu
1588   Steward of Aberconwy lands

       1588 William Morgan's translation of the Welsh Bible
             Spanish Armada

1589   appointed Deputy Attorney General, North Wales
1591   appointed to Quora of Caernarvonshire and Merioneth
      appointed Anglesey Commission of the Peace
1595   Steward of Bishop of Bangor lands

       1595-1601 Irish Wars

1596   appointed Attorney General, North Wales
1597   Anglesey's Knight of the Shire (MP) in 1597 Parliament
1601   appointed Member of the Council in the Marches
1602   becomes Treasurer (i.e. head) of Lincoln's Inn

       1603 James I's accession
       1605 Gunpowder Plot

1609   appointed Chief Justice of Ireland
      Hugh Hughes dies in London

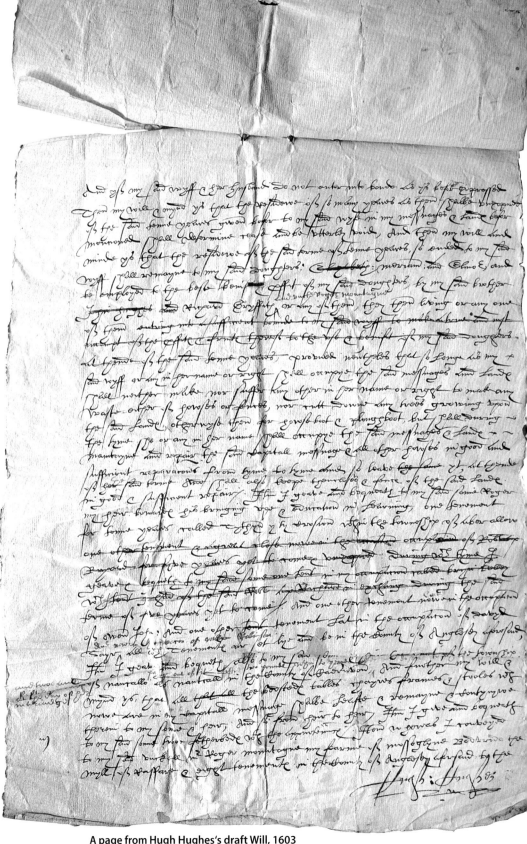

A page from Hugh Hughes's draft Will, 1603

Appendix B

Hugh Hughes's Will

This Appendix contains a transcription of the Last Will and Testament of Hugh Hughes of Plas Coch, dated 20 June 1603. A copy of the draft is held in the Bangor University Archives, as Plas Coch 173. The transcription also refers to amendments added by Hugh in the days before his death on 6 June 1609, and held in the National Archive as a second version of the Will, proved by the Prerogative Court on 21 August 1609. Specific alterations from the original are shown italicised in square brackets.

The Will was drafted by Hugh personally. His signature appears at the bottom of each of the five individual pages (though the last page is missing in the Bangor version).

The original (1603) will's contents include detailed future financial provision for Hugh's wife Elizabeth and three daughters Elizabeth, Miriam and Eleanor, over and above the bequests to his son and heir Roger. Posthumous gifts to various patrons, professional colleagues, and personal friends are also specified. Considerable pains are taken to provide for an apparently equitable distribution of assets amongst his wife and female children during their lifetimes. Hugh and Elizabeth having married in 1588, the three daughters were still in their minorities in 1609.

However, most of the italicised (1609) amendments involve redistribution of specific assets away from the eldest daughter Elizabeth, towards her younger sisters. The likely explanation is that at some point between 1603 and 1609, this Elizabeth married her husband, David Lloyd of Llwydiarth, and hence was judged no longer in need of paternal support.

There are also repeated mentions in the will of Hugh's male Montagu relations-by-marriage — Roger particularly, though also Henry and Edward. Roger's role in supervising his niece Elizabeth's future security is especially notable. However, the final sentence (here translated from the Latin of the probate) notes that, perhaps contrary to Hugh's expectation, Roger decided to 'renounce' his role as executor, for 'certain reasons influencing him and his soul'. Though renunciation of an executor's role was not uncommon in this period, research is on-going for clues as to precisely why he took this decision, he and Hugh having previously been on good terms for two decades at least (as shown in chapters four and six above).

Of incidental local interest is the mention in the will of 'bryn kelly' (Bryn Celli Ddu) as a property in Hugh's possession at the time of his death.

Testamentum Hugonis Hughes

In the name of James Kyng of England Fraunce and Ireland and of
Scotland the Six and thirtieth defender of the fayth. I Hugh Hughes of
Lincolnes Inne, being at this present whole in mynde and of perfect
memory (thankes be to God) doe make and ordayne this my present
Testament and last will in manner and forme following.

Fyrst I commende my Soule to Jhesus Christe my Creator Redeemer and
mediator : And my body to be buryed in such place as shall please myne
executors, and my buryall to be in such decent sort as shall please them.
I give and bequeathe towardes the reparation of the Chappell of Llanedwyn
twenty shillinges : And to the poore of the sayd parish fortie shillinges, to be
payd within half yeare after my deceasse.

Item I give and bequeathe to my welbeloved wife Elizabeth Hughes all my
messuages landes Tenementes and Hereditamentes sett lyeng and being
within the Towneship of Porthamall within the Countie of Anglesey in as
large and ample
manner as now they are in myne owne occupation, to have and to hould to
my said wife for the terme of Tenne yeares, to begynne after my deceasse :
And my will and meaning is that the sayd Terme of Tenne yeares shall end
and expyre at the feast of St Michael the Archangell upon the expiration of
the Terme of Tenne yeares : yeelding and paying to my Sonne and heyre
Roger Hughes the yearely rent of fortie shillinges at the feast of All Saynctes
yearely during the sayd Terme of Tenne yeares. Further my will and mynde
is, that yf my sayd wief happen to marry within the Terme of tenne yeares,
then her husband and she with sufficient sureties, to the number of two shall
enter within one monthe after the sayd mariage into bond of fower hundred
poundes to my unckle Mr Roger Mountague *[struck out in the original, 'my
brother'; the name John Hughes is not struck out, but a note in Hugh's own hand
over his name states 'he ys dead'; in the margin, Written under 'my owne two
phrindes' 'Richard gruff ys living']* yf he then be lyving and my brother in lawe
Richard Gruffith or to any of them to pay the somme of two hundreth
poundes within two yeares next, following after the ensealing and deliverie
of the sayd bande to the handes of my said unckle Mr Roger Mountague (yf
he then be lyving) or ells to the handes of my sayd brother Richard *[text
struck through by HH in 1609: 'such of my said bretherne as then shal be lyving']*
to the use and benefitt of my daughters *['Elizabeth' struck through]* Myriam
and Ellenor Hughes or to such or so many of them as then shal be lyving
equallie to be devyded.

And yf my sayd wife and her husband doe not enter into bande as is before
expressed : Then my will and mynde is, that the residue of so many yeares as
then shal be unexpyred of the sayd Tenne years given before to my sayd wief
in my Messuages and landes before mentioned shall determine cease and be
utterly void.

And then my will and mynde is that the residue of the sayd terms of Tenne years so ended to my sayd wief shall remayne to my said daughters *['Elizabeth' struck through]* Myriam and Elenor and be ymployed to the best benefitt and proffitt of my sayd daughters by my said Brother *['John Hughes' struck through]* Mr *[Mr is not in the original]* Richard Griffith and unckle Roger Mountague, or any of them they then lyving or any one of them *[text struck through: 'entring into a sufficient bounde to my said wyff to make a true and just accompt of the proffites & fruites thereof to the use & benifit of my said doughters at the ende of the said tenne yeares,']*. Provided nevertheless that so longe as my sayd wief of any in her name or right shall occupie the sayd Messuages and landes shall nether make nor suffer any other in her name or right to make any waste either of houses or fences nor cutt downe any trees growing upon the sayd landes otherwise then for houseboote and ploughboote but shall duringe the tyme she or any in her name shall occupy the sayd Messuages and landes maynteine and repayre the sayd Capitall Messuage and all other houses in good and sufficient reparations from tyme to tyme and so leave it at the end of the *[original: 'her']* sayd Terme, and shall also keepe the incloses and fences of the sayd landes in good and sufficient repaire.

Item I give and bequeathe to my sayd sonne Roger my Heire towardes his bringing up and education in learning, one tenement for Tenne yeares called tythyn y ty Croision within the Towneship of Aberalawe *[struck through: 'one other tenement & a great close nowe in the occupation of Robt ap Richard for fyve yeares yet to come & unexpired : during which tyme I geave & bequeth to my said sonne one tenement in my occupation called bryn kelley which tenement I had of the said Robt ap Richard in exchange during the said terme of fyve yeares yet to come]*, and one other Tenement late *[original: nowe]* in the occupation of Owen John, and one other Tenement late in the occupation of David Sayre and now in the occupation of William Robinson. All which tenementes are sett lye and bee in the Countie of Anglesey aforesayd.

Item I give and bequeathe also to my sayd Sonne and Heire the Towneship of Nantcallo alias Nantcall in the Countie of Carnarvan payeng out of it fiftie two poundes within two yeares after my deceasse to my daughter Myriam and two and fiftie poundes at the day of her mariage.

And further my will and mynde is that all the bedstedes tables Chaires frames and stooles which now are in my Capitall messuage shal be left and remaine and contynue therin to my sonne and Heire and so from Heire to Heire.

Item I give and bequeathe to my sayd sonne two fether beddes with th'appurtenaunces

Item wheras I conveyed to my sayd unckle Mr Roger Mountague my ferme of Mosseglyn Bodvrida the mill of Rosfayre and eight tenementes in the Countie of Anglesey aforesayd to the use and benefitt of my sayd wief yf she did happen to survive me : My will and true intent is that my sayd wife shall have and enjoy the rentes yssues and proffittes of my sayd ferme during the naturall lief of my said wife. And after her decease my will and mynde was and is that my sonne and Heire (if He be then lyving) shall have and injoy the sayd ferme : And if my sayd sonne and Heire be not then living : then my will is that *[struck through: 'the next heire named in this will shall have & enyoy the residewe of the terme or termes of yeares of my said fearme']* the residue of the sayd Terme unexpired upon the sayd fearme shall be and remayne at the tyme of the deathe of my sayd wife. And in such sort aforesayd to my other daughters and Heires successively to enjoy the same fearme that ys to say *[struck through: 'fyrst to my doughter Elizabeth And yf she dey within my said terme Then']* to my daughter Myriam, And if she dye within the sayd terme of yeares Then my will and mynde is that my sayd wief shall have the one half of all my goodes Jewells plate household stuff, except such as is before mentioned and reserved to be left in my Capitall House to my Heyres.

Further I give and bequeathe to my daughter Myriam *['Elizabeth' struck through]* Hughes my estate interest and terme of yeares which I have nowe in the fearme and parsonage of llanedwen and Chappell therof so called within the Towneship of Porthamall with all tithes oblations offeringes proffittes and commodities therunto belonging whatsoever for and during my terme of yeares yet to come, payeng the rent of five shillinges to Sir William Harbertes daughter and Heire for all manner of rentes and services.

[Struck through: **Item** *I geave & bequeth to my said doughter Elizabeth over & besydes the said parsonage the somme of twoe hundred markes to be payed her at the tyme of her mariage yf she doth followe the advyse of her mother in the bestowing of her sellfe X Also]* I give and bequeth my towneship of nantcallo alias nantcall with the appurtenances to my doughter meriam Hughes, for the tearme of fourtenne yeares next after the experation forfiture or other determination of a lease for yeares graunted befor my purchach by the Late abbote of Conwey

Item I give and bequeath to my sayd daughter Myriam *['…terme of xiij yeares' struck through, some text hidden in fold]* the somme of fortie poundes to be payd her at the tyme of her mariage

Item I give and bequeath to my daughter Elenor Hughes the Somme of one hundreth poundes to be payd her by my executors at the tyme of her mariage or the age of eightene yeares which shall first happen : And my desire is that the benefitt therof shalbe answered by my executors towardes her mayntenaunce in the meane tyme. *[struck through: 'said some of one hundred poundes may be employed to her use in such Lawfull sort as shall seeme good to my executors during the mynoryty of my said doughter Ellinour']* And my will and meaning is that yf any of my sayd two daughters die before their mariage or the age of eighteen yeares then ech others portions and legacies shal be and remayne to *[struck through: 'equally devided amongst']* the survivour*[s]* of them.

And if it please God that they all die before their mariage or age of eighteene

yeares, then my will and mynde is, that my wife and my sonne and Heire
shall equally have all their portions and legacies before mentioned and given
unto them. Further I give devise and bequeathe to my sayd sonne and Heire
and to the heires of his body lawfully begotten all Reversion and Reversions
of all my Capitall Houses Messuages Towneships and landes whatsoever
within the sayd Towneships of Porthamall Bodlewe Nantcall alias Nantcall
Aber alawe llanberies, or are scituate lyeng and being in any other place
parish or Hamlettes within the Counties of Anglesey and Carnarvan after
the expiration of such terme or termes of yeares herein devised and given to
such persons herein named :And if my sayd Sonne and Heire happen to dye
without yssue of his body lawfully begotten Then I give devise and
bequeathe all the sayd Messuages landes Reversion or Reversions
tenementes and Hereditamentes within the sayd places and Counties to my
said daughter Elizabeth Hughes and to the Heires of her body lawfully
begotten if my sayd daughter doe well and truly pay or cause to be payd the
somme of fower *[struck through: 'Twoe']* Hundreth poundes of lawfull money
at my now dwelling house in Porthamall aforesayd to my other two
daughters Myriam and Ellenor to ech of them two *[struck through: 'a']*
Hundreth poundes a peece within eighteene monethes after the deceasse of
my said sonne Roger Hughes dyeng without yssue of his body lawfully
begotten wherby my sayd daughter Elizabeth may enter into the aforesayd
premisses by force of the Remaynder to her herein lymited and appoyncted
if my sayd daughters Myriam or Ellinour be then lyving.

Otherwise my will and mynde is that the sayd somme of fower Hundreth
poundes shal be equally devided among their Children if they or any of
them happen to have any. And if any of my sayd two daughters be then dead
without yssue, that then the sayd fower hundred poundes shal be payd in
manner and forme aforesayd by my sayd daughter Elizabeth or her heires to
the Survivour of them.

Also my will and mynde is that if my sayd daughter Elizabeth dye without
yssue of her body then I give and bequeathe the aforesaid mentioned
premisses to my sayd daughter Myriam Hughes and to the Heires of her
body lawfully begotten so that she or her heires doe well and truly pay the
somme of three *[struck through: 'one']* hundreth poundes of lawfull money to
my daughter Ellenor Hughes within Twelve monethes after the decease of
my sayd daughter Elizabeth dyeng without yssue of her bodye lawfully
begotten, the sayd somme to be payd at my now dwelling house in
Porthamall aforesayd in the sayd Countie of Anglesey. And if my sayd
daughter Myriam die without yssue of her body then I give devise and
bequeathe all the before mentioned premises to my daughter Ellenor
Hughes and to the Heyres of her body lawfully begotten, and for default of
such yssue of her body lawfully begotten Then I give devise and bequeath
the sayd premises before mentioned to my right heires for ever performing
such conditions as are named and specified in this my last will and
Testament provided alwayes and my true intent and meaning is to settle and

erect the said severall estates of intayles of all the sayd premisses by way of
Remaynder herein expressed for the preservation and contynuance of my
House in my name and bloud.

Therfore yf any person or persons to whom any estate or estates in
possession reversion or reversions Remaynders above herein or hereby is
bequeathed or lymitted shall goe about to doe any act or actes thing or
thinges to sell alien bargayn devise or devises of the sayd premisses or any
part therof except making of leases in possession for one and Twentie yeares
of the sayd premisses or any part therof wherupon the auncient rent or
rentes shal be reserved That then the estate or estates of such as shall so
offend shall cease extinguish and be utterly voyd as though he or shee or any
of them weare utterly and naturally deade, and then the aforesayd premisses
to remayne to him or her that are next in Remainder having committed any
such acte or offence to discontynue the sayd estates of intayles before
expressed.

And further my desire is of my blessing that ech of my sayd Children shall
and will regard my true intent request and meaning herein expressed as I
trust they and every of them will performe. [*Plas Coch MS version ends here*].

And further my will and mynde is that wheras the late Quene Elizabeth by
her gratious letters patentes bearing date the six and twentith day of
November in the fortith yeare of her late reigne amongst other things in the
sayd letters Patentes mentioned hath demised and graunted unto me the
sayd Hugh Huges myne executors and Assignes the Towneships of
Mosseglyn, Bodrida, the Mill of Rosfaire and eight Tenementes or Frithes
within the Hundred of Menai in the Countie of Anglesey for the Terme of
One and Twentie yeares to commence in the yeare of our Lord God One
thowsand Six Hundreth and eightene, I give and bequeathe the use and
occupation of the sayd recited landes mill and eight tenementes with the
appurtenaunces to my sayd wief Elizabeth Hughes during her lief yf she
happen to be lyving after the expiration and determination of my first
recyted lease and terme of yeares which I now have in possession of the sayd
Towneships Mill and landes being to her first bequeathed I n this my will To
Have and to Hould the use and occupation of my sayd towneships mill and
eight Tenementes with the appurtenaunces to my sayd wief during her life.
So that she doe no act to prejudice my sayd sonne and Heire or Heires to
Have the residue of the sayd Terme of One and Twenty yeares into the said
premisses that shall happen to be unexpired therof at the time of her
deceasse. And if it happen my sayd wief to dye before the expiration or
determination of the sayd terme of one and Twenty yeares, then my will and
mynde is and I give and bequeathe the sayd terme of One and Twentie
yeares into the sayd Towneships mill and landes to my Sonne Roger His
Executors and Assignes.

Further for token and remembrance of my good will towardes my freindes
First and especially I give and bequeath to the right honorable the Lord

Chauncellor a Ring of the value of three poundes in remembraunce of my good will and dutie towardes His Lordship.

Item I give and bequeathe my sister Ellenour and her husband to ech of them a ring of twenty shillinges. Item to my loving freind Mr John Deycrowe a ring of fortie shillinges.

Item my request and desire is to my loving wief that she be good to my ould unckle Thomas Hughes for his keeping and mayntenaunce.

Item I give and bequeath to my Cozen Mr Thomas Wood a ring of Twentie shillinges.

And touching the nomination of my executors I doe by this my last will and Testament nominate constitute and ordayne my said loving wief and my sayd loving uncle Mr Roger Mountague myne executors to execute and performe all thinges that ap pertayneth to Executors. And I give to my sayd uncle and executor for his good will and paynes a ringe of fyve poundes. And further I desire the right worshipfull Mr Justice Warberton to be my Overseer for the performance and accomplishment of this my last will and Testament and for his worships good will and paynes therin I give him fyve poundes.

Also I desire Sir Henry Mountague Knight Recorder of London to be one other of my Overseers of this my will, and for his paynes and good will for the accomplishment therof I give him a ringe of the value of three poundes. And all other former willes by me heretofore made and all estates and legacies therin given by me to any person or persons, I doe hereby revoke frustrate and make voyde. In witnes wherof I have hereunto subscribed my name and put my seale the day and yeare above written in the presence of the witnesses hereunder named.

Hugh Hughes

Memorandum that is the last will of the sayd Hughe Hughes conteyning five sheetes of paper all written upon one side and every leafe subscribed with his owne hande and by him sealed published and delivered this two and twentith June a thousand six hundred and three for his last will and Testament in presence of us:

> Johes waren Scr. lre. Curialis *[writer of court hand]* London.
> Rob Steele. Kenelme Harrison. Tho: Hodgeson.

Memorandum that this will was corrected and newly published the sixt day of Jun in the yeare of the raigne of our Soveraigne Lord James by the grace of God King of England Scotland Fraunce and Ireland viz of England Fraunce and Ireland the Seaventh and of Scotland the two and fortith in the presence of the witnesses subscribed Anno Domini A Thowsand six Hundred and Nine. Roger Jenkins: John Hughes: fulke lee haberdasher. William Thomas.

Probate sentence, translated from the Latin:

The above written testament was proved at London before the venerable lord John Benet, Knight, Doctor of Laws, Master, Warden or Commissary lawfully constituted of the Prerogative Court of Canterbury, on the twenty first day of August in the year of the Lord 1609, by the oath of Elizabeth Hughes, relict of the said deceased, and one of the executors nominated in such testament, to whom was committed administration of the goods, rights and credits of the said deceased, having been sworn upon the holy gospels of God to well and faithfully administer the same, by force of a commission issued elsewhere in this behalf, Roger Mountague, the other executor nominated in the said testament, for certain reasons influencing him and his soul, expressly renouncing the burden of execution of such testament, just as appears by the Act Book.   Examined.

I am grateful for the contribution of Peter Foden, who transcribed, annotated, and assisted in the interpretation of the document.

Appendix C

The Plas Coch Estate after Hugh Hughes

Brief mention should be made of the way in which the Plas Coch estate evolved in the centuries following Hugh, if only to gauge the longer-term impacts of the latter's efforts on behalf of the Hughes family.

The surviving estate papers suggest that Roger, his son and heir, though called to the bar at Lincoln's Inn, was a paler character than his father, content to live a relatively uneventful Anglesey life on the estate till his death in 1646. The same appears to have been true of several further generations of his successors, beneficiaries of a by-now complacent 'age of the gentry'. A painted Plas Coch family genealogy dated March 1697, shown on pages xxii-xxiii above, bears the inscription *'The Pedigree* [sic] *of Roger Hughes Esq of Plas Coch in Anglesey drawn by Mr Owen Hughes his brother'*, thus confirming both that the family was by then overwhelmingly English-speaking (the Roger in question being the grandson of Hugh's son), and that pride in the family's ancient Welsh roots continued to prevail.

The Brynddu–Plas Coch connection was established in 1765, with the marriage of Hugh Hughes (the third) to Anna Wright, granddaughter and heiress of the celebrated diarist, William Bulkeley of Brynddu. This added Brynddu's then–2,200 acres to Plas Coch's 1,500, an increase in resources which did not prevent colossal mismanagement, sweeping sell-offs of key farms, and looming bankruptcy by Hugh and Anna's playboy son, Sir William Bulkeley Hughes (1766-1836), who as a Bath habitué owed his knighthood in 1804 to an acquaintanceship with the Prince Regent. It was Sir William's son, William Bulkeley Hughes,[777] best known as MP for Caernarfon Boroughs (for forty years during the period 1837-82) who retrieved the position, expanding the Plas Coch–Brynddu portfolio to more than 5,000 acres by the mid-nineteenth century.

William Bulkeley Hughes apart, Hugh's descendants did not repeat his pattern of public accomplishments. Nevertheless, fragments of the modest estate he consolidated have survived in family hands into the twenty-first century.

The present-day Plas Coch mansion is now owned and maintained by Park Leisure as the centrepiece of a thriving holiday park business.

---

777 *Dictionary of Welsh Biography*, p.394.

... occupied ... of Rosthern
... During ... same ...
... occupied called ... toller
... dwelling ... the ...
... tenement now in the occupation
... the occupation of Dabyd
the county of Anglesey aforesaid,
... grant of the ... to
... And further my will is
... frames & stooles wh
... to romayne & contynewe
... Item I gyve and bequeath
... Howe & howes ... rowboyd
... is ... Bodewida the
... of Anglesey aforesaid by the

Hugh Hughes

Bibliography

A Original sources : unpublished

1 *British Library, London*
BL Harleian MS 6686.
BL Lansdowne MS 155.
BL Hargrave MS 254.
BL Collections, 1379.h.10

2 Huntington Library, California
E1 Ellesmere MSS 1763.

3 *The National Archives, Kew*
EXCHEQUER

E 123/12
E 123/19
E 133/8/1126
E 134/35 & 36 Eliz/Mich 18
E 179/219/4
E 179/219/5
E 179/219/6
E 179/219/13
E 179/219/16
E 179/219/17

AUGMENTATIONS COURT RECORDS

E 310/41/16

SPECIAL COLLECTIONS, MINISTERS & RECEIVERS ACCOUNTS

SC 6/1152/4
SC 6/1152/5
SC 6/1170/5
SC 6/1227/7
SC 6/1233/1

STATE PAPERS DOMESTIC, ELIZABETH I

SP 12/38
SP 12/195

STAR CHAMBER PROCEEDINGS

STAC 4/4/57
STAC 5/G6/18
STAC 8/197/29
STAC 8/215/20

4 National Library of Wales
Carreglwyd MSS 135.

5 *Bangor University Archives and Special Collections*
  Plas Coch MSS
  Baron Hill MSS

6 **Northamptonshire Records Office**
  Letters of the Montagu Family 1537-1644, Boxes 13/1-6.

7 **Brynddu, Llanfechell**
  Hughes family records, *Pedigree of Hughes of Plas Coch* (1869) (uncatalogued).
  Plas Coch estate maps, 1805 and 1875 (uncatalogued).

B Original sources : published

Acts of the Privy Council (J.R.Dasent ed.),Vols 12, 14, 15, 16 & 28 (London, HMSO, 1896-1898).

I. Bowen (ed), *The Statutes of Wales* (London, Fisher Unwin, 1908).

Calendar of State Papers Domestic: James I, Vols 32 & 57 (M.A.E.Green (ed) (1857), in National Archive).

Calendar of the Patent Rolls 1416-1422 & 1557-8 (HMSO, London 1908).

Calendar of Wynn Papers 1515-1690 (Cardiff, UWP, 1925).

Letters & Papers, Foreign and Domestic, of the Reign of Henry VIII, Brewer, J.S., Gairdner, J. & Brodie, R.H. (eds),Vol 2 (London, 1862-1932).

Sir John Davies, *Le Primer Report des cases in Law Courts del Roy* (Dublin 1615), translated as *A Report of Cases and Matters of Law Resolved and Abridged by the King's Courts in Ireland* (Dublin 1762).

Sir Antony Fitzherbert, *La Nouvelle Natura Brevium* (London 1553).

Lincoln's Inn, *The Black Books – The Records of the Honorable Society of Lincoln's Inn,*Vols 1 & 2 (Lincoln's Inn, 1897).

Lincoln's Inn Admissions Register 1420-1799, Vol 1 (Lincoln's Inn, 1896).

Sir Thomas Littleton, *Littleton's Tenures* (London 1557).

Humphrey Llwyd, *Commentaroli Descriptionis Britannicae Fragmentum* (Cologne 1572) tr. Thomas Twyne, *The Breviary of Britayne* (London 1573), fo. 606.

Sir S.R. Meyrick, *Lewis Dunn's Heraldic Visitations of Wales (folio)* Vol 2 (Llandovery,Welsh Manuscript Society, 1846).

John Nichols, *The Progresses and Public Processions of Queen Elizabeth* (London, 1823).

NLW MS 1610, F II – reproduced in 'A Merioneth Wage Assessment', *Journal of Merioneth Historical & Record Society,*Vol 2, Part 3 (1955), pp.204-208.

Owen, H. (ed), 'The Diary of Bulkeley of Dronwy, Anglesey, 1630-36', in *TAAS* 1937, pp.26-172.

George Owen, 'The Dialogue of the Government in Wales', in H.Owen (ed), *The Description of Penbrokshire by George Owen of Henllys, Lord of Kemes* (London, Bedford Press, 1906).

Thomas Phaer, *A Boke of Presidentes Exactly Written in Maner of a Register* (London, 1550).

Edmund Plowden, *Les Comentaries* (London, 1571).

William Rastell, *A Colleccion of Entrees* (London, 1566).

Revd. Henry Rowlands, 'Antiquitates Parochiales XII & XIII', *Arch.Camb.* 4, (1849).

William Shakespeare, *Henry IV Part I* (London, Penguin, 2005 edn.).

William Staunford, *An Exposicion of the Kinges Prerogative* (London, 1567).

Dafydd Wyn Wiliam (ed), *Y Canu Mawl i Deulu Mysoglen* (Llangefni, O.Jones, 1999).

Dafydd Wyn Wiliam (ed), *Y Canu Mawl i Deulu Myfyrian* (Llandysul, Gwasg Gomer, 2004).

Dafydd Wyn Wiliam (ed), *Y Canu Mawl i Rai Teulueodd o Gwmwd Menai* (Llandysul, Gwasg Gomer, 2007).

Sir John Wynn, *History of the Gwydir Family*, edited by J. Gwynfor Jones (Llandysul, Gwasg Gomer, 1990).

C **Secondary sources**

Aaron, J., 'Postcolonial change', in *New Welsh Review* 67 (2005), pp.32-36.

Anderson, B., *Imagined Communities: Reflections on the Origin and Spread of Nationalism* (London, Verso, 1983).

Andrews, L., Letter in *New Welsh Review* 69 (2005), pp.106-107.

Archer, I.W., 'City and Court Connected: The Material Dimensions of Royal Ceremonial *ca* 1480-1625', *Huntington Library Quarterly* 70 71/1 (2008), pp.157-179.

Ashcroft, B., Griffiths, G., & Tiffin, H., *Post-Colonial Studies: the Key Concepts* (London, Routledge, 2000).

Ayres, G., *History of the Mail Routes to Ireland until 1850* (www.lulu.com, 2017)

Bagehot, W., *The English Constitution* (Oxford, OUP, 2011 edn).

Baker, J.H., *Readers & Readings in the Inns of Court and Chancery* (London, Selden Society, 2000).

Baker, J.H., *An Introduction to English Legal History* (Oxford, OUP, 2007 edn).

Baker, J.H. (ed.), *The Men of Court, 1440-1550: A prosopography of the Inns of Court and Chancery and the Courts of Law*, 2 vols (London, Selden Society, 2012).

Barber, H. & Lewis, H., *The History of Friars School, Bangor* (Bangor, Jarvis & Foster, 1901).

Bartley, J.O. & Richards, M., 'The Welsh Language in English Plays', *Philological Quarterly* 12 (1933).

Bartrum, P.C., Welsh Genealogies AD 300-1400, Vol 3 (Cardiff, UWP, 1974).

Bate, J., *Soul of the Age: the Life, Mind and World of William Shakespeare* (London, Penguin, 2008).

Benbow, R.M., *Index of London Citizens Active in City Government 1558-1603* (London, Centre for Metropolitan History, Institute of Historical Research, 2010).

Beverley Smith, J., 'Crown and community in the Principality of North Wales in the reign of Henry Tudor', *WHR* 3 (1966), pp.145-171.

Beverley Smith, J., 'Owain Gwynedd', *TCHS* (1971), pp.8-17.

Beverley Smith, L., 'The gage and the land market in late medieval Wales', *Economic History Review* 29 (1976), pp.537-541.

Bhabha, H., *The Location of Culture* (London, Routledge, 1994).

Bindoff, S.T. (ed), *The House of Commons 1558-1603*, Vol 2 Members (London, Secker & Warburg, 1982).

Bouwsma, W.J., 'Lawyers and Early Modern Culture', *American Historical Review* 78 (1973), pp.303-327.

Bradbury, J. & Andrews, R., 'State Devolution and National Identity: Continuity and Change in the Politics of Welshness and Britishness in Wales', *Parliamentary Affairs* 63 (2010), pp.229-249.

Bradshaw, B., 'The Tudor Reformation and Revolution in Wales and Ireland: the Origins of the British Problem', in Bradshaw B. & Morrill J., *The British Problem c.1534-1707: State Formation in the Atlantic Archipelago* (London, Macmillan, 1996).

Brady, C., 'Comparable Histories? Tudor Reform in Wales and England', in Ellis, S. & Barber, S. (eds), *Conquest and Union: Fashioning a British State 1485-1725* (London, Longman, 1995) pp.65-85.

Brayshay, M., *Land Travel and Communications in Tudor and Stuart England: Achieving a Joined Up Realm* (Liverpool, Liverpool University Press, 2014).

Brooks, C.W., *The Law, Politics & Society in Early Modern England* (Cambridge, CUP, 2008).

Brooks, C.W., *Pettifoggers and Vipers of the Commonwealth: the 'Lower Branch' of the Legal Profession in Early Modern England* (Cambridge, CUP, 1986).

Bullock, P.J., 'An Early Election Contest in Anglesey', *TAAS* (1976-77) pp.25-35.

Canny, N., *Making Ireland British 1580-1660* (Oxford, OUP, 2001).

Carr, A.D., *Medieval Anglesey* (Llangefni, Anglesey Antiquarian Society, 2011 revised edn).

Carr, A.D., *The Gentry of North Wales in the Later Middle Ages* (Cardiff, UWP, 2017)

Carr, A.D., 'The Extent of Anglesey, 1352', *TAAS* (1971-72), pp.150-272.

Carr, A.D., 'Maredudd ap Cynwrig: a medieval public person', *TAAS* (1988) pp.13-21.

Colley, L., *Britons: Forging the Nation 1707-1837* (Newhaven, Yale University Press, 1992).

Collinson, P., 'The Monarchical Republic of Queen Elizabeth 1', *Bulletin of the John Rylands Library* (1987), pp.394-424.

Cope, E.S., *The Life of a Public Man: Edward, First Baron Montagu of Boughton 1562-1644* (Philadelphia, American Philosophical Society, 1981).

Davies, J., *A History of Wales* (London, Penguin, 1994).

Davies, R.R., *The First English Empire: Power and Identities in the British Isles 1093-1343* (Oxford, OUP, 2000).

Davies, R.R., *The Revolt of Owain Glyn Dŵr* (Oxford, OUP, 1995).

Dawson, J.E.A., 'William Cecil and the British dimension of Early Elizabethan Foreign Policy', *History* 74 (1989), pp.196-216.

Dictionary of Welsh Biography (Oxford, Blackwell / Hon Soc of Cymmrodorion, 1959).

Dodd, A.H., *Studies in Stuart Wales* (Cardiff, UWP, 1952).

Dodd, A.H., 'The Pattern of Politics in Stuart Wales', *THSC* (1948), pp.8-35.

Dodd, A.H., 'Wales's Parliamentary Apprenticeship, 1536-1625', *THSC* (1942) pp.8-72.

Dodd, A.H. & Williams, J.G. (eds), *Aspects of Welsh History* (Cardiff, UWP, 1969).

Dyfnallt Owen, G., *Elizabethan Wales* (Cardiff, UWP, 1986).

Dyfnallt Owen, J., *Wales in the Reign of James I* (London, Royal Historical Society / Boydell Press, 1988).

Edwards, I ap O., *Catalogue of Star Chamber Proceedings relating to Wales* (Cardiff, Board of Celtic Studies & University Press Board, 1929).

Edwards, J.G., The Principality of Wales, 1267-1907 (Caernarfon, Caernarvonshire Historical Society, 1969).

Edwards, P.S., 'Cynrychiolaeth a Chynnen: Agweddau ar Hanes Seneddol a Chymdeith-asol Sir Fôn yng Nghanol yr Unfed Ganrif ar Bymtheg', *Welsh History* Review 10 (1980/81), pp.43-68.

Ellis, S., *The Making of the British Isles: the state of Britain and Ireland 1450-1660* (London, Routledge, 2007).

Ellis, S. & Barber, S. (eds), *Conquest and Union: fashioning a British State* (London, Longman, 1995).

Ellis, S., 'Tudor State Formation & the Shaping of the British Isles', in Ellis & Barber op cit.

Elton, G.R., *The Tudor Constitution: Documents and Commentary* (Cambridge, CUP, 1960).

Elton, G.R., 'Parliament in the Reign of Elizabeth I', in Haigh, C. (ed) *The Reign of Elizabeth I* (Athens, Georgia University Press, 1985).

Emery, F. E., 'The Farming Regions of Wales: Regional Economies', in Thirsk, J. (ed) *The Agrarian History of England and Wales* Vol IV 1500-1640 (Cambridge, CUP, 1967).

Evans, G., *The Fight for Welsh Freedom* (Talybont, Ceredigion, Y Lolfa Cyf, 2000).

Evans, N., *Religion and Politics in Eighteenth-Century Anglesey* (Cardiff, UWP, 1937).

Figes, O., *Natasha's Dance: A Cultural History of Russia* (London, Penguin, 2003).

Flenley, R., *A Calendar of the Register of the Queen's Majesty's Council in the Dominion and Principality of Wales and the Marches of the Same (1569-1591)* (London, Hon.Soc. of Cymmrodorion, 1916).

Foster, R.E., *Modern Ireland 1600-1972* (London, Allen Lane, 1988).

Foster, R.E., *The Oxford History of Ireland* (Oxford, OUP, 2001).

French, P.J., *John Dee, the World of an Elizabethan Magus* (London, Routledge & Kegan Paul, 1979).

Grant, A. & Stringer, K.J., *Uniting the Kingdom? The Making of British History* (London, Routledge, 1995).

Graves, M.A.R., 'Thomas Norton the Parliament Man: An Elizabethan MP, 1559-1581', *The Historical Journal* 23 (1980), pp.17-23.

Graves, M.A.R., *Elizabethan Parliaments, 1559-1601* (Harlow, Pearson Education, 1996).

Gray, M., 'Mr Auditor's Man: the Career of Richard Budd, Estate Agent and Crown Official', *WHR* (1985), pp.307-323.

Gresham, C., *Eifionydd: a Study in Landownership from the Medieval Period to the Present Day* (Cardiff, UWP, 1973).

Gresham, C., 'The Aberconwy Charter', *Arch.Camb.* XCIV (1939), pp.124-144.

Griffith, W.P., *Civility and Reputation: Ideas and Images of the 'Tudor Man' in Wales* (Bangor Studies in Welsh History, 1995).

Griffith, W.P., *Learning Law and Religion: Higher Education and Welsh Society c.1540-1640* (Cardiff, UWP, 1996).

Griffith, W.P., *Power, Politics and County Government in Wales: Anglesey 1780-1914* (Llangefni, Anglesey Antiquarian Society, 2006).

Griffith, W.P., 'Schooling and Society', in Gwynfor Jones, J. (ed) *Class, Community and Culture* op cit.

Griffith, W.P., 'Welsh Students at Oxford, Cambridge and the Inns of Court' (Bangor University, PhD thesis, 1981).

Griffith, J.E., *Pedigrees of Anglesey & Carnarvonshire Families* (Horncastle Lincs, W.K. Morton & Sons, 1914).

Gwynfor Jones, J., *Wales and the Tudor State* (Cardiff, UWP, 1989).

Gwynfor Jones, J., *The Welsh Gentry 1536-1640: Images of Status, Honour and Authority* (London, Routledge, 1990).

Gwynfor Jones, J., *Early Modern Wales c.1525-1640* (Basingstoke, St Martin's Press, 1994).

Gwynfor Jones, J., *Law, Order and Government in Caernarfonshire 1558-1603: Justices of the Peace and Gentry* (Cardiff, UWP, 1996).

Gwynfor Jones, J. (ed), *Class, Community and Culture in Tudor Wales* (Cardiff, UWP, 1989).

Gwynne Jones, E., 'Anglesey and Invasion 1539-1603', *TAAS* (1947), pp.26-37.

Gwynne Jones, E., 'Some Notes on the Principal County Families of Anglesey in the

Sixteenth and Early Seventeenth Centuries', *TAAS* (1939), p.66.

Habermas, J., *The Structural Transformation of the Public Sphere* (Cambridge Mass, MIT Press, 1991).

Haigh, C., 'Politics in an age of peace and war, 1570-1630', in Morrill, J. (ed), *The Oxford Illustrated History of Tudor and Stuart England* (Oxford, OUP, 1996).

Ham, R.E., 'The Four Shire Controversy', *WHR* 8 (1977), pp.381-399.

Hartley, T.E. (ed), *Proceedings of the Parliaments of Elizabeth I – Vol III, 1593-1601* (Leicester, Leicester University Press, 1995).

Hasler, P.W. (ed), *The House of Commons 1509-58*, Vol 2 Members (London, Secker & Warburg, 2006).

Hechter, M., *Colonialism: the Celtic Fringe in British national development, 1536-1966* (London, Routledge & Paul, 1975).

Hindle, S., *The State and Social Change in Early Modern England, 1550-1640* (Basingstoke, Palgrave, 2002).

Hoare, Q. & Nowell-Smith, G., *Selections from the Prison Notebooks* (Antonio Gramsci) (New York, International Publishers, 1999).

Hurstfield, J., *Freedom, Corruption and Government in Elizabethan England* (London, Jonathan Cape, 1973).

Jenkins, G. (ed), *The Welsh Language before the Industrial Revolution* (Cardiff, UWP, 2001).

Jenkins, G.H., *Concise History of Wales* (Cambridge, CUP, 2007)

Jones, D.C., *The Bulkeleys of Beaumaris* (Bangor University, MA thesis, 1957).

Jones, G., *Exchequer Proceedings Concerning Wales: Henry VIII – Elizabeth* (Cardiff, UWP, 1939).

Jones, G.P., 'Notes on Some Non-Dynastic Anglesey Clan-Founders', *TAAS* (1923), pp.35-48.

Jones-Pierce, T., 'Landlords in Wales', in Finsberg, H.P.R. (ed) *The Agrarian History of England and Wales* Vol 5 (Cambridge, CUP, 1969).

Jones-Pierce, T., 'Medieval Settlement in Anglesey', *TAAS* (1951), pp.1-33.

Jones-Pierce, T., 'Some Tendencies in the Agrarian History of Caernarvonshire during the later Middle Ages', *THCS* (1939), pp.18-36.

Jones-Pierce, T., 'The Clennenau Estate', in Jones-Pierce, T. (ed), *Introduction to Clennenau Letters and Papers in the Brongyntyn Collection*, NLW Supplement Series Pt I (Aberystwyth, 1947).

Judt, T., *The Memory Chalet* (London, William Heinemann, 2010)

Knafla, L.A., *Law and Politics in Jacobean England* (Cambridge, CUP, 1989)

Knafla, L.A., 'The Law Studies of an Elizabethan Student', *Huntington Library Quarterly* (1969), pp.221-240.

Leith, M.S., 'Governance and Identity in a Devolved Scotland', in *Parliamentary Affairs* 63, No 2 (2010).

Lewis, C.W., 'The Decline of Professional Poetry', in Geraint Gruffydd, R. (ed), *A Guide to Welsh Literature 1530-1700*, Vol 3 (Cardiff, UWP, 1992).

Lewis, D., 'The Court of the President and Council of Wales and the Marches from 1478 to 1575', *Y Cymmrodor* Vol XII (1891).

Lewis, T.H., 'The administration of justice in the Welsh county in its relation to the organs of justice, higher and lower', *THSC* (1966), pp.158-159.

Loades, D., *The Cecils: Privilege and Power behind the Throne* (London, TNA, 2007).

Longley, D., 'Medieval Settlement and Landscape Change in Anglesey', *Landscape History*

23 (2001), pp.39-60.

Lord, P., *Words with Pictures: Welsh Images and Images of Wales in the Popular Press, 1640-1860* (London, Planet, 1995).

MacCulloch, D., *Reformation: Europe's House Divided 1490-1700* (London, Allen Lane, 2003), pp.286-358.

Macfarlane, A., 'The Origins of English Individualism', *Theory and Society* 6 (1978), pp.255-277.

Maclure, M., *The St Paul's Cross Sermons 1534-1642* (Toronto, Univ of Toronto Press, 1979).

Madgwick, P.J., 'Reviews', in *Welsh History Review* 8:1 (1976-77), pp.241-244.

McDiarmid, J.F., *The Monarchical Republic of Early Modern England: Essays in Response to Patrick Collinson* (Oxford, Ashgate, 2007)

McGurk, J.J.H., 'A Survey of the Demands made on the Welsh shires to supply soldiers for the Irish wars 1594-1602', *THSC* (1983), pp.56-67.

Miller, E.J., 'Wales and the Tudor Drama', *THSC* (1948), pp.170-183.

Morton, S., *Gayatri Spivak: Ethics, Subalternity and the Critique of Postcolonial Reason* (Cambridge, Polity, 2007).

Morrill, J., 'The Fashioning of Britain', in Ellis & Barber (eds) op cit, p.26.

Morrill, J. & Bradshaw, B., *The British Problem c.1534-1707: State Formation in the Atlantic Archipelago* (London, St Martin's Press, 1996).

Neale, J.E., *Elizabeth and Her Parliaments*, Vols I & II (London, Jonathan Cape, 1957).

Neale, J.E., *The Elizabethan House of Commons* (London, Jonathan Cape, 1949).

Nicholl, C., *The Reckoning* (London, Vintage, 2002).

Nichols, J., *Progresses of Queen Elizabeth*, Vol I (London, John Nichols & Son, 1823), pp.149-169.

O'Day, R., *The Professions in Early Modern England 1450-1800: Servants of the Commonweal* (London, Pearson Education, 2000).

Offering, L.H., 'Puchasing Power of British Pounds from 1284 to the Present' ('MeasuringWorth', 2011, www.EH.net)

Oxford Dictionary of National Biography (Oxford, OUP, 2004)

Owen, H., 'The Plea Rolls of Anglesey 1509-1516', *TAAS* supplement (1927).

Palliser, D.M., *The Age of Elizabeth: England under the Tudors, 1547-1603* (London, Longman, 1983).

Parry, G., *A Guide to the Great Sessions in Wales* (Aberystwyth, NLW, 1995).

Pawlisch, H.J., *Sir John Davies and the Conquest of Ireland: A Study in Legal Imperialism* (Cambridge, CUP, 1985).

Pettit, P.A.J., *The Royal Forests of Northamptonshire, a Study in their Economy, 1558-1714* (Gateshead, Northumberland Press, for Northants Record Society, 1968).

Pevsner, N., *Northamptonshire* (London, Penguin, 1961).

Phillips, J.R.S., *The Justices of the Peace in Wales and Monmouthshire 1541 to 1689* (Cardiff, UWP, 1975).

Powell, N.M.W., 'Crime and Community in Denbighshire during the 1590s: the Evidence of the Records of the Court of Great Sessions', in Gwynfor Jones, J. (ed), *Class, Community and Culture in Tudor Wales* (Cardiff, UWP, 1989).

Powell, N.M.W., 'Near the Margin of Existence? Upland Prosperity in Wales during the Early Modern Period', *Studia Celtica* 41 (2007), pp.37-62.

Prest, W.R., *The Rise of the Barristers: A Social History of the English Bar 1590-1640* (Oxford, Clarendon, 1986).

Prest, W.R., *The Inns of Court under Elizabeth I and the Early Stuarts, 1590-1640* (London, Longman, 1972).

Prest, W.R., 'Legal Education of the Gentry at the Inns of Court, 1560-1640', *Past and Present* 38 (1967), pp.20-39.

Raffield, P., *Images and Cultures of Law in Early Modern England,: Justice and Political Power, 1558-1660* (Cambridge, CUP, 2004).

Rees, W., 'The Union of England and Wales', *THSC* (1937), pp.27-100.

Richards, H.F., *New Kalendars of Gwynedd* (Denbigh, Gwasg Gee, 1994).

Roach, J.P.C., *A History of the County of Cambridge and the Isle of Ely.* Volume 3: *The City and University of Cambridge* (London, University of London, 1959).

Roberts, G., 'The Anglesey submissions of 1406', *BBCS* 15 (1952).

Roberts, P.R., 'A Breviat of the Effectes devised for Wales *c.*1540-41', *Camden Miscellany* 26 (1975).

Roberts, P.R., 'The Welsh Language, English Law and Tudor Legislation', *THSC* (1989), pp.19-75.

Roberts, P.R., 'Tudor Legislation and the Political Staus of 'the British tongue', in Jenkins, G.H., *The Welsh Language before the Industrial Revolution* (Cardiff, UWP, 1995), pp.123-152.

Rouse Ball, W.W. & Venn, J.A. (eds), *Admissions to Trinity College* (London, Macmillan, 1911).

Royal Commission on Ancient & Historical Monuments in Wales and Monmouthshire, *An Inventory of the Ancient Monuments in Anglesey* (London, HMSO, 1937).

Russell, C., *The Crisis of the Parliaments – English History 1509-1660* (Oxford, OUP, 1971).

Seel, G. & Smith, D., *Crown and Parliaments 1558-1689* (Cambridge, CUP, 2001).

Shapiro, J., *1599: A Year in the Life of William Shakespeare* (London, Faber & Faber, 2005).

Sharpe, J., *Geographies of Postcolonialism* (London, Sage, 2007).

Sharpe, K., *Image Wars: Promoting Kings and Commonwealths in England 1603-1660* (Newhaven & London, Yale University Press, 2010).

Sharpe, J., 'Social strain and dislocation, 1585-1603', in Guy, J. (ed), *The Reign of Elizabeth I: Court and culture in the last decade* (Cambridge, CUP, 1995).

Shrewsbury, J.F.D., *A History of Bubonic Plague in the British Isles* (Cambridge, CUP, 1970).

Skeel, C.A.J., *The Council in the Marches of Wales: a study in local government during the sixteenth and seventeenth centuries* (London, 1904).

Skyrme, T., *History of the Justices of the Peace* (Chichester, Barry Rose, 1991).

Smith, D., *The Stuart Parliaments 1603-1689* (London, Hodder, 1999).

Sommerville, J.P., *Royalists and Patriots: Politics and Ideology in England, 1603-1640* (London, Longman, 1999).

Stephens, M., *The New Companion to the Literature of Wales* (Cardiff, UWP, 1998).

Stephenson, D., *The Governance of Gwynedd* (Cardiff, UWP, for Board of Celtic Studies, 1994).

Stone, L., *The Family, Sex and Marriage in England 1500-1800* (London, Pelican, 1979).

Stone, L., 'The Educational Revolution in England 1560-1640', *Past and Present* 28 (1964), p. 67.

Strong, R., *The Cult of Elizabeth: Elizabethan Protraiture and Pagentry* (London, Thames & Hudson, 1977).

Suggett, R., 'The Welsh Language and the Court of Great Sessions', in G. Jenkins (ed), *The Welsh Language before the Industrial Revolution* (Cardiff, UWP, 2001).

The Spenser Encyclopaedia (Toronto, University of Toronto Press, 1990).

Thirsk, J. (ed), *The Agrarian History of England and Wales*, Vol IV 1500-1640 (Cambridge, CUP, 1967).

Thomas, D., 'Leases in Reversion on the Crown's Lands, 1558-1603', *Economic History Review* 30 (1977), pp.67-72.

Thomas, D.L., 'Further Notes on the Court of the Marches, with Original Documents', *Y Cymmrodor* XIII (1900), pp.97-164.

Thomas, G., *Eisteddfodau Caerwys* (Cardiff, UWP, 1968).

Thomas, H., *A History of Wales 1485-1660* (Cardiff, UWP, 1991).

Thomas, K., *The Ends of Life: Roads to Fulfilment in Early Modern England* (Oxford, OUP, 2009).

Thorne, S., 'Tudor Social Transformations and Legal Change', *New York University Law Review* 26 (1951), pp.10-23.

Thornton, T., *Cheshire and the Tudor State* (London, RHS / Boydell Press, 2000).

Turner, R.C., 'Robert Wynn and the building of Plas Mawr, Conwy', *National Library of Wales Journal* 29 (1995-96), pp.177-203.

Updike, J., *Memories of the Ford Administration* (London, Hamish Hamilton, 1992).

Williams, E., 'Sir William Maurice of Clennenau', *THCS* 24 (1983), pp.78-97.

Williams, G., *Religion, Language and Nationality in Wales* (Cardiff, UWP, 1977).

Williams, G., *Recovery, Reorientation and Reformation: Wales c.1415-1642* (Oxford, OUP, 1987).

Williams, G., *Religion, Language and Nationality in Wales* (Cardiff, UWP, 1979).

Williams G.A., 'The Bardic Road to Bosworth: a Welsh View of Henry Tudor', *THSC* (1986), pp.7-31.

Williams, G.A., *When Was Wales?* (Bury St Edmonds, Black Raven Press, 1985).

Williams, P., *The Later Tudors: England 1547-1603* (Oxford, OUP, 2002).

Williams, P., 'The Attack on the Council of the Marches, 1603-1642', *THSC* (1961, Pt II), pp.10-14.

Williams, P., *The Council in the Marches of England and Wales under Elizabeth I* (Cardiff, UWP, 1958).

Williams, W.L., 'The Union of England and Wales', *THSC* (1907-8), pp.54-56.

Williams, W.L., 'The King's Court of Great Sessions in Wales', *Y Cymmrodor* XXIV (1916), pp.44-45.

Williams, W.O. (ed), *Calendar of the Caernarvonshire Quarter Sessions Records, 1541-1558* (Caernarfon, Caernarvonshire Historical Society, 1956).

Williams, W.O., 'The Survival of the Welsh language after the union of England and Wales: the first phase, 1536-1642', *WHR* 2 (1964-5), pp.67-93.

Williams, W.O., *Tudor Gwynedd* (Caernarfon, Caernarvonshire Historical Society, 1958).

Williams, W.R., *The History of Great Sessions in Wales 1542-1830* (Brecknock 1899).

Wyn Wiliam, D. (ed), *Y Canu Mawl i Deulu Mysoglen* (Llangefni, O.Jones, 1999).

Wyn Wiliam, D. (ed), *Y Canu Mawl i Deulu Myfyrian* (Llandysul, Gwasg Gomer, 2004)

Wyn Wiliam, D. (ed), *Y Canu Mawl i Rai Teuluoedd o Gwmwd Menai* (Llandysul, Gwasg Gomer, 2007).

Young, R., *Postcolonialism: An Historical Introduction* (Oxford, OUP, 2001).

Acknowledgements

I'm grateful for the kindness and insight of two particular individuals who helped me bring this book to fruition – Nia Powell, who gave consistently stimulating guidance in the research stages, and my dearest wife Helen.

It's a pleasure also to thank many friends and colleagues who've given help and support on relevant matters over recent years, including Ian Archer, Mary Aris, the late Ann Benwell, Margaret and Robert Bradbury, Glenda and the late Tony Carr, Tony Claydon, Carl Clowes, Andrew and Jo Davidson, David Devalle, Shaun Evans, Wil Griffith, Eryl Rothwell Hughes, Jerry Hunter, Gareth Huws, the late Chas Parry Jones, Gerallt Llewelyn Jones, Frances Lynch Llewelyn, David Longley, the late Patrick Lyndon, George Meyrick, Rev Emlyn Richards, Sara Elin Roberts, Michael Senior, Einion Thomas, the late Glyndwr Thomas, Rev Dafydd Wyn Wiliam, and the late Paul Woddis.

I also thank Elen Simpson and Ann Hughes of Bangor University Archives, and staff at the Lincoln's Inn Library, London Library, and Northamptonshire Public Records Office, for invaluable assistance.

Finally I record my sincere appreciation of the many contributions of Robert Williams in the design and publication stages of the book.

ROBIN GROVE-WHITE

Index

Page numbers in *italics* indicate illustrations.
Numbers with the suffix 'n' indicate footnotes.

Astudiaethau Hanes Môn / Studies in Anglesey History

1   *Copper Mountain*, John Rowlands 1966

2   *Natural History of Anglesey*, edited by W Efion Jones 1966

3   *Prehistoric Anglesey* *The archaeology of the island to the Roman conquest*
   Frances Lynch 1970

4   *Ships & Seamen of Anglesey 1558-1918*, Aled Eames 1973

5   *Two Centuries of Anglesey Schools 1700-1902*, David A Pretty 1977

6   *Medieval Anglesey*, A D Carr 1982

7   *Portraits of an Island* *Eighteenth century Anglesey*
   Helen Ramage 1987, ISBN 0 9500199-5-X

8   *A New Natural History of Anglesey*
   edited by W Efion Jones 1990, ISBN 0 9500199-6-8

9   *Prehistoric Anglesey* *The archaeology of the island to the Roman conquest*
   Frances Lynch. Second edition 1991, ISBN 0 9500199-7-6

10 *Portraits of an Island* *Eighteenth century Anglesey*
   Helen Ramage. Second edition 2001, ISBN 0 9500199-8-4

11 *Power, Politics & County Government in Wales* *Anglesey 1780-1914*
   W P Griffith 2006, ISBN 0 9500199-9-2

12 *Medieval Anglesey*
   A D Carr. Second edition 2011, ISBN 978-0-9568769-0-4

13 *A Prism for his Times* *Late-Tudor Anglesey & Hugh Hughes of Plas Coch*
   Robin Grove-White 2020, ISBN 978-0-9568769-1-1